Lucifer Ascending

Lucifer Ascending

The Occult in Folklore and Popular Culture

BILL ELLIS

THE UNIVERSITY PRESS OF KENTUCKY

Publication of this volume was made possible in part by a grant
from the National Endowment for the Humanities.

Scholarly publisher for the Commonwealth,
serving Bellarmine University, Berea College, Centre
College of Kentucky, Eastern Kentucky University,
The Filson Historical Society, Georgetown College,
Kentucky Historical Society, Kentucky State University,
Morehead State University, Murray State University,
Northern Kentucky University, Transylvania University,
University of Kentucky, University of Louisville,
and Western Kentucky University.
All rights reserved.

Editorial and Sales Offices: The University Press of Kentucky
663 South Limestone Street, Lexington, Kentucky 40508-4008
www.kentuckypress.com

08 07 06 05 04   5 4 3 2 1

Library of Congress Cataloging-in-Publication Data

Ellis, Bill, 1950-
  Lucifer ascending : the occult in folklore and popular culture / Bill
Ellis.
    p. cm.
  Includes bibliographical references (p.   ) and index.
  ISBN 0-8131-2289-9
  1. Satanism. 2. Occultism. 3. Superstition. I. Title.
BF1548.E44 2003
133.4—dc21   2003008810

This book is printed on acid-free recycled paper meeting the requirements of the
American National Standard for Permanence in Paper for Printed Library Materials.

Manufactured in the United States of America.

 Members of the Association of
American University Presses

Lucifer, the Light-bearer!
Strange and mysterious name to give to the Spirit of Darkness!
Lucifer, the Son of the Morning!
Is it he who bears the Light. . . ? Doubt it not!

—*Albert Pike*

Contents

Acknowledgments

After publishing *Raising the Devil,* a book born from the same dark journey as this one, I received the following message from an alumnus of Penn State University:

> If you think that Satan is not alive and an ever present threat to Christians, then you are either (A) not a Christian or (B) a dupe of Satan himself. To say that "Satanism scares belong to the realm of folklore and are generally harmless" [a quote from a press release about my book, not my actual words] is to say that you do not believe in Satan and his evil power. How can you ignore his evil work with drugs, sex, murder and violence that abound in today's culture? Maybe you are (A) above, in which case I pray for your soul. But if, by chance, you are actually (B) above, then I pray for your students and for your removal from your position. Your efforts to desensitize good people at the college level is inexcusable.

At the same time, a number of academic reviews, while generally favorable toward the book, commented on the way in which I had professed my faith in God and my status as a practicing member of the Evangelical Lutheran Church in America, finding it unnecessary and perhaps defensive. An on-line review on the message board *alt.satanism* also found some value in its description of how the media and some religious commentators negatively stereotyped satanic movements but felt it was "of little value for those who wish to learn about Satanism as practiced by many individuals or groups."

Although I do include some information on the satanic movement begun by Anton LaVey in this book, I fear that the same could be said about this book: it does not really attempt to portray the practices of the many "witchcraft" and "satanic" alternative religions that have emerged in the Anglo-American world during the last four decades. My goal here is somewhat different: to look at "witchcraft" and so-called "black magic" as it was actually practiced on the grassroots level by many people at many times who did not set themselves apart from Christianity or wish to start a separate religious movement like Wicca. This continues the objective of *Raising the Devil:* to look at Christian responses to satanism from an academic point of view. This perspective, however, is influenced on many levels by my own choice of faith, as I have served on Church Council and Stewardship Committees, volunteered in charitable activities, and on occasion taught adult Sunday school and led services. My daughter went to a Catholic-affiliated school from kindergarten to her high school graduation. As noted before, I am regularly called on to publicly "reject sin, the devil, and all his empty promises." Therefore I am inclined to respect those who express faith in Jesus Christ and follow His commandments to love God and neighbor.

On the other hand, as an academic, I regularly teach and collaborate with people of other denominations and faiths, and I find their personal integrity and good will far more important to me than the form their religious expression takes. Many of my close professional friends are Jewish and Islamic, and some are members of the Neo-Pagan movement. I deeply respect both their beliefs and the actions they have taken based on them, and see my primary role in books like this as trying to discern the truth as objectively as I can, even when it includes some harsh criticisms of fellow Christians and challenges to some definitions of church doctrine. I think this is a stand that is professionally responsible for an academic, and I also feel it is compatible with Scripture.

In this regard, I often feel like J.K. Rowling, whose *Harry Potter* books have been part of my household for several years, just like the Christian-influenced fantasy books of her predecessors, C.S. Lewis and J.R.R. Tolkien. During an AOL Live on-line chat, she was asked for the umpteenth time whether she *believed* in the magic about which she wrote so vividly. Rowling first responded with an "on-line sigh," then said, "Well, as it happens, I believe in God, but there's no pleasing some people!" (Drennan 2000). Just as the battle of good and evil is central to Christianity and many other related religions, so, too, the debate over what *is* godly and what "satanic" seems an eternal debate, and too often the question divides communities that ought to work together. For this reason, I have used "Lucifer," or "The Lightbearer," in the title of this book. Historically, the name has been a synonym for Satan, "The Adversary," but many thoughtful commentators have wondered if an entity or concept that brings light, enlightenment, or knowledge had to be by definition diabolical. So this book is about debate between those who feel that the magical realm is worth exploiting in the name of God, and those who feel that such activities are intrinsically dangerous.

As it happens, I believe in God. I do not perform the magic that I describe. I respect the ideas of the fundamentalists whom I study, even if I feel they are sometimes mistaken or misled. In the end, though, Satan (whether this names an entity outside the personality or the human tendency to disobey God and Scripture and choose to hate one's neighbor) has more to gain through co-opting the activities of Christians and inducing them to attack each other in the name of Jesus Christ than through any direct appeal to do evil in the name of evil. This occurs, of course, but it is less dangerous than the activities of institutions that appeal to holiness as an end that justifies meanness.

As before, I owe a debt to those who helped me through the lonely time during which *Raising the Devil* and this book were researched, written, and rewritten. Their support sustained me, even though they knew that such assistance might be misconstrued as lending support to a book that would outrage religious sensibilities. On a professional level, Penn State University made basic groundwork for this research possible with a one-semester sabbatical in the spring of 1992 that allowed me to visit a number of folklore archives and locate many ephemeral sources from the 1960s and 1970s. Penn State was also generous in providing travel money that allowed me to present versions of some chapters at international meetings and at the same time consult archives in Great Britain. During my stays there, Jacqueline Simpson was especially kind in sharing her own rich knowledge of British legends and related rituals, and for walking me up Chanctonbury Ring so that I could circumambulate this notoriously uncanny site for myself.

Richard Tyce and Kathy Stone of the Penn State Hazleton Library were both untiring in locating many extremely rare books and periodicals through interlibrary loan, and the late Charles Mann allowed me to access many books in the Occult Collection of the Rare Books Department of the Pattee Library. Philip Jenkins of the Religious Studies Program shared with me many clippings and ephemera documenting the rise of interest in the occult in Great Britain. Colleagues and friends assisted me materially in finding rare sources and making it possible to visit archives on an extremely limited budget by sharing their homes and sofas with me. Daniel Barnes and Linda Milligan of Ohio State, Janet

Langlois of Wayne State, and Ruth Stotter of Dominican College, San Francisco, provided help at especially needful times.

Even with the material in hand, this book would not have been completed had it not been for the encouragement given me by others. Chief among these has been Anne Lafferty of the Memorial University of Newfoundland, who allowed me to see much of her own research into the history and significance of the Dumb Supper among the Neo-Pagan community. Michael Aquino of the Temple of Set and the late Anton LaVey of the Church of Satan were also kind enough to respond to my requests for background information on *The Satanic Bible*. Professors Stephen Mitchell of Harvard University and William Harman of the University of Tennessee at Chattanooga allowed me to discuss my previous book with their classes and try out some of the material in this book on them. I thank Philip Johnson of the Presbyterian Theological Centre, Sydney, Australia, for noting the relevance of my work to the *Harry Potter* books and alerting me to the flap caused by the *Onion* satire. I appreciate the faith and patience of Leila Salisbury, zig Ziegler, and Jennifer Peckinpaugh of the University Press of Kentucky in helping me find ways to bring this dark project to term.

Finally, I again thank my wife and my daughter for the support they have given me, even though the intellectual path I chose was one that has exposed them to social and professional hardships.

As before, none of the individuals or institutions mentioned above should be held responsible for the opinions I present or the conclusions I reach. These are mine alone, and beyond the assistance acknowledged above I have not been offered or given any consideration or promise of consideration from any organization, be it academic, political, religious, or occult.[1]

Chapter One

ꟽizards ꟊs. ꟽuggles

A Long-Standing Debate

The publication of *Harry Potter and the Philosopher's Stone* in 1997 quickly made Britain's J.K. Rowling a world-famous author. This children's novel (retitled *Harry Potter and the Sorcerer's Stone* in its U.S. release) was followed by four best-selling books and two successful movies. In the process, the story of Harry Potter's rise, from being a despised orphan living underneath the stairwell at his reluctant adoptive parents' house to a successful student of magic at the Hogwarts School of Witchcraft and Wizardry, became common knowledge among both young readers and their parents throughout the English-speaking world. In the process, the novel once again brought to light the issue of whether it was safe to allow young people to become involved in the occult.

Rowling's quick rise to prominence brought sharp criticism from some Christian commentators. The *Harry Potter* books, they claimed, are spiritually dangerous to children because they present the occult in a positive light and can encourage young people to dabble in diabolical practices. Warnings proliferated, particularly on the Internet, where tracts and critiques of the books could travel freely across national borders and be copied from one site to another. One site concedes that the world of Hogwarts is, admittedly, a fiction, but adds, "the timeless pagan practices it promotes are real and deadly" (Kjos 2002). Another, a tract by David J. Meyer, an ex-occultist turned Pentecostal minister, described the *Harry Potter* books as "orientational and instructional manuals of witchcraft woven into the format of entertainment," adding that "[u]ntold millions of young people are being taught to think, speak, dress, and act like witches by filling their heads with the contents of these books" (Meyer 2000a).

Even from a Christian point of view, painting the *Harry Potter* books as "satanic" seemed unnecessary. A *Christianity Today* "Opinion

1

Roundup" reported broad consensus from religious leaders and publications that the books were at worst unrelated to real religious issues and even promoted wise ethical decisions, in a fantasy vein previously exploited by explicitly Christian authors such as G.K. Chesterton, J.R.R. Tolkien, C.S. Lewis, and Madeleine l'Engle (Olsen 1999). And the crusade often backfired with the young audience that was allegedly at risk. An especially embarrassing moment in the anti-Potter crusade was the wide circulation among Christian youth counselors of a chain letter that alleged that Rowling's books had inspired millions of children to join satanic organizations. The chain letter's allegations were supported by passages from a news article, containing many validating quotes from both children and concerned Christians. Ashley Daniels, a third-grader from Lock Haven, Pennsylvania, was described using "an ancient spell to summon Cerebus [*sic*], the three-headed hound of hell,"[1] while commenting, "I used to believe in what they taught us at Sunday School. . . . But the *Harry Potter* books showed me that magic is real, something I can learn and use right now, and that the Bible is nothing but boring lies." Organized satanic groups were overwhelmed by young converts, the article continued, so children were forced to create their own impromptu covens. One Texas eleven-year-old was said to have founded his own group, named "Potterites to Destroy Jesus." Initiates had to curse God, have a lightning-bolt scar cut into their foreheads, and pay a membership fee of $6.66. "When I grow up," the Potterites' founder was quoted as saying, "I'm going to learn Necromancy and summon greater demons to Earth."

The article also cited a representative from a Denver religious concern called Focus on Faith as saying, "These books do not merely depict one or two uses of magic spells or crystal balls. We're talking about hundreds of occult invocations. The natural, intuitive leap from reading a Harry Potter book to turning against God and worshipping Satan is very easy for a child to make. . . . These books are truly magical and therefore dangerous" (*Harry Potter* Books Spark Rise in Satanism 2000). Many of those forwarding the chain letter added comments supporting this Christian message. One warned readers: "Now if you have been sitting back in your little 'comfortable Christian bubble,' IT'S TIME TO FACE REALITY! This is really happening out there! . . . Innocent little kids are being lied to by the ultimate father of lies. Their parents are either completely ignorant of the dangers these books pose, don't care, or are encouraging them to pursue destruction and death" (Porter 2000). "What a sad day it is when pastors have the discernment level of a fence post," another evangelist said, adding, "These books are a curse on our nation" (Meyer 2000b). A third asked readers "to become involved in getting the word out about this garbage. Please forward to every pastor, teacher, and parent you know. . . . Pray also for the Holy Spirit to work in the young minds of those who are reading this garbage that they may be delivered from its harm" (Harry Potter Books 2001). Yet another cautioned parents that "God's charge to parents everywhere is that we do not allow our children to be subjected nor persuaded by demonic influence. We must familiarize ourselves with what they are reading and the practices in which they are engaging. To ignore this equals nothing short of child suicide" (Wright 2003).

The problem is that most Web-savvy youngsters recognized that the article quoted came from the *Onion,* a popular on-line satire journal that posts daily parodies of news articles. The information contained was bogus, and none of the children or adult interviewees existed. When the chain letter containing quotes from the article was reproduced and handed out by well-meaning adult leaders of youth groups among those supposedly targeted for satanic indoctrination, its recipients immediately saw that their elders, blissfully ignorant of their on-line reading habits and practices, had fallen for an obvious hoax. One teenager recorded such an event in his on-line journal:

> Something happened at church this Sunday that made me angry. Well actually, it more made me sad. The director of the children's ministry passed out copies of this article from some Christian talking about how Harry Potter is evil. And it had all these examples and quotes, and asked us to pray.
>
> The thing is, all the quotes and examples were from a single article from a website, a copy of which was attached and handed out. And the website was The Onion.
>
> Maybe you don't know it, but that site is probably the most well known satirical site on the web. . . . And the Potter article in question was clearly satire. Just so way over the top. I thought it was funny. Like, it talked about how children were forming black magic clubs with names like "Potterites to Destroy Jesus" and stuff like that. . . . Obviously satire.
>
> I guess not so obvious. It just makes me sad that Christians are so hypersensitive and touchy that they can't even recognize when something is a joke. It really disturbed me. This article in

question was distributed by the children's ministry director's relative's pastor. The article is a joke! Can't you see that?

And we wonder why Christians get a bad rep. Anyway, my claim is that Christians should just not talk about pop culture unless they have any clue what they're talking about. (Chai 2000)

The *Onion* flap was duly recorded as a "hoax" on a variety of websites documenting urban legends, chain letters, and other forms of frequently forwarded misinformation (e.g., Astor 2000, Buhler 2000, Mikkelson 2001). Nevertheless, as William Blake observed (appropriately enough, in a list of "Proverbs of Hell"), "Every thing possible to be believ'd is an image of truth" (1970: 36). This and similar beliefs about the *Harry Potter* books cannot be fully understood without looking at a still larger body of thoughts, beliefs, and activities that are deeply embedded in the world shared by Rowling's fans and detractors.

In my previous work, *Raising the Devil*, I discussed how the Anglo-American Satanism Scare of the 1980s and 1990s grew out of a complex network of religious and political beliefs that I described as a *contemporary mythology*. Attempting to debunk an individual rumor or claim that devil-worshipers were responsible for a given crime or social problem, I showed, was ineffective unless one fully understood the intellectual and social contexts that informed them. This is no new insight for social scientists, however. As early as 1960, the social anthropologists Charles White and J.C. Chinjavata warned that African beliefs dealing with magic and the supernatural should not be seen merely as "discrete superstitions," but as "part of a systematic body of beliefs." It is important to see, they continue, "that the basis of many African beliefs is essentially pragmatic. They are not so much philosophies about the nature of the universe or about metaphysical problems as answers to the more practical questions which affect the daily lives of individuals. . . . In short, then, Africans are much concerned to relate their beliefs to the total social situation within which they live and this often determines their essentially pragmatic nature" (56). For this reason, White and Chinjavata pointed out, simply showing that a given belief or piece of alleged information is false will not make it disappear from the culture. The fallacy in approaching "urban myths" with such an assumption, they concluded, "is that though they may be illogical and not in accordance with established facts, they are not comparable to illogical and systematic superstitions. On the contrary they are built into a systematic body of thought and belief about a given social system within which individuals live" (1960: 57).

Similarly, anthropologist Joseph William Bastien stresses that amulet-making in a Bolivian tribe he studied must be examined "in terms of the place of these amulets *in the total tapestry of customary beliefs and practices*" (1982: 354; emphasis added). Rather than being the result of ignorance and prescientific thinking, he finds, such objects reflect, in tightly condensed ways, a whole range of religious and cultural beliefs. "By fabricating an amulet and anointing it at ritual," he comments, "they are bringing out what is already there" (1982: 358).

In the same way, the *Onion* parody took information that was "already there" among fundamentalist Christian circles, particularly among Pentecostals, and simply pushed it a step further. For those who found the anti-Potter message intrinsically absurd, the parody simply made it the more so; but for those who already had reasons for finding Rowling's work spiritually dangerous, the exaggeration was too slight to be noticed. For instance, Pastor Meyer had already discerned a series of eerie significances in July 8, 2000, the release date of *Harry Potter and the Goblet of Fire:*

> On July 8 at midnight, bookstores everywhere were stormed by millions of children to obtain the latest and fourth book of the series known as "Harry Potter and the Goblet of Fire." These books were taken into homes everywhere with a real evil spirit following each copy to curse those homes. July 8th was also the 18th day (three sixes in numerology) from the witches' sabat of midsummer. July 8th was also the 13th day from the signing of the United Religions Charter in San Francisco.[2] Now we have learned that the public school system is planning to use the magic of Harry Potter in the classrooms making the public schools centers of witchcraft training.

The year 2000, Meyer had noted, was popularly associated with the beginning of the Apocalypse, and now "all of the foundations for occultism and witchcraft are in place" (Meyer 2000a).

While the figures quoted above for new child members in satanic groups were obviously fantastic, other sources reported that the Pagan Federation, a coalition of Wiccan and New Age movements, had indeed observed an increased number of inquiries from young readers of the

Harry Potter books. The report stressed that the federation did not allow anyone under eighteen to join, and sought parental consent before even issuing basic information about itself. Still, it reported receiving about a hundred inquiries per month from youths "who want to become witches" and added that Rowling's books were well received in Wiccan circles (Buffy Draws Children to Witchcraft 2000). Even Rowling admitted that she had received letters from children addressed to Professor Dumbledore, the fictional headmaster at Hogwarts, asking if they could be admitted to the wizardry school. "Some of them are really sad," she told a reporter. "Because they want it to be true so badly they've convinced themselves it's true" (Jones 2000: 58). While it was not true that the books led children to turn against Christian beliefs, it was certainly true that the role of magic in the *Harry Potter* books spoke very strongly to some deeply-felt need in their personalities.

So there are two sides to this controversy, just as there are implicitly two sides to the enigmatic figure of "Lucifer." Traditionally a synonym for Satan, the devil, the Prince of Darkness, the name paradoxically means "light-bearer," and the story of his expulsion from Heaven parallels the divine punishment given Prometheus, the rebellious god who brought fire to mankind against the Olympian gods' wishes. Hence, playing with magic often has been equated with playing with fire, particularly when youngsters with limited knowledge of the spiritual and practical world are involved. But magic has also provided socially tolerated opportunities for individuals to empower themselves in the face of institutionalized power structures. Both perspectives need to be understood to see why the occult appeals to some people and repels others.

This book will survey the social roles played by occultism in Great Britain and North America from the Early Modern period of the witch-hunts to the present. As we shall see, the *Harry Potter* dispute is only the most recent expression of a long-standing dispute, in which "magic," however defined, including as fictional or as a form of play, in fact functions as a way of subverting power structures. For this reason, it is often associated with adolescents, particularly females, whose power roles in adult society are precisely the most debatable. In and of themselves, the practices defined as "magical" may not be politically threatening, but the fact that such traditions gave people on the margins a context to entertain the possibility of inverting social roles made them dangerous enough for many observers.

We will first examine the background of the real, documentable practices that were defined as "witchcraft" in Anglo-American circles, along with the essentially pragmatic concerns that gave them life. We will then look at several closely related traditions of fetishism, ranging from the common (rabbit's feet, chain letters) to the esoteric occult (spell books, human body parts). This will lead us into the poorly understood supernatural play activities of children and adolescents, and the ways in which these "games" have regularly been corrupted into social panics. This survey of grassroots occult traditions will illustrate three essential principles:

- Folk traditions of magic and witchcraft are by no means fictional or part of the distant past.
- Self-consciously occult rituals have been a common element in children's and adolescents' folk culture for a long time.
- One motive for becoming interested in the occult is to participate directly in the mythic realm, in spite of organized religion's efforts to institutionalize it.

A common response to occultism is to present it as part of a conspiracy, directed either by diabolical forces or by the folk devils that represent them in this world. Hence it is no surprise that Pastor Meyer presents the *Harry Potter* books as part of a global plan orchestrated by the Illuminati, a secret society dedicated to bringing the world under complete satanic control. This work, like my previous one, *Raising the Devil*, does not deny that there are well-organized media and alternative religious networks devoted to promoting images of witchcraft. However, it argues that interest in folk magic is not *created* by these networks, however much they may *exploit* the attraction of the occult for certain groups. What drives this phenomenon, rather, is the way in which magic provides a potent symbol for individuals' desire to take control of the religious world.

This desire does not necessarily include a craving to overturn the moral code of institutional religion. As the Christian leaders cited in *Christianity Today* note, Harry Potter's actions are based on altruistic motives that most religions would admire as righteous in nature. Similarly, most documented practitioners of the occult have said that their actions are intended to benefit their communities and to combat the same moral and social evils that organized religion opposes. The occult, in other words, is usually seen not as an alternative to Christianity but rather as an appropriation of its underlying powers by ordinary people.

Paradoxically, the religious factions that are most prone to see private involvement in the divine realm as spiritually dangerous are not the mainstream denominations with the most to lose through this process. Rather, as *Raising the Devil* showed, the strongest concern about the "satanic" influence of the occult comes from alternative religious movements like Pentecostalism that have historically been involved in a parallel effort to restore the miraculous "gifts of the spirit" to the common person.

For this reason, the penultimate chapter of this book will look at magical practices in the context of an especially influential event in alternative Christianity, the Welsh Revival of 1904–5. This revival brought together occultism, conspiracy, and mythmaking, and its aftereffects powerfully influenced the development of Pentecostal religion. As a classic contact point between institutional religion and folklore, it will provide an illustration of how the former appropriated the latter, in a way that helped create a mythology of satanism that proved influential among conservative religious movements. Yet, at the same time, the Welsh Revival also demonstrated how folk traditions expressed political positions, particularly concerning the role of women in organized religion, that were powerfully subversive. This episode shows how beliefs that might have been channeled into some form of witchcraft in a previous day actually influenced the creation of alternative religions, which have since been troubled by their problematic kinship with the occult.

This point of view gives us some ways in which we can see contemporary phenomena, such as the debate over the *Harry Potter* books, in the light of long-range historical trends. As a prelude to the more detailed discussion, let's look at how each of the premises listed above help us bring together issues raised by the witch trials of the fifteenth and sixteenth centuries with contemporary concerns.

My first premise is that folk traditions of magic are by no means fictional or part of the distant past. The modern debate over the "reality" of witchcraft dates to the early decades of the previous century, the immediate catalyst being Margaret Murray's influential *The Witch-Cult in Western Europe* (1921), one of a series of postwar books that attempted to reconstruct a pre-Christian religion through historical records. (Sir James George Frazer's *The Golden Bough* and Jessie L. Weston's *From Ritual to Romance* were others.) Murray argued that the record of the witch trials reflected Christianity's efforts to stamp out the stubborn remains of an underground nature religion. Confessions and accusations preserved in trial records presented, for her, evidence of a fertility cult that met regularly to worship a god and goddess through frequently orgiastic rituals. Her thesis, however, brought a harsh response from the Rev. Montague Summers in *The History of Witchcraft and Demonology* (1926); he countered that the evidence in the trials was often literally accurate, and that the accused witches were part of an obscene and subversive conspiracy. "Miss Murray," he argued, "does not seem to suspect that Witchcraft was in truth a foul and noisome heresy . . . none other than . . . the worship of Satan. . . . It is true that in the Middle Ages Christianity had—not a rival but a foe, the eternal enemy of the Church Militant against whom she yet contends to-day, the dark Lord of that city which is set contrariwise to the City of God, the Terrible Shadow of destruction and despair" (1956: 32). Furthermore, Summers said, the "hideous cult of evil" imperfectly destroyed by the witch-hunters was still very much alive. Clandestine groups of devil-worshippers, he claimed, still carried out "the black mass," a blasphemous ceremony often including child sacrifice and cannibalism. "In many a town, both great and small," he concluded, "they congregate unsuspected to perform these execrable rites" (1956: 151).

In reaction, Murray developed and strengthened her argument for witches as part of a diabolized nature religion in *The God of the Witches* (1931). Her argument gained a widespread following among academics, and her *Encyclopaedia Britannica* entry on "Witchcraft" was reprinted without revision for several years. Adherents included Pennethorne Hughes, who paraphrased Murray's thesis in a frequently reprinted Pelican paperback, *Witchcraft* (1965). A more influential supporter was Gerald Gardner, whose popular books on the living traditions of "Wica" (later corrected as "Wicca") that he claimed to have found in the New Forest region of England were crucial to beginning the Neo-Pagan movement. However, Murray's reliance on evidence drawn from trial records has since been challenged by a number of rationalist historians, such as H.R. Trevor-Roper (1969) and Norman Cohn (1975). They felt it much more likely that "confessions" produced under torture or threat of execution reflected more what witch-hunters wanted to hear than what alleged witches had actually done. They argued that the witch craze was simply a revival of earlier persecutions of Jews and heretics and showed only the inner fears of authorities.

Such a critique, not surprisingly, is rejected by antioccult crusaders who have, like Summers, argued that witchcraft accusations were simply too prevalent in the 1600s to be nothing more than hysterical illusions.

Evangelist Nicky Cruz cautioned, "don't think all these witches brought to trial in the Middle Ages were innocent, sweet old ladies. . . . witchcraft itself is and always has been a horrible mixture of paganism, blasphemy, and cruelty" (1973: 108–9). And Jess Pedigo, in his influential 1971 tract, *Satanism: Diabolical Religion of Darkness*, also argued that at least some of the confessions drawn from females indicated the attraction that occult power had for them. He continues, "Is it at all possible that the multitudinous covens of witches and adherents to the satanic churches presently scattered across America are bearing the stigma, the ostracism from society, the persecution of their peers, for nothing at all; no power, no experience, no sensation or reward above the ordinary?" (4).

More recent attempts to reconstruct the social setting underlying the witch crazes have suggested a judicious middle ground between these two extreme positions. More recent research by Carlo Ginzburg (1990, 1992) and Gustav Henningsen (1990) into records of Italian trial proceedings has found evidence that in some areas highly organized and coordinated societies of shamans had indeed practiced an ecstatic religion. These included dream-journeys to banquets that resembled what later emerged in witch trials as the witches' Sabbath. The adherents of these religious societies presented themselves as agents of good to inquisitors, and only after extensive questioning and threats from priests did they renounce their activities. Ginzburg and Henningsen conclude that the tradition of the vile rites of witches developed directly out of such activities rooted in village folk culture, which elite authority figures interpreted as a religious movement hostile to Christianity.

In fact, "cunning folk," or village experts who specialized in such occult traditions, have operated in rural areas of both the United States and Great Britain into recent times, and while the tradition appears to be on the decline in Britain, it apparently is alive and well in North America. Some of these "experts," especially women, have always been viewed with suspicion by the representatives of organized religions, who may have encouraged others to define them as potentially evil in nature. Muggles, that is, have always distrusted wizards, even in times and places where their role in folk medicine and local justice was seen as necessary.

In sum, we should not be so naive as to assume that "there were no witches" or "there are no satanists." Occult practices have existed for many centuries, and they provide a ground for the more sensational claims that emerge from time to time. But crusades have always exaggerated the number and seriousness of crimes committed by witches or satanists, as well as the numbers said to be involved. Further, as social historian Julio Caro Baroja concluded, the information obtained during such crusades even from "confessing witches" presents a complex mixture of what real witches said and did, and what crusaders interested in building a legal case against them *wanted* them to say they said and did. Of the information taken down at the time, he concludes, two-thirds—perhaps more—is utterly unreliable as a guide to genuine traditions of witchcraft. As a result, he admitted, "it is easier to find out what is said to have occurred than what really happened" (1965: 242–43). Still, we cannot ignore the one-third that describes the genuine occult practices of the time; the trick is to discern what is real and what is the projection of crusaders' anxieties.

My second premise is that self-consciously diabolical rituals have been a common element in children's and adolescents' folk culture for a long time. This is a point often missed by modern commentators on the occult scene, who tend to define the alleged threat of witchcraft as a new threat to society. Evangelist Berit Kjos (1999), for instance, puts the threat embodied by the *Harry Potter* books in the context of a recently departed age of Christian stability:

> Unlike most children today, their parents and grandparents were raised in a culture that was, at least outwardly, based on Biblical values. Whether they were Christian or not, they usually accepted traditional moral and spiritual boundaries. Even the old fairy tales I heard as a child in Norway tended to reinforce this Christian worldview or paradigm. The good hero would win over evil forces *without* using "good" magic to overcome evil magic. Social activities didn't include Ouija Boards, Séances, and an assortment of popular occult role-playing games. Nor did friends, schools or Girl Scouts tempt children to alter their consciousness and invoke the presence of an "animal spirit" or "wise person." Occult experimentation was not an option.

But, as we will see in the middle chapters of this book, occult experimentation has been an option for children and adolescents at least since the time of the witch trials. We should not forget that the notorious panic that occurred in Salem, Massachusetts, in 1692 was focused on a group of "afflicted girls," the oldest of whom were teenagers and the youngest only eight years old. While it is now difficult to discern what specifically sparked the outbreak that made adult observers believe that these girls had been afflicted by witchcraft, contemporary records left by the Puritans allow us to identify a number of occult rituals carried out by young girls. The record of teenagers' ritual visits to uncanny sites is even more extensive, dating at least to medieval times and possibly farther. Traditions surrounding Stone Age monuments in Great Britain and Brittany repeatedly allude to customs involving trips by courageous youths to challenge the power of the supernatural. Thus we can trace a lengthy history of occult play activities like Ouija boards and séance rituals.

My final premise is that one motive for becoming interested in the occult is to participate directly in the mythic realm, in spite of organized religion's effort to institutionalize it. This is a more debatable thesis, but my previous book concluded by suggesting that "raising the devil" raises those who raise him; that is, allowing individuals access to divine beings (even diabolical ones) allows them to resolve their doubts about religious beliefs through direct experience. Hence the occult may not be an adversary of organized religion, but an alternative way of validating its dogmas. In this book, we will investigate this proposition more fully. Mircea Eliade, a leading authority of comparative religion, likewise criticized scholars who saw the earlier crusade against witchcraft as merely "a creation of religious and political persecution." The practices alleged against witches, real or imaginary, suggest for him "a radical protest against the contemporary religious and social situations." Satanic elements, he conceded, may well have been imposed by authorities onto witnesses' and defendants' testimony, but their content also indicates "a religious nostalgia" in which cultures express "a strong desire to return to an archaic phase of culture" (quoted in Ankerloo and Henningsen 1990: 191–92). If witchcraft is, as Eliade suggests, a form of protest against social and religious norms, the rebellious stages of adolescence are, psychologically, the place to expect an attraction to the occult. This is particularly true among circles of women at times when they saw the adult roles they were beginning to assume as repressive in nature.

It is clear that much occult literature is best seen as an expression of protest against religious norms. The prominent American Freemason Albert Pike often appears as a bogeyman in antioccult conspiracy theories, as the leader of a nineteenth-century satanic movement with world domination as its goal. Many of the quotes and opinions attributed to him are frankly bogus, having been fabricated by the notorious Leo Taxil as part of his "Luciferian Masonry" hoax (Medway 2001: 11–12).

Nevertheless, Pike's authentic writings included many subversive opinions that challenged institutional Christianity. His magnum opus, the *Morals and Dogma of the Ancient and Accepted Scottish Rite of Freemasonry*, repeatedly argued that "Lucifer" was not a name for the devil but an emblem of the illuminating force of reason. To the initiated, Pike says, Satan is "not a Person, but a Force, created for good, but which may serve for evil. It is the instrument of Liberty or Free Will. [The initiated] represent this Force, which presides over the physical generation, under the mythologic and horned form of the God PAN; thence came the he-goat of the Sabbat, brother of the Ancient Serpent, and the Light-bearer or Phosphor, of which the poets have made the false Lucifer of Legend" (1947: 102). Later, Pike poetically apostrophizes this principle of liberty: "LUCIFER, the Light-bearer! Strange and mysterious name to give to the Spirit of Darkness! Lucifer, the Son of the Morning! Is it he who bears the Light, and with its splendors intolerable blinds feeble, sensual, or selfish Souls? Doubt it not!" (1947: 321). Then as now, occultism may have been not so much a heresy as a protest against the way orthodox Christianity limited the common person's ability to contact and participate in divine forces.

When we move to the contemporary realm, we can see similar dynamics working. The crusade against the *Harry Potter* books makes little sense in terms of the contents of the books themselves, which define the magical craft as simply one of many academic subjects like mathematics or biology, and in any case limit such education to those who inherit a gift for sorcery. Wizardry, as taught at Hogwarts, is not defined as a rival or enemy to Christianity or any other religion: it is simply what people go to school to learn. But this in itself is a heretical idea for many fundamentalist Christians, who resent the intrusion of science into realms, such as the origins of mankind and of the universe, that previously were under the purview of myth. Attempting to rationalize the supernatural world as well as the natural world is, from this point of view, a similar attempt to replace God with blind scientific laws. The *Onion* satire, in fact, slyly referred to this resentment when it added Darwin's *The Origin of the Species* to a list of satanically inspired books that Rowling's works were encouraging young people to read.

Again, Albert Pike's genuine writings on occultism foresaw the "scientific" teaching of magic in Hogwarts. He, like the fundamentalists who demonized him, argued that supernatural phenomena were undoubtedly real, and he continued, "There is in nature one most potent force, by means whereof a single man who could possess himself of it, and should know how to direct it, could revolutionize and change the face of the world." This natural force (which he associated with the "animal magnetism" supposedly discovered by the disciples of Mesmer) was what lay behind "the elemental matter of the great work [of alchemists] . . . it was adored in the secret rites of the Sabbat or the Temple, under the hieroglyphic figure of Baphomet or the hermaphroditic goat of Mendes." Once it could be grasped by scientists, not religious specialists, then, he predicted, "it will be possible to change the order of the Seasons, to produce in night the phenomena of day, to send a thought in an instant round the world, to heal or slay at a distance, to give our words universal success, and make them reverberate everywhere" (1947: 733–34). This force is magic, he later concludes, and far from being mystical in nature, it "is that which it is; it is by itself, like the mathematics; for it is the exact and absolute science of Nature and its laws" (1947: 841).

With subversive ideas such as these at the heart of the *Harry Potter* books and also implied by many forms of occult folklore, we can well understand why many groups would find both threatening. Further, as Amanda Cockrell observes, Rowling herself portrayed the "muggles" in her books in a form that uncomfortably resembled religious antioccult extremists. The Dursleys, Harry's adoptive parents, loath magic in all its forms, refusing to even speak the word in the house, and Cockrell suggests that they are intended to be satirical portraits of those who, like religious conservatives, are convinced "that they know evil when they see it, and know it only by its difference from themselves" (2002). Indeed, the force of this satirical portrait was not lost on some antioccult crusaders, such as Berit Kjos (1999), who commented on the topsy-turvy world created by Rowling:

> Harry Potter's author does it by creating a captivating world where strength, wisdom, love, hope—all the good gifts God promises those who follow Him—are now offered to those who pursue occult thrills. Likewise, her main characters demonstrate all the admirable traits our God commends: kindness, courage, loyalty, etc. But the most conspicuous muggles (ordinary people who are blind to these mystical forces) are pictured as mean, cruel, narrow and self-indulgent. These subtle messages, hidden behind exciting stories, turn Truth upside-down. But fascinated readers rarely notice the deception. This power-filled realm with

its charms and spells soon becomes normal as well as addictive to those who immerse their minds with [*sic*] its seductive images.

In fact, Kjos observes, Harry and his friends do not actually behave in an ethical manner, but repeatedly violate the rules of their academy and carry out their plans by deceiving their teachers and prefects. A better way to describe Rowling's intent, she concludes, is to "model how to lie and steal and get away with it."

This is a fair point, even according to Rowling's own text: Harry succeeds in defeating his evil antagonist Voldemort *because* (as Professor Dumbledore freely admits) he is willing to break "a hundred school rules into pieces along the way" (1999: 328). Rowling, according to Cockrell, seems to be suggesting that defining "Truth" in terms of a static "given" revealed in one religious point of view is constricting and dangerous, potentially a greater evil than the speculative world revealed by the occult. But presenting rule-breaking wizardry as a source of spiritual strength risks stereotyping Christianity as a narrow-minded evil, Kjos seems to retort.

This is not a new dispute, as we shall see. Exploring it in an objective, evenhanded way will allow us to make sense not only of the historical record, but of the way in which this Luciferian dialectic continues to emerge in contemporary culture.

Chapter Two

𝕎hat 𝕎ere 𝕎itches 𝕽eally 𝕃ike?

This question is problematic for most readers who have grown up on popular culture images of evil witches who dress in black, ride broomsticks with black cats (their familiar spirits), and brew poisonous potions in order to prey on little children. Witches have been domesticated as Halloween decorations, alongside similar stereotypical images of vampires, goblins, and werewolves, each deriving from its own tradition of once-lively but now-extinct beliefs. Similarly, the counterculture image of the witch as priestess of a persecuted nature religion, as promoted by the Neo-Pagan movement, likewise derives from a twentieth-century stereotype imposed on the complex mixture of real tradition and conspiracy theory revealed in the records of the witch trials.

The *Harry Potter* image of witches and wizards draws from both these traditions: like the Halloween witch, Harry and his friends are trained to ride magic broomsticks and mix up potions of deadly potency. They wave wands, change shapes, communicate by means of their familiars (in this case, owls and rats), and engage in a whole range of supernatural acts. At the same time, though, Hogwarts resembles the image of the esoteric tradition promoted by Wicca. The lore taught by the professors derives from a complex of secrets generated during medieval times and passed down to a select few. True, only those who have inherited a tendency toward magic are entitled to become wizards and negotiate the loopholes in space, invisible to all muggles, that lead to Diagon Alley and Platform Nine-and-Three-Quarters, from which the train to Hogwarts departs. The magical tradition in Rowling's books is an alternative to normal life, not a rival to it.

Still, the image of "good" witches and wizards learning rituals and incantations resembles contemporary workshops on techniques and details of "the Craft" (as Wiccans refer to it). "Untold millions of young people are being taught to think, speak, and act like witches by filling their heads with the contents of these books," claims Pastor Meyer, himself a reformed astrologer and Wiccan (2000a).

The truth is that real witches thought, spoke, and acted in ways that only superficially resembled any of these stereotypes. However, to get at the reality of this tradition, as it existed (and presumably still exists) in rural contexts, we have to look critically at material collected by many persons, some more sympathetic to their informants than others. And we need to keep Julio Caro Baroja's caution in mind: probably two-thirds of the material collected about witches reflects the anxieties of the teller rather than the reality of the tradition. When we do this, however, we find that there were in fact many positive functions played by self-proclaimed witches. Even though they expressed an alternative to social and religious norms, they functioned as an integral part of village culture, disapproved by the power structure, but (in most times and places) tolerated. Still, while their rituals rivaled institutional religion, medicine, and legal systems, they did not themselves constitute institutions. The notion of witchcraft as an underground, invisible religion is misleading, as magic functioned best when it was done (for better or for worse) in plain sight of everyone concerned.

Myth, Legend, and Fetish

To look objectively at the folk traditions concerning witchcraft, we need to examine them using academic terms that define ways in which all cultures describe magic and the supernatural. To do this, we must refer to the *legends, fetishes,* and *mythologies* of folk magic. Briefly, legends and fetishes are ways of *naming* something uncanny, finding a tangible, sharable form for something that would otherwise be difficult to grasp. As we have seen, a mythology is a *system of ideas* that helps give meaning to individual traditions, much as syntax gives meaning to individual words.[1]

All three terms, however, have been widely abused in the popular press. "Legend" and "myth" have often been used vaguely to mean "something that *we* know is not true," while as early as 1889, the British scholar William Robertson Smith said that "fetish" was "merely a popular term, which conveys no precise idea, but is vaguely supposed to mean something very savage and contemptible" (quoted in Ellen 1988: 215). This attitude, however, assumes that we scholars *know* what is true or civilized, and those we study do not. But to understand witchcraft beliefs, even if we feel they are not true, we need to begin by examining why they are *credible*. We need to be careful to use these terms precisely, as a means of understanding the reasons a legend, fetish, or myth was popular, and not as a way of implicitly disparaging such beliefs as irrational. So it is important to begin by being as clear as possible about what we mean by these three terms.

What is a legend? A legend is *a story that embodies some controversial element of a culture's worldview.* Folklorists have often disagreed about whether a legend is "true" or not, or whether people "believe" it or not, but both criteria have inevitably broken down over their intrinsic subjectivity. Many such stories contain situations and details that are verifiably realistic, though the way in which they circulate tends to exaggerate other details for the sake of vividness and memorability. Still, it is impossible for folklorists to debunk every such story, and, as Patricia A. Turner (1993) has pointed out, even if a story is not factually verifiable, it may express politically realistic insights. It is also naive to assume that such stories circulate because those who pass them on "believe" them. Kenneth Pimple also warns us that "belief" is an internal mental state not directly observable to an outsider, and not always easy for the alleged "believer" to verbalize (1990: 15).

However, legends clearly do function in discourse, by initiating debate or discussion of current topics. As such, they help those who circulate and discuss them to "name" some social reality accurately and conveniently. A legend is also a way of territorializing a poorly defined cultural anxiety by "naming" it, reducing it to "tellable" (or quantifiable) form. Once such a narrative has taken shape, it gains status within the accepted belief-language of a culture, representing an allegedly unique and extraordinary historical event in reproducible language. As the legend gains power, it may itself become a social factor that influences or manipulates people's behavior.[2]

What is a fetish? The term "fetish" refers to the fabrication, acquisition, and use of a material object invested with extraordinary spiritual forces. It implies a practice that operates in a gray realm of folk religion, which comprises the beliefs and practices that operate "apart from and alongside the strictly theological and liturgical forms of the official religion" (Yoder 1974). That is, a fetish is the product of an unofficial magical or religious practice that involves making or using some power object.

Such a practice is not necessarily by design opposed to official religion, but neither is it sanctioned, and it therefore inhabits a liminal realm in the interstices of society.[3]

Like the legend, a fetish is a way of capturing a single, intensely meaningful experience within an object that can be commodified and owned. That is, the fetish is a physical object that is shaped in order that we may comprehend a spiritual or personal value that would otherwise be difficult to grasp. Thus, it, like the legend, is a way of gaining control over complex social relationships through a kind of narrative. When this happens, the fetish occupies a dialectical place in culture, functioning in terms of the culture's belief-language and at the same time offering its users an opportunity to challenge the culture's social codes.

Contemporary Descriptions of "Witches"

A number of evangelical books published during the Satanism Scare of the 1970s and 1980s gave vivid descriptions of evil witches as actively at work in the contemporary world. "Ann," a member of an urban American, man-hating coven, loved to look at construction workers out of her office window and "silently chant a spell to make [them] fall," according to Nicky Cruz (1973: 110). Another of Cruz's accounts tells how "Barbara" was found in her apartment meowing and acting like a cat. After she was removed to a mental institution, authorities found a diary in which she recorded how she had learned to change places with her pet cat by performing a sixteenth-century witchcraft rite. One night, while roaming in her cat's body, she was run over by a truck, leaving "Barbara's" body inhabited by the cat's spirit (1973: 146–47). Cruz, however, does not explain where he obtained these stories, which seem stereotypical and secondhand.

More compelling were the firsthand accounts given by Jess Pedigo, another prominent antioccult crusader of the 1970s, of how he had met many persons who had used their own blood to sign pacts offering themselves and their children to the devil. While supervising an evangelical church camp during the summer of 1970, he relates, he met two youths who confessed to selling their souls to the devil. One seventeen-year-old boy worshipped an image of Satan nightly to gain enough power to curse his enemies; another seventeen-year-old girl said she had given her body to the devil and at first insisted she could only be released by having sex with a minister (1971: 49).

Another important firsthand account is by Victor H. Ernest, who was raised in a spiritualist family in Minnesota but renounced spiritualism in 1929 to enter the Baptist ministry. His autobiography, *I Talked with Spirits* (1970), describes how during his antioccult ministry he frequently suffered baffling psychological blocks during his services, which he blamed on attacks from local witches. In 1948, he felt one such attack during a service at a Minnesota church. Ten days later he was contacted by a local woman who claimed to be a witch and who admitted that she and a friend "had turned on satanic power" during Ernest's service. The two of them met on the banks of the Mississippi River to worship Satan and pray to be chosen to bear the Antichrist. When they failed to stop Ernest's message, she attempted suicide and her friend was committed to a mental hospital. Ernest exorcised her successfully, and two weeks later she publicly renounced her magic in Ernest's church—though, the pastor reports, she had "many ensuing battles with Satan" (60–61).

We can add to these the testimony of self-confessed witches that shows up in collections of folklore compiled in the early twentieth century, though folklorists have tended to minimize their importance by treating them as the ramblings of senile women. Emelyn Gardner, who collected many traditional witch legends in upstate New York, briefly relates an encounter with a "poor, wretched, half-crazed old woman" whom rumor blamed for the murder of several family members, and who, it seems, derived a "fiendish joy . . . from relating her experience" (1937: 45–47). Ozark folklorist Vance Randolph likewise tells of interviewing three women who freely admitted that they had sold themselves to the devil for magical powers: he comments that they "were quite mad, of course" (1947: 265).

Such people might well have been "half-crazed" or "quite mad" from the establishment point of view; nevertheless, such women existed into modern times in many rural areas in the United States, and they played functional roles provided them by folklore. Even if they were psychotic, that is, they drew their delusions from a repertoire of legends and beliefs that their culture provided. "The point is," as Randolph admits, "that their neighbors did not regard them as lunatics, but as witches" (1947: 265).

Such firsthand contacts challenge the rationalist point of view, and we could try to explain them away as fabrications by the crusaders or by the alleged witch. In the first set of cases, identifying information is vague enough to make us suspect that the stories have been invented or embroidered to fit an evangelist author's purposes. But the folklorists, for their part, might well concede that *some* of these cases reflect underlying traditions that rivaled and even reacted against mainstream Christianity. Thus, we need to understand the mythological context that gave people complex motives for adopting the self-defined role of witch within such a community.

Witchcraft in Rural Folklore

First of all, we need to clarify what roles documentably existed in rural folk culture. "Witch" tends to be an exoteric term, one used to label a person that one considers blasphemous and/or spiritually dangerous. Some people accepted this term with pride; others would have considered it at best an ignorant misconception, and at worst an actionable insult. In many cases, the term "witch" was simply thrown at persons who had chosen to specialize in magical traditions of folk medicine and fortune-telling. Anne Llewellyn Barstow, in her *Witchcraze: A New History of the European Witch Hunts* (1994), notes that traditions of healing and divining were passed down predominantly by women in European cultures, and "village experts" in such crafts were at risk when a witch-hunt began. As accused witches were four times more likely to be women than men, she argues that the persecutions were often efforts to control the social power that such supernatural talents gave them. Today, supernatural experiences are experienced by both sexes evenly, according to random surveys, but are three to four times more frequently *volunteered* by women, suggesting that contact with the "irrational" is more in line with social stereotypes of women than of "rational" males. Hence an attempt to diabolize folklore would have the effect—perhaps would be intended to have the effect—of diabolizing women more often than men.

But if women were not (despite a common institutional belief) simply more prone to the supernatural than men, then their disproportionate *choice* to practice folk magic therefore implies, on some level, an individualistic protest against institutional religion. In his study of witchcraft and folk healing in rural South Germany, Hans Sebald noted that the practitioner normally defined her work in terms of orthodox church dogma, but continued: "And yet there was another element involved. She expressed the age-old individual claim on magic that asserts authority on the basis of personality and not on the basis of a formal institution, such as the Church. Insofar as she was her own magical authority, she perpetuated an element of the pre-Christian sorceress" (1978: 85–86). Interestingly, whether such magic-workers defined themselves as "white" or "black" witches, they tended to be female by a 10–1 ratio; the *Hexenmeister*, or witch-finder, whose job it was to expose and neutralize witches on behalf of society, was by contrast *always* male. Barstow also observes the explicitly pornographic nature of many charges against witches, and indeed the ways in which accused witches were examined and tortured. She suggests that these were violent efforts of a patriarchal power structure to maintain power over females.

Whether the witch-hunts were indeed a "war against women," as Barstow suggests, the historical witchcraft claims were grounded in real female-oriented folk traditions, which called the power of male-specific institutions into question. The epidemic of witch prosecutions occurred at a moment when occultism became politically threatening to institutions for many reasons, among them a redefinition of women's place in society or as part of what Robert Muchembled calls "the conquest of the West European countryside by the forces of law and order" (1990: 139). However, in the process, legal and religious authorities overinterpreted widespread and often quite consistent folk traditions, many of which remain vital in contemporary times. That is to say, most of the persons accused of and executed for participating in alleged witch conspiracies were clearly not guilty of the charges against them; but these charges (and similar ones made in our time) were credible to law enforcement agents and judges because they were made against a ground of genuine occult practices.

These traditions were certainly more complicated than authorities gave them credit for being. The widespread distinction between "black," "white," and "gray" witches is, as British folklorist Owen Davies (1998: 41) has shown, misleading and characteristic of academics' attempts to describe folk magic. In any case, most practitioners of occult crafts claimed to be doing good, while most institutional critics held that the use of magic, even to do good, was dabbling with satanism and therefore "black." For this reason, Davies argues for the more neutral term "cunning-folk," drawn from English rural folklore, to describe practitioners of folk magic. Such persons offered a variety of occult services: telling fortunes; providing charms intended to secure or keep a person's love;

detecting and punishing a thief. In some cases, they treated mysterious illnesses, either of humans or livestock, by diagnosing them as caused by witchcraft. For a fee, they would remove the spell and send it back on the person responsible.

Because the role of cunning-folk shaded over into folk medicine, priests and other institutional representatives often confused them with charmers, persons who simply had (or had inherited) a "gift" for treating a specific condition. As Davies (1998) points out, they were seen within communities as being more "ordinary" than cunning-folk: they usually specialized in treating only a single "natural" ailment such as warts or accidental burns. Thus, while cunning-folk interpreted illness as the result of witchcraft or demonic attack, charmers tended to see the cases they treated as simply an opportunity to exercise a specialized gift given them by God. However, in the eyes of many representatives of institutional Christianity, the two were equal rivals to priests in their exercise of supernatural power.

Kurt E. Koch's Catalog of Modern Witchcraft

One of the most complete records of charmers and cunning-folk made in the twentieth century came from the antioccult crusader Kurt E. Koch (1913–1987), whose influence on the Satanism Scare was detailed in my previous work (Ellis 2000). A Lutheran pastor in the German province of Baden, on the Swiss border, Koch specialized in counseling young people suffering from depression and other psychosomatic and mental illnesses. Becoming convinced that folk magic lay at the roots of many of these cases, Koch made a practice of interrogating those he counseled about the specific practices they or their parents had been involved in. Such acts, he reasoned, involved an implicit contract with the devil, which in turn left both the practitioners and their children open to demonic attack. In the course of his work, Koch compiled a huge file of cases from Germany, Switzerland, and Austria, which formed the basis for a series of influential works for antioccult counselors, including *Between Christ and Satan* (1962) and *Christian Counselling and Occultism* (1972). While Koch's books presented these as examples of satanic practices that Christian pastors ought to seek out and destroy, for folklorists his books (like analogous works from the Early Modern period of witchcraft panics) provide many detailed accounts of rural charming and folk magic.

As detailed as Koch's files are, we still cannot accurately place his cases into the context of rural Germany and Switzerland without having more information on the role occultism played in everyday life. We are thus fortunate that Hans Sebald (1978) has produced a detailed ethnography of modern witchcraft beliefs in the nearby district of Franconia. Such information is often sensitive and difficult for casual folklorists to document: the two most detailed American collections, by Randolph and Gardner, were compiled after years of cultivating friendships with informants. Sebald was born into a Franconian family with extensive experience with supernatural traditions, and when he returned to conduct his fieldwork, he found that his clan alliance with a family already reputed to be witches encouraged many informants to share their knowledge and feelings more openly.

This tradition of witchcraft beliefs, he found, was culturally functional, an insight echoed by other ethnographers. First, witchcraft is rarely distinguishable from private supernatural healing. In Franconia, as elsewhere, the witch who used evil spells was counterbalanced by the healer or spell-caster who used similar rituals for good. But "good" was usually defined in terms of clans or factions within the community, so the two roles are often difficult to distinguish. Nevertheless, Sebald found, no matter how intense antiwitch feelings grew in the area of Franconia he studied, violence never emerged. That is, the competition involved in casting spells and counterspells seems to have been a valid substitute for physical reprisals when rivalries or disputes between powerful clans surfaced. Whatever we may think about the scientific or religious implications of folk magic, then, we have to concede that on a social level malicious witchcraft was an integral, indeed an essential, part of rural culture.

Some of the incidents reported by Koch reflect story types documented in witchcraft lore for many years. Typical are accounts of the "dairy witch," which show up most often as "fabulates," compelling narratives that are long on dramatic detail and short on confirmation. Since they are similar in structure to stories found in many cultures over many centuries, folklorists have tended to assume that they survive less because they are based in historical truth than because they are good stories. Here is one of Koch's: "A farmer discovered that the milk of one of his cows had blood in it. He took the milk and just before midnight he heated it up. At the same time he thrust a sickle into it murmuring a magic spell. The next day a woman who lived nearby had some facial

injuries, and the farmer was thereby convinced that this woman had bewitched his cow" (1962: 81).[4] And here is another: "A man dabbled in
black magic for many years. He specialized in stealing milk from the
neighbouring farmers. He would tie a towel to a door knob, then mur-
mur his magic phrases and squeeze the milk out of the towel" (1962:
59).[5] Significantly, Koch adds, "I have heard of similar examples in my
counseling work but I was unable to investigate them personally." In a
later book, however, Koch was more sure of the essential truthfulness of
such anecdotes. Summarizing stories he had heard in Switzerland about
cats, he explains, "There are some powerful mediums, capable of materi-
alization, who can split off energy when in a state of trance, and transfer
this energy over to a cat which they then send out to annoy one of their
neighbors. Milk and butter can disappear. Cows can be milked dry, and
other things. If someone catches the cat and beats it, the blows affect the
medium" (1978: 147).[6] Koch comments, "I was asked years ago to publish the story of these Swiss cats. I dared not." First, he says, the stories
were irrelevant to his concern with "the pastoral aspect of the problem";
second, he feared ridicule. Nevertheless, the story was for Koch more
than a tall tale, for he mentions that he had heard three confessions from
mediums who claimed to be capable of such activities.

A number of women confessed to having even stronger powers.
One "boasted of having caused the deaths of her husband and daughter"
and, in an inversion of the usual repertoire of healers, said she could
cause "eczemas, diarrhoea, heart trouble, itching, stomach pains, swell-
ing of the body and other things." After killing off her entire family, Koch
reports, this woman, rather oddly, became a district nurse (1962: 83).
Another told Koch that she was responsible for "several murders which
the police had been unable to solve" and was working on the mental
collapse of a local minister; Koch confirmed that the man had in fact
been quite ill (1962: 78–79).

Before entering counseling, Koch felt that blood pacts—written
contracts selling one's soul to Satan for a specific sum of money—were
legends from the medieval past. But, when he entered counseling, he
found the phenomenon widespread in rural Germany, and dealt with
over a hundred cases. In one instance, he describes a woman who came
to him after an evangelistic meeting and confessed having subscribed
herself to the devil in her own blood to gain mediumistic powers. "She
belonged to a spiritistic circle with a membership of 15 people who consciously used to summon the devil to appear," Koch relates. "Each time

this happened a horrible figure manifested itself, and the members then indulged in an orgy." Koch referred the woman to a prayer group and a group of Christian psychiatrists, but also comments that blood subscriptions were very difficult to heal: in only two cases in his experience had such persons been delivered (1970: 25–27).

In Toggenburg, Koch relates, several persons confessed to having the power to kill livestock (1962: 60). He offers a lengthy account of one such person who admitted to two different ministers that he had used sorcery to kill thirty-two of his neighbors' pigs because he was annoyed at the noise their children made. The story calls to mind many literary accounts of sorcerers like the legendary Doctor Faust: after studying books of magic, this sorcerer confessed, he went to a crossroads on a Friday night and there drew up a contract with the devil, who appeared as "a black curly headed figure with blood-red eyes and a small snout . . . dressed in rather old-fashioned clothes." Despite the literary trappings of this story, however, Koch confirmed it by speaking with the two ministers, the victimized farmer, and the veterinarian, who produced a certificate from the Biological Institute in Zurich saying that no natural cause of death could be determined for the animals (1962: 136–38).

Members of such devil cults were capable of horrifying crimes against children, as well, and by 1978 Koch offered this allegedly authentic case in point: "A young couple was asked by an American family to come and baby-sit. When the parents came home, they found that the young couple, who belonged to a satanic cult, had roasted the baby on a gridiron. The horrified parents had entrusted their child to two 'young devils'" (1978: 198). This final story is recognizable to folklorists as a variant of the widely distributed "Hippie Babysitter," who, high on drugs, gets the instructions for cooking the *turkey* and putting the *baby* to bed confused (see Brunvard 1981: 65–69, 72–73). Variations on this story have been found not only in European, but Latin American and African cultures, as well, never in a verifiable form.

Koch presented these stories with names and identifying details omitted, insisting on the secrecy both of the confessional and of the doctor/patient relationship. Nevertheless, he stressed that such narratives were true to the stories presented to him and consistent with many others related to him by fellow pastors and counselors. On the other hand, the rationalist is committed to disregarding *all* these accounts as hearsay or hysteria. Can folklore provide a reasoned middle ground for sifting this body of evidence?

Folkloristic Approaches to Witchcraft Claims

We can identify several more specific social functions for circulating legends about evil witchcraft in communities with strong supernatural healing and witch-finding traditions.

1. Witchcraft legends may "name" experiences for which institutions do not provide convenient language.
2. Witchcraft beliefs could provide a socially acceptable way to scapegoat cultural Others.
3. Conversely, witchcraft practices could provide such marginalized persons with ways to vent their own social aggression.
4. Witchcraft legends may demonize folk traditions, such as magical healing, that challenge institutions.
5. Witchcraft legends may validate the practices of witch masters and their modern equivalents.

Thus we have a field of reference in which "real" satanism stories can be located. On the one hand, accounts of real witches' activities may act as legends, which are often stories told to make a social point but not intended to convey a directly verifiable event. On the other, we may be looking at ostensive legend-telling—that is, storytelling as a purposive action founded on existing legends. By adopting the roles of legendary witches and satanists, a certain number of occult "experts" may have gained and held considerable status in their communities. We might add that, if these experts later chose to convert to mainstream religion, their old status as witches might well have carried over into their new roles as witch-finders. Let us return to Koch's valuable corpus of witchcraft narratives and integrate it more fully into the folklore record from Europe and America, according to our five-fold field of reference.

1) Witchcraft legends may "name" experiences for which institutions do not provide convenient language. Direct experience of the supernatural is often associated with "credulous" individuals or cultures that accept "irrational" beliefs and then project them into reality. But, in fact, events that are perceived as paranormal apparently occur more frequently than one might expect, even in the absence of an explaining folk tradition. A 1973 survey of the National Opinion Research Center found that 58 percent of the American population had experiences that they characterized as paranormal, ranging from precognition to communication with the dead. Fully 24 percent reported several such events, and 8 percent said they occurred "often" (Greeley 1975). Similarly, in 1991, the Roper Organization polled Americans on "unusual personal experiences": 55 percent reported at least one anomalous experience; 5 percent reported four or more (Hopkins et al. 1992).

Neither poll found any connection between high rates of supernatural contact and psychological problems, while both suggested that the "psychic" sector of the population was more politically active and less likely to be prone to racism than the "normal" sector. Interestingly, surveys based on information *volunteered* by informants show that women come forward with such accounts three times more often than men. But those based on a randomly chosen population report no significant difference between men's and women's paranormal experiences.

The stubborn prevalence of the supernatural in the face of a rationalistic point of view that denies its credibility suggests that anomalous experiences are a given in cultures of whatever kind. It follows that legends do not *create* such experiences, but provide convenient language to help cultures *express* them. Thus, the concepts communicated by legends are not only givens in such cultures, they are necessities.

In an important case study, folklorist David Hufford found that about 20 percent of individuals in several cultures had experienced some form of "the Old Hag," a paralysis attack that includes perception of some evil supernatural intruder. Informants in Newfoundland regarded such an event with little concern, because the event had a name and carried with it a variety of folk magical practices designed to avert any recurrence. But victims in the United States, where a folk term was much less common, were more likely to be traumatized by the event and to keep silent for fear of being ridiculed or termed mentally ill. Hufford comments:

> When one has an experience and is aware that others have had a similar experience, that knowledge is generally accompanied by the availability of words and phrases understood to describe the experience or some of its aspects. . . . Such language allows a great many complex operations and experiences to be indicated quickly and conveniently. The same is true with experiences that are considered supernatural. . . . Not only does general knowledge allow for convenient language, but the presence of convenient

language indicates the presence of a consensus, which in most cases provides assurance that one's experience is not somehow monstrous. (1982: 51–52)

Hufford subsequently found "hagging," under a variety of names, in many widely distributed reports of witchcraft throughout the world. Sebald found it as "*Hexendrüken*" (being smothered by a witch), one of the most widely known witchcraft experiences in Franconia. Many of the accounts he cites allude to the fact that the phenomenon ends as soon as the victims move any part of their bodies. One advises throwing a pillow on the floor to make the witch sit on it instead; another suggests trying to grab hold of the entity sitting on one's chest, in order to learn the witch's identity (1978: 66).[7]

Allusions to this phenomenon are common in early anticult crusaders' writings. Koch's childhood experience may be a variation on the Old Hag, and he gives a clear description of it while recounting his later evangelical work in Canada. A believer in Saskatoon, he says, "saw in the night a figure coming towards her. She was crippled and could not move. The black figure reached out towards her. Then from the other side came another hand and pushed the black figure away with the words: 'She is my child.' This brought the attack by the powers of darkness to an end, and Mrs. B. could again pray and move her body" (1973b: 81). His mentor, Alfred Lechler, likewise describes a case, successfully treated by exorcism, in which a woman "sometimes heard footsteps coming up to her bed and had the feeling that a figure was approaching her trying to squeeze her throat or put its hands on her chest" (Koch and Lechler 1970: 180).[8] In such cases, the concept of witchcraft brought a common but unpredictable and terrifying experience within the ken of social experience. Unlike the rationalist-dominated United States, members of such communities could both talk about the event and take decisive action to ward it off in the future. Failing that, tradition provided ways of interpreting the next occurrence in a way that assured the victim that the "hagging" could be brought to an end and the person responsible identified and supernaturally punished.

2) *Witchcraft beliefs could provide a socially acceptable way to scapegoat cultural Others.* A similar dynamic motivated legends that focused on some kind of physical ailment that resisted treatment or otherwise seemed part of an unexplained pattern. A variety of sicknesses, both in animals and infants, were explained in terms of witchcraft, and one com-

mon element in treatment was identification of a person who might have cast the spell. Often, the person was said to be identifiable as the next person to call, or to ask to borrow something. Often, identifying the source of the hex was all that was necessary to dispel it; in other cases, a counterspell was recommended; in still others, the counterspell itself served to identify the guilty party. One complex of legends mentioned by Koch identifies the regular violent crying of babies at set times during the night as the result of a hex. Whatever the remedy, the crucial element is the exposure of a person as an evil agent.

One woman who came to Koch for pastoral counseling complained of persistent melancholy and added that her child had a similar affliction. "At night the child would cry out at exactly 12 P.M. At 1 A.M. the voice of the mother-in-law, living fifty miles away would be heard saying 'Quiet!' Immediately the child would be silent." This mother-in-law, the woman added, owned the grimoire *The Sixth and Seventh Books of Moses*, and Koch comments that, in his experience, such incidences of "remote influence" almost always appear linked with persons who have this volume (1972: 148–49).

In a more elaborate incident, Koch tells of a mother, desperate because her child cried every night between 11 P.M. and 1 A.M., went to a charmer and was told to place a knife, fork, and scissors under the child's pillow. The witch responsible, she was told, would thus injure herself on the next visit. "The next day the maid had a bandage on, and the mother was convinced that she had been the cause of the nightly disturbances" (1962: 81). A similar phenomenon and explanation was offered by Pat Brooks, an American pioneer in the antioccult movement. She describes how her youngest son, Billy, would wake up screaming in terror at 2:45 A.M. every morning, a regular event that they had been unable to stop with prayer. A friend "who understood spiritual warfare" suggested that such a pattern "was the result of occult bondage somewhere in the family line." After the friend led the Brookses in a prayer breaking demonic influence caused by relatives, the child's nightmares stopped and never recurred (Brooks 1972: 75–76; 1978: 32–33).[9] Such cases are paralleled by a contemporary folk narrative from northern Germany, in which a baby regularly began screaming at 11:00 P.M. The family suspected a neighbor thought to be a witch, and one of them slipped up to her window at exactly eleven "and allegedly witnessed the woman spanking the bare bottom of a doll to transfer the pain to the child" (Sebald 1978: 67).

We could also see the situation as a way of displacing anxiety over the child's problem (which in the case of children experiencing colic may in fact *be* the source of the ailment). Once the focus of the problem is the accused witch and not the child, the infant's ability to sleep nights may well be restored. But the more crucial point here, as Sebald comments, is that witchcraft is never *random*: the agents were intimate neighbors or relatives and the motives were well-known quarrels and envy. Such an approach defines the mysterious ailment in terms of understandable family and community conflicts.

The aggrieved parties may respond with supernatural or social sanctions. If they have contact with a sympathetic healer (or even, as we will see, a self-identified rival witch), they may respond with a counterspell. This does not counteract the effects of the first hex, but if the healer or witch is powerful enough it may harm the witch to the extent that she may be persuaded to withdraw the effects of her own spell (Sebald 1978: 83–84). Alternatively, the family may simply refuse to have anything to do with the suspected party or denounce her to the community as a witch. Sebald notes, however, that such an act might be grounds for a slander lawsuit, so more often the response takes the form of covert counteractions.

In fact, some members of the community, well aware that they are not on good terms, may act in accordance with the tradition when their neighbors define them as witches. For example, one Pennsylvania resident told folklorist Richard Shaner that, when her infant refused to eat for no reason, she consulted a local expert who identified "Aunt Annie" as the witch responsible. He advised the mother to make a circle of salt around the house and wait for Annie to make her usual rounds selling produce. As soon as the woman reached the trail of salt, the story goes, "without any ado—Annie turned around and never returned again. The following day the child regained its appetite" (1972: 40). Seen from within the tradition, the experience confirmed the definition of Aunt Annie as a witch; but, since the test involved leaving a visible and well-known sign, Annie might have sensibly taken the ring of salt as a notice that her visits were no longer welcome.

A similar hint was given unwelcome visitors in the Ozarks, according to Randolph. "When a witch comes into the house, raw onions that have been cut up and peeled are supposed to sour instantly and become poisonous. I have seen a housewife, when another woman entered the room, ostentatiously remove some raw onions from the table and throw them out into the yard. In this case the housewife did not really believe that the visitor was a witch, but she wanted to *behave* as if she believed it" (1947: 282).

Witchcraft legends are particularly apt to express aggression, as Sebald notes, when familial or community norms normally restrict one's freedom to express overt hostility. Envy of someone's better fortune, for instance, was not normally acceptable, but accusations of witchcraft could become "an expressive guise for getting back at the envied person, perhaps the only feasible way to express animosity and inflict punishment" (1978: 188).

This was apparently true in historical witch-hunts, such as the notorious Salem witch craze. While some of the persons implicated may have dabbled in the witchcraft beliefs of the time, detailed research into legal records from the years preceding the panic showed that most participants had in fact quarreled before over such mundane topics as taxes, boundary lines, and inheritances. More detailed studies of historical witch-hunts might well discover a background of clans or factions whose relationships had grown dangerously sour even before a witchcraft claim crystallized these suspicions.

3) Conversely, witchcraft practices could provide such marginalized persons with ways to vent their own social aggression. The presence of openly "confessing witches" in many communities suggest that a certain number of people encouraged others to see them as evil witches and enjoyed the notoriety they thus received. Victor C. Dieffenbach of Bethel, Pennsylvania, recalled one nearby healer who encouraged people to believe that he had the sinister "Dairy Witch" powers. "He always said that he could go to the towel hanging on the wall in their kitchen and there at the corners of the towel, he could milk any and every cow in the entire township. He would take the corners of the towel as though they were a cow's teats; but whenever we kids would gather there to hear him discourse on such matters, and asked him to demonstrate, he said he was too tired—it was the wrong sign of the Zodiac, etc., etc." (1976: 37). The brother of "Old Miz Akers," a reputed witch who lived in Kanawha County, West Virginia, was less bashful about his demonstrations:

Old Miz Akers, she had three cows, she wouldn't give her brother no milk.
He said, "Come in, John." Dad, he went in, see what he wanted. He set there and they was eating dinner.

Said "John," said, "You like milk?"

He said, "Yeah, I like milk."

Well he said, "I'll just milk some." He retch over and got a hold of an old hand towel a-hanging agin the wall and said he gave that hand towel a few squirts and he said the milk just flew out of there just like milking it out of a cow.

He said, "John," said, "That's good milk."

[John] Said, "That's a dirty towel."

He said, "Wait a minute," he said, "I'll milk you some clean milk," and said, "I want you to taste it, see if it ain't milk."

Said he retch over and got an old dry rolling pin a-laying there, and said, he just took a hold of it, that little old rolling pin, and commenced squeezing that rolling pin, and he said that milk flew out of the rolling pin, and Dad said, "I tasted it," and he said that was just warm sweet milk like you suck right out of a cow. (Milspaw 1978: 78–79)

Since the story is secondhand, it is impossible to verify exactly what happened here. Similarly, Koch's story about the German black magician who stole milk by milking a towel tied to a doorknob just might be based on a real event. But the dynamics of the event suggest that the milking was intended as an ostensive performance in a semi-humorous vein, "witchcraft" of a legendary sort being used to poke fun at a woman who was reputed to do dairy witchcraft of a more serious type. Certainly, the invitation to taste the liquid being produced to "see if it ain't milk" implies that both performer and audience were considering the event a stage trick of a high order. Certainly, the conclusion of the story bears this out: the witness does indeed taste the milk and chooses not to take action against the milker, which would be unlikely if John genuinely believed the man to be a potentially dangerous witch.

Other kinds of signs—probably similar illusions or stage tricks—are described in memorates about reputed witches. Richard Shaner's Aunt Annie, who lived in a rural area near Kutztown, actively participated in many local witchcraft beliefs. When a neighbor visited and stayed too long, she showed her impatience by making the iron plates on top of her stove "pop high into the air," reportedly by magic (1972: 40). In much the same way, the cunning-folk George Pickingill, who gave himself out to be the "Master of Witches" in a small Essex town, discouraged visitors by opening the door a crack to show everything in the room behind

moving, apparently by magic. "The clock and ornaments might be solemnly dancing on the mantelpiece," a visitor reported, "chairs and table
waltzed elegantly together and this would continue until the Master had
had enough of it when, with one gesture, he would bring the mad masque
to an abrupt halt" (Maple 1964: 173–74). Old Miz Akers likewise had a
trick to get unwelcome visitors out quickly:

> One time your great-grandpa was going through the hills,
> stopped into a house to warm, and he stopped at the old lady
> Akers' house, asked her about warming.
>   And [she] said, "Yeah," said, "Come on in."
>   Said, just had a little bit of old fire in there, said not enough
> to even get warm by.
>   I said, he asked her for a drink of water.
>   Said, "Yeah," said, "Right there sets a bucket of water."
>   Said, a bucket of water setting there on a little stand. He took
> him a tin of water, and drunk that water.
>   And said he was a standing up close to the fire, and he said,
> she said to step back a little bit, said, "I'll show you something."
>   Said she dipped out a tinful of water out of that bucket
> where he just drank out of, throwed it on that fire, and he said it
> just flashed up like gasoline. Boy, he said, right then, said, "I
> moved out of that house," said, "I was afraid of her. I left."
> (Milspaw 1978: 77)

What motivated women (and a lesser number of men) to take on
such roles in rural cultures? First, women in marginal situations might
have taken on the aura of supernatural threat as a form of self-defense.
Historians of the witch-hunts have noted that many targets of accusations were beggars or paupers, scraping out a bare existence on the fringes
of rural communities. Aunt Annie, crippled early in life, hobbled around
the countryside with the help of a cane, selling produce door-to-door on
foot. To protect herself from thieves, she carried both a revolver and a
magical amulet. Thus, one motive for taking on the persona of a "witch"
might be to deter potential robbers. Folklorist Yvonne J. Milspaw makes
a similar comment on West Virginia witches, whom she found to be old,
poor, unmarried, and cast out by male blood relatives who normally
would take on the job of protecting and caring for them. Such women
may appropriate the witch's legendary ability to punish with magic those

who try to harm or cheat her. Such an act, Milspaw notes, appropriates "a traditional male role in Appalachia" (1978: 82).

A second reason might be as a form of social self-defense. The threat of a supernatural reprisal for an insult or slight might have ensured respect and inclusion in functions from which a scapegoated person would otherwise be excluded. The Rev. John R. Crosby gave a detailed description of Marie Kountzik, one such marginal figure in Western Pennsylvania. An adherent of the Thondrakian sect, a splinter Armenian Orthodox denomination, she was assumed to have made a pact with the devil, like all her female ancestors. Rather than challenging this prejudice or withdrawing from society, Kountzik encouraged this belief by calling herself "the Black Witch," and keeping black cats and a raven, which she allowed were her familiars.

Rev. Crosby tells how, offended at not being invited to a christening ceremony, Kountzik stormed into the ceremony with her familiars, snatched the baby's cap, and announced that she would cast a spell that would make the child "wither away." Called in for help, Rev. Crosby tactfully found a way to break the spell without offending either side. He began by improvising an amulet and encouraging the parents to continue to nourish the child, then convinced Kountzik to participate in a counter-ceremony. "At my suggestion, the old lady burned the cap she had taken from the child and I compelled her to drink the ashes in a cup of blessed salt and water." The ceremony "greatly impressed the community," Rev. Crosby noted, "and appears to have had an excellent effect in moderating the activities of the enchantress." But the pastor's participation in this ceremony probably *added* status to Kountzik's role as witch.

He also records that the community believed that an enemy could be injured by stealing a piece of clothing, performing a ceremony over it, then taking it to "the Black Witch" for safekeeping. "This custom seems to be extremely popular," Rev. Crosby observed, "and . . . as the enchantress's hut resembles a clothing store . . . I suppose there must be some results to justify the continued faith" (1927: 304–7).

It is not said whether Ms. Kountzik charged a fee for her participation in the curse. But the custodians of the infamous "cursing well" in Wales maintained a parallel tradition up to the end of the nineteenth century, and were said to earn nearly £300 a year from the fees charged. A person wishing to place a curse on a neighbor wrote the victim's name on a piece of slate and placed this in the well while the custodian read "Biblical passages." The well's owner could also arrange to have one's name removed from the well, though the fee charged was somewhat larger (Bord and Bord 1986: 84–86).

We can thus add a third and perhaps most important reason for adopting the role of a witch. While such people were feared by the rest of the community, even in modern times they were also quietly encouraged, even admired by those who understood the tradition. Milspaw observes that two Appalachian witches actively implied through comments and ostensive tricks that they had made a pact with the powers of darkness. "The implication here is that the women are in control. They are manipulating the society." But this relationship is complex and reciprocal, she also notes, with some surprise:

> The community is apparently affecting their behavior not by attempting to maintain the status quo, but by providing them with a culturally patterned role to follow. This thematic content is curious; it is not what we are supposed to find. . . .
>
> In Appalachia, at least, there is an awareness, apparent in the narratives, that witchcraft belief was used by people—particularly old, eccentric, unprotected (i.e. without kin) women—to manipulate the community around them. . . . Existing beside this awareness there is a lack of any real malevolence directed toward the witches. Rather there appears to be a somewhat grudging admiration extended toward the cleverness and self-reliance of these otherwise misfit people. (1978: 82–83)

Such individuals were also patronized by those members of the community who felt that a witch was more useful than a healer in carrying out certain requests. This was demonstrated when Richard Shaner arranged an exhibit for the 1961 Kutztown Folk Festival, in which he described his family's involvement in witchcraft: at once he was approached by several dozen people who wanted to make use of his powers. Of these, several wished to borrow his copy of the grimoire, *The Sixth and Seventh Books of Moses* (to be discussed later in detail), so that they could rid themselves of problems caused by neighbors or in-laws with the help of an evil spell (1961).

This function of witchcraft precisely complements the previous one: if an otherwise suppressed social grudge could sometimes surface *implicitly* in the form of a witchcraft charge, then the same kinds of grudges could be mediated *explicitly* by an individual who was not afraid to take on the responsibility of handling such matters. Just as healers specialized in ailments with a strong psychosomatic element and did not attempt to cure every disease, so, too, the scope of the witch's activity was limited by tradition. Her specialty largely lay in handling negative interpersonal affairs, such as exposing thieves and exacting supernatural revenge for real or perceived slights. We might therefore see the real witch as embodying a complex role whose functions mediated religious, medical, and legal responsibilities in precisely those situations in which families or small towns preferred not to call in institutional help. In short, the witch was feared, but resorting to her may have been seen as a valid alternative to calling in a priest, medical doctor, or sheriff, whose institutional solutions might have been seen as still more threatening to the traditional norms of a rural community.

4) Witchcraft legends may demonize folk traditions, such as magical healing, that challenge institutions. Thus, we could see self-identified witches as to some degree a necessary evil, supported by communities as a reaction to institutional norms that were being imposed from outside. The efficacy of witchcraft, after all, mirrored and justified that of the "good" healer.

But for Koch, like many representatives of institutional religion, the cunning-folk were also a diabolical threat to the community. Even though they nominally supported institutional norms, the fact that they, like the witch, used magical powers derived from individual, not official, sources, made them an even more insidious danger to the Church. Alongside his self-identified witches, Koch gives equal attention to the healers he had contacted, and notes that their powers were communicated as family secrets. One Bukowina woman described a family corpus of charms, all characterized as "white" magic and signified as such by ending in the Three Highest Names, or the Trinity. These "could heal any type of disease in both animals and human beings" and had been passed down within the family for several generations. Koch expresses surprise that this tradition of folk magic expertise was preserved "in spite of a family tradition of church-going" (1962: 73).

Not that Koch felt that miraculous healing was intrinsically wrong: from the beginning of his pastorate he himself practiced a ritual derived from James 5:14 ff. that involved group prayer and anointing with oil (Ensign and Howe 1984: 10; cf. Reimensnyder 1989: 6). But, like many previous ordained ministers, he was concerned by the extent to which Scripture and holy names were combined with overtly pagan deities and practices. In departing from biblical and liturgical precedents, such beliefs fell into a gray area, not overtly diabolical but no longer clearly Christian. He records several elaborate rituals prescribed by village cunning-folk, such as this one: "A farmer's son suffered repeatedly from a severe pain in his knee. He took the advice of a magic charmer and carried out the following procedure. On a night when the moon was on the wane he went out into a field. He then invoked the Trinity, repeated a magic charm, anointed his knee with oil and finally threw kisses at the moon. Afterwards the pains left him!" (1962: 85–86).[10] The hint at moon-worship in this rite suggested a linkage of pagan goddesses with the Trinity, a thought that horrified the doctrinaire Koch.

Several cases Koch encountered suggested that healing was not as benign as it seemed. One nurse told Koch how she was attending a woman suffering from ulcers and shingles, when the woman called her over and asked her for help. "I want you to put your hands on the places on my body which are diseased," the woman told the nurse. "Then I want you to make three crosses over them, and to mention the names of the Trinity together with a little verse that I will tell you." Although frightened, the nurse complied, and the patient was completely well within five days. However, in a denouement that Koch came to expect, the nurse was unsettled by participating in this form of magic, found herself dizzy and unable to pray, and eventually went to the minister for counseling—a victim, in his eyes, of demon-oppression (1962: 74–75). Hence, Koch concluded, much of alleged "white" charming was actually witchcraft in a thinly disguised form.

Koch was hardly breaking new ground in attacking "white" magic of this sort. Clerical comments on cunning-folk's activities similarly characterized them as, at best, a sign of ignorance. William E. Raber, a Pennsylvania minister, wrote in 1855, "Wording it over people belongs to Paganism, from whence it came, and is unworthy of an enlightened, leaving out of the question, a Christian community." He asked, "To cure by words and manipulations would be performing a miracle, and where would that supernatural power come from?" To assume that God would give a common person such powers, he concluded, was "too much for any sane man, woman, or even child of common understanding, to believe. Satan is in the whole matter" (quoted in Yoder 1965/66: 45, 47). Rev. Daniel Weiser added in 1868 "that great ignorance and implicit confidence in [magical charming] are mostly associated in one and the same person. We never yet found a single educated mind, and not unbalanced, given to its miserable follies." Like Raber, he added that not only did participants often become wicked, or at least indifferent toward sacred duties, but frequently they became physically "hideous and repulsive," in the well-known stereotype of the hag (1954: 14).

Barbara Reimensnyder, in studying folk healing in a Pennsylvania rural area, found that most residents had at least been told that such power came from the devil, but few credited it, except in cases in which the healer was also notorious for swearing and other sins (1989: 21–22). Still, the practice carried with it the taint of witchcraft, and still generated some degree of fear. One source admitted, "People are afraid of their power. Wouldn't you be afraid if you touched someone and they were healed?" (1989: 18). So, even in communities where folk magic was accepted as functional, it was usually seen as ambiguous, and narratives emerged that suggested that the same person who promised to heal could and often did use the same powers to harm.

A second aspect of the rural healing tradition that made many uneasy was the secretive way in which it was handed down. Most reports note that charms had to be passed down face-to-face, often under strictly observed rules. In some cases, males could only teach females and vice versa; in other cases, the person taught had to be a family member, or, in still others, *not* a blood relative. In most instances, healers could pass a charm on to only one person, or at most three, before losing the "gift" themselves. Hence, healers would wait as long as possible before relinquishing a charm, but would be anxious to find a successor if they believed death to be near. Folklorists like Barbara Reimensnyder see such rules as built-in checks on the social power involved in a charm, which one person, family, or sex might otherwise attempt to monopolize.

Koch, however, saw this tradition as a diabolical parody of the apostolic succession of ordained priests, and argued that even if the charming tradition was nominally good, children still might suffer in time from their parents' occult dealings. He followed a widespread anti-cunning-folk belief that those holding such charms could *not* die peacefully until they had passed on their magical abilities to their eldest son or daughter. If such children do not accept this responsibility, he said, the charmer's death "can drag on over a period of weeks till the office of 'succession' has been settled" (1962: 62–63). Alternatively, the witch may die in horrible agony: "A minister told me of the way someone in his parish had died. The man in question had the reputation of being a magician. Two weeks before his death, as he lay in bed seriously ill, he began to groan,

'Take the charm away from me, take the charm away from me.' The relatives had gone to the minister for advice, but he had warned them against doing as the man requested. The magician finally died in terrible agony. The minister told me that the man looked as black as coal when he had seen him in the coffin" (1962: 88).

Again, Koch was following folk tradition, in which the normal orderly apprenticeship through which white-magic charms were passed on was mirrored by a black-magic inversion. An English fabulate describes a blacksmith who, having sold his soul to the devil, could not die until he gave his powers to a successor. As he spoke, the legend says, "his imps, all white mice, solemnly marched up the bedspread and sat in a row facing him." In due time, his daughter agreed to accept the imps, and the man died, satisfied that she "had inherited the powers of a witch" (Maple 1964: 176). Such beliefs were taken seriously enough, Richard Shaner notes, that when his Aunt Annie fell fatally ill in 1960, rumor was so strong that she had evil powers that, when she beckoned family members to come close to her bed, they refused. "Fearing that she wished to pass on her 'powers' to one of them, her bedroom door was closed and she died in solitude" (1972: 41).

5) Witchcraft legends may validate the practices of witch masters and their modern equivalents. In the above cultures, as in others supporting witchcraft beliefs, the self-identified witches complemented self-identified healers. The two, in fact, were often difficult to distinguish, since a variety of misfortunes, ranging from personal illness to accident, could be the result of evil spells cast intentionally or unintentionally by neighbors. For this reason, one common role of the cunning-folk was to determine whether or not such problems were the result of an evil spell and to perform the appropriate counterspell. Since this was a form of interpersonal revenge, it was thus a form of harmful witchcraft. As Sebald found it expressed, the power to heal implied the potential power to harm,[11] and since a private pact with the devil could be concluded at any moment, it was practically impossible to distinguish the healer from the witch.

Such a state of affairs was another necessary evil that the Franconian villagers were, on the whole, content to endure. But a certain number found it more appropriate to reject the whole folk tradition and expose rather than challenge witches. This brought about the rise of a certain number of "*Hexenmeistern,*" or "witch masters," who specialized in detecting and accusing individuals of such practices. Such a figure was often itinerant, had a rich but flexible knowledge of "signs" of witchcraft, and used cautionary legends to illustrate both the potential danger of hexes and the ease with which they could be removed if you had the right knowledge. Significantly, Sebald found, while the dualistic witchcraft/healing tradition was dominated by women, the witch master was almost always male. We could see this as a reaction to the implied matriarchy of folk magic, a grassroots patriarchal effort to efface the tradition or at least to ground it more fully in the male authority of the priest and legal authorities.

Many of the stories collected by Koch, since they were contributed by fellow ministers with antioccult interests, could be compared with the cautionary stories of male "witch masters." One of Koch's "Dairy Witch" narratives, for instance, is paralleled by an Ozark legend collected by Randolph (1947: 296).

> Old Granny Bryant, of Reeds Spring, Missouri, used to tell of a family whose cow suddenly began to give bloody milk. they talked the matter over and called in a witch doctor. "Put some of that bloody milk in a fryin' pan," said he, "an' bile it over a slow fire. While the milk's a-bilin', beat on the bottom of the pan with a hickory stick." These instructions were carried out, and people who went to the local witch's cabin said that her back and buttocks were a mass of bruises, so sore that she could not walk for several days. The spell was dissipated, and the cow gave no more bloody milk.

Another anecdote, attached to a woman rumored to be the antagonist of "Cunning Murrell," a famous Essex witch master, had it that the witch's son arrived just after her death, took the box containing her imp, and burned it, saying, "The power has been destroyed. At last I'm free" (Maple 1964: 168–69). This story contains a significant change in gender from the one above, implying that a male heir could theoretically free himself from the powers of a female ancestor, but a daughter could only agree to carry on the evil tradition.

The witch master himself, because he challenged both sides of this oral tradition, had to contend with considerable opposition from communities. Even during the British witch-hunts, the "witch finder" Matthew Hopkins was forced to publish a pamphlet defending his methods, during which he repeats many of the charges raised against him. Many suspected him of inflating the numbers of practicing witches, since he was paid a fixed sum for each witch he exposed. But others argued that, even if his identifications were accurate, the only way he could succeed was by having concluded his own cynical bargain with the devil for the power of recognizing witches. Thus, the witch master had to compile a convincing case, since he had to satisfy both the rationalist and the believer in witchcraft. It therefore follows that the witch master, alone of the roles we have surveyed, would resort to print both as a means of argument and a vehicle for pursuing his efforts.

how Do We Assess Witchcraft Reports?

This brings us back to the dilemma we faced earlier. When we survey print sources for witchcraft, we are operating in the world of the witch master, who had powerful reasons to choose and shape his materials to justify his dubious function: to combat witchcraft in the name of God and reason.

Koch, in counseling his parishioners, demanded that they renounce all forms of charming and folk magic. When his patient could not recall any occult activity, he sought the source of illness in an older *female* relative. In one case of a suicidal Bible school student, he confidently diagnosed the problem as resulting from the family's occult involvement. When he challenged the student to check, Koch relates, "A single phone call was sufficient. His grandmother admitted that the family had indeed practised certain forms of occultism in the past." With this knowledge, Koch was able to carry out the Christian ritual necessary to deliver the student from his demonic burden (Koch and Lechler 1970: 104).

We are left to reconstruct, with the help of scattered archival and ethnographic surveys, the actual culture behind the crusaders' reports of "real" satanism, and to do so with care, since even in oral tradition we may have a plurality of reasons for telling about witchcraft. For instance, we have Randolph's famous account of a rural witchcraft "coven's" initiation rites, which has since been circulated by Neo-Pagans as evidence that their rites are in fact direct survivals of the underground religion inferred by Murray.

When a woman decides to become a witch, according to the fireside legends, she repairs to the family buryin' ground at midnight, in the dark of the moon. Beginning with a verbal renunciation of the Christian religion, she swears to give herself body and soul to the Devil. She removes every stitch of clothing, which she hangs on an infidel's tombstone, and delivers her body immediately to the Devil's representative—that is, to the man who is inducting her into the "mystery." The sexual act completed, both parties repeat certain old sayin's—terrible words which assemble devils, and the spirits of the evil dead—and end by reciting the Lord's Prayer backward.

The ceremony, according to Randolph, is witnessed by two other nude initiates and is repeated on three consecutive nights. Such an account sounds suspiciously like the erotic fantasies favored by historical witch-finders, which Barstow argues derive from a patriarchal fantasy intended to reduce the roles of witch and healer to that of whore. Yet Randolph concludes, "I am told by women who *claim to have experienced both,* that the witch's initiation is a much more moving spiritual crisis than that which the Christians call conversion" (1947: 267–68; emphasis added).

Does this last comment refer to the ceremony described before? If so, why is the authority for that account given as "fireside legends," not the admitted witches' testimony? Or did Randolph assume that the witches who claimed to have undergone such an initiation were "quite mad, of course"? Using our five-part folklore paradigm, we could suggest that the truth lies somewhere in a field of reference that included witchcraft as a living and functional tradition.

1) Randolph's sources might have been referring to a form of the "Hag" event that involves an erotic or sexual experience. The "incubus" form of sleep paralysis has been widely found and well documented. Likewise, women who contact spirits through Ouija boards or automatic writing have suffered frightening aftereffects that are empirically experienced as intercourse with a demon. Such an event might well have a more profound effect on the victim than institutionally channeled religious feelings.

2) The story might have been circulated by institutional authorities as a "horror story," discouraging youngsters from graveyard rites like those we will discuss in chapter 5. By diabolizing the way in which folk magic traditions were in fact passed on in the Ozarks, the story suggests that all such rites were essentially erotic/satanic in nature. (The "infidel's

gravestone," in particular, sounds like a detail added by a fundamentalist Christian source.)

3) Granting the above, individuals displeased with the repressive role of the area's fundamentalist religion may well have chosen to participate in diabolical activities as a form of social protest. These activities might include a graveyard ritual patterned along the lines of the "forbidden" ritual. Antiwitch propaganda might have brought such a "coven" into existence. That is, official Christianity, by continuing to warn people against practicing witchcraft, may have served unintentionally as the conduit preserving the details of such practice over the years.

4) Or the story may have been a way of diabolizing a living tradition of fertility customs that involved nudity and ritual intercourse. A few years later, Randolph published accounts of women who banned witches by running three times around a cabin in the nude while shaking an apron or white rag over their heads. (1953: 335; cf. Randolph 1947: 285). He also found accounts, within living memory, in which families had carried out a planting ritual to protect crops: both partners stripped and ran around the newly planted field three times, "then [the husband] would throw her right down in the dirt and have at it" (1953: 334). The power of such sex rites might have suggested an evil orgy/ initiation, as a mirror image of such "white" magic practices.

5) Or there might have been families or groups who initiated new members in much this way. Randolph admitted that he had once predicted that magical folkways were dying rapidly, and commented, "I wouldn't make such a statement today. . . . The ceremonies associated with witchcraft are secret, but nature worship is not dead, and I believe that men and women still dance naked in certain secluded groves. A great body of folk belief dies slowly, and some vestige of the ancient landmarks may be with us for a long time to come" (1953: 339).

Folklorists cannot make the final judgment on which of these interpretations is "factual," though some are easier to fit into what we know about rural cultures than others. It is not likely that fiercely independent folk groups like the Franconian Germans or the Ozark mountaineers simultaneously adopted a super-secretive, super-authoritative religion like the witch cult described by contemporary evangelists and Neo-Pagans. But as a form of protest against the perceived authoritarianism of Christianity, such a tradition may well have survived and flourished.

Likewise, folklorists cannot say for certain whether evil witchcraft "really" works, although we must concede that real people, outside of

Hogwarts and horror movies, "really" did cast malicious spells. If magical healing produces medically observable positive results, we can infer that witchcraft could empirically produce sickness, particularly in situations when such practices were believed and feared. Koch and his fellow crusaders, to that extent, had warrant for their cautions. But the system in which witchcraft worked had complex checks and balances that, like the rules of wizardry mastered by Harry Potter and his associates, needed to be carefully learned. Hexes could not be randomly cast, but needed to follow a community's implicit sense of justice. Victims of hexes, for their own part, had avenues open to strike back with spells of their own, without violating the community's sense of propriety. And the system seems to have worked in most communities at most times: while some acts of physical violence were motivated by witchcraft rumors within rural cultures, these were the exception rather than the rule. So long as an increasingly rationalistic theology ignored such folkways, witchcraft continued to be passed on and practiced among families and small groups.

Chapter Three

Black Books and Chain Letters

A particularly robust motif in the lore of witchcraft is the importance of the *grimoire,* or magic book, an essential tool for occultists to cast spells. Evidence presented in witchcraft trials regularly mentioned two such volumes: One was a "large black book" owned by the devil or by the head of the witches' coven, in which the names of witches were signed, often in blood. Another was a "Black Bible" or "Devil's Missal," from which the devil or his servants read during their rituals. Some seventeenth-century accounts describe this as a version of the orthodox Missal, with blasphemous changes (such as "Satan" replacing "God" throughout); others say the reader mumbled so that no one could understand it; still others suggest that it was in a completely unknown language. "Possibly," Montague Summers suggests, "this blasphemous volume is the same as that which Satanists to-day use when performing their abominable rites" (1956: 85–87). Such a book, one assumes, can give the owner amazing powers. Even *owning* such a volume, in some cultures, was said to be lucky, for the devil would bring the owner good fortune so long as it was in his possession.

But, if used unwisely, such a book could put even a godly person at risk. J.K. Rowling's character Ron Weasley was well aware of this, for when his friend Harry Potter is about to pick up a mysterious black book, he warns him, "It could be dangerous. . . . Some of the books the Ministry's confiscated—Dad's told me—there was one that burned your eyes out. And everyone who read *Sonnets of a Sorcerer* spoke in limericks for the rest of their lives. And some old witch in Bath had a book that you could *never stop reading!* You just had to wander around with your nose in it, trying to do everything one-handed" (1999: 230–31).

Rowling's description is comic, but based on a real folk tradition.

"They say that book is printed in black and red, black pages with white letters," a Pennsylvania Dutch source said. This book was extremely dangerous to *read*, as one could "sich fast lesen" or "read oneself fast." Some legends present this quite literally: once one had begun reading, one would "finally come to a point beyond which one could not continue; one would 'lose himself' among the words and become confused and puzzled like a fly entangled in a spider's web." The only remedy would be to "read oneself free" (*sich frei lese*) by reading the text *backwards*, retracing one's steps to the beginning. "If this is not done, the devil will appear, and seek to lay hold of the reader" (Dorson 1964: 111–13).

An elaborate nineteenth-century North German version tells of a man who went one day to a Hamburg church and found a strange book at the back of the altar.[1] Curious, he opened it up and

> he began to read, and went on reading and reading, till he at
> length *read himself fast*. He strove to release himself and to give
> his thoughts another direction, but in vain; he was obliged to
> stand reading on and on, while a cold sweat stood on his fore-
> head and he trembled in every limb; he would have died, had he
> not been observed by an old man, who, it is said, was a Catholic
> priest, who guessing what had befallen him, advised him to read
> the whole backwards; for that only by so doing he could release
> himself. (Thorpe, 1851: 3:14)

Some versions of this legend interpret this warning metaphorically: one Pennsylvania healer suggested that being "read fast" meant simply that once you had dabbled with evil spells, "you could not keep from using the power for evil" (Snellenburg 1969: 44). Another suggested that a son who looked into evil books inherited from his father "read so much that he came under the power of the devil. He lost his peace of mind; he could not eat by day, nor sleep at night." In this case, the son was "read free" by a healer who performed a sort of exorcism by reading the magic book in reverse by proxy (Dorson 1964: 113).

The idea that reading forbidden works can entrap the unwary has continued to inform contemporary beliefs and legends. During the Satanism Scare of the 1970s and 1980s, possession of an alleged grimoire was a particularly damning piece of evidence for "cult cops" (police officials who specialized in finding allegedly dangerous devil-worshiping cults behind teenage activity). One of the most persistent beliefs is that the act of reading such a "satanic" book is the first step to becoming ensnared in devil-worship. The potential dangers were illustrated graphically in *Jay's Journal* (1979), purportedly the journal of a teenage suicide victim, edited by anticult author Beatrice Sparks. This book describes the fate of a naive sixteen-year-old who falls under the control of a local coven. At the book's climax, the coven leaders direct an initiation rite for Jay and two friends out of their "little black books . . . white writing on black paper, [from which] they demanded that each thing had to be done with precision and exactness." After undergoing a baptism in blood, Jay describes entering a "zombie" state during which "I couldn't stop myself from saying and doing things I didn't want to say and do." The ritual turns out to be an invocation of Satan through a perverted version of the Lord's Prayer, while "a strange flickering orange kind of light" in the room signals a demonic presence. The initiates are thereafter slaves to the devil. "It's like I'm a puppet," Jay writes toward the end. "Like I'm controlled and I don't want to be controlled! . . . Actually the occult movement is kind of a Pied Piper sort of thing: we want to go but we don't want to go . . . in the end we have no choice . . . we've just got to see what's in that mountain" (111–12).

Robert Hicks (1991) found that the works of Aleister Crowley and Anton LaVey were frequently mentioned as a sign that the possessor was about to commit criminal acts; they should be confiscated whenever possible, some argued, and a few even suggested attempting to trace users through public library records (50–56). Many books were defined as "dangerous" simply because of their alleged occult content or even because the word "devil" or "witch" appeared in the title. For example, the satirist Ambrose Bierce's book *The Devil's Dictionary* showed up in the "evidence" collected during one Pennsylvania cult raid. Hicks found, when he actually read modern "occult" books like the *Necronomicon* (a pastiche of anthropological sources in honor of H.P. Lovecraft's science fiction), that they were in fact New Age spoofs or in-jokes. However, given the potential dangers of looking at such books, many cult cops felt that it was safer to act out of ignorance rather than put themselves into spiritual or physical danger by looking at such "evidence" carefully. One guide to occult dangers quoted by Hicks gives a warning similar to Ron Weasley's: "note: intense study of resource books and materials by occult sources or practitioners is hazardous. Preferred is studying overviews and synopses by credible authors who have studied the occult traditions. The unknown realm of the occult beckons with many lures. Study and/

or experimentation are to be avoided" (quoted in Hicks 1991: 55). Deliverance expert Don Basham makes an even more inclusive warning: "Fascination with psychic phenomena is a subtle trap. Even as we were researching *Christian* literature renouncing occult experiences, it was a struggle not to become intrigued. Therefore, repress any inclination to further inquiry into any of these practices" (1974: 114).

What "little black books" lie behind such stories? We can find in folklore a wealth of belief that ritual magic, especially the kind that involves writing, leads to a contagious, practically irreversible fascination with evil. It is useful to survey this lore to see what real practices and texts can be documented behind such warnings. Indeed, a long and virtually unbroken tradition of occult use of writing can be traced from the age of the witch trials up to contemporary works. This chapter and the next will survey several sides of this tradition, ranging from the esoteric tradition of using Latin and Hebrew texts as magical spell books to the modern practice of copying and distributing chain letters. Such a survey will show, among other things, how the occult has maintained an unsavory link with ethnic hatred, and how the use of writing to gain luck and fortune for oneself is often linked with the act of ritually cursing one's friends and neighbors.

The Written Word as Fetish

The dynamic that motivates this body of lore, interestingly, focuses on writing not as something to be *read*, much less as something used to express the writer's original ideas, but as a *fetish*, an object that has magical properties in itself. What is a fetish? While this term has been appropriated to refer to a wide variety of activities (usually described as illogical or psychopathic by nature), in its most objective sense "fetish" refers to the fabrication, acquisition, and use of a material object invested with extraordinary spiritual forces. It implies a practice that operates in a gray realm of folk religion, which includes beliefs and practices that operate "apart from and alongside the strictly theological and liturgical forms of the official religion" (Yoder 1974). That is, a fetish is the product of an unofficial magical or religious practice that involves making or using some power object. The use of written words as fetish objects is ancient. Some of our oldest Biblical texts come from silver amulets bearing the Shema, or oath of allegiance to Yahweh, in ancient

Hebrew lettering (Deuteronomy 6:4–5; Weinfeld 1991: 342). The use of written texts, baked into clay tablets or written on scraps of papyrus kept in leather pouches, was common throughout the ancient Middle East (see Budge 1978).

At the oldest historical levels, when literacy was a rare and somewhat mysterious craft, a common set of terms applied to both conjuring and reading (the latter word originally meant "seeking advice," as one would in consulting a soothsayer). "Spell," originally a dialect term for a kind of oral narrative, became associated, on the one hand, with being able to write out words correctly, letter by letter, and on the other hand with being able to perform magic (casting a "spell") with the help of the skill of reading aloud from a book. Likewise, "grammar," the art of being able to parse sentences and understand relationships between words, became a dialect term for the "ability to perform magic," a usage that survives in the French *grimoire*, or "book of spells," and also in the phonic variation "glamor," originally an illusion of beauty created through black magic. This ambiguity survives in an Anglo-American ballad usually titled "Lady Gay" (Child 79), in which a woman sends her children to "th North Count-try/For t' learn their grammer-ree" (Riddle 1965). She seems at first to be simply a normal mother sending her children off to boarding school to learn to read and write, but in fact in many versions she is also a witch. When her children die, she uses a spell of her own to draw their spirits from the grave and attempt (unsuccessfully) to have them stay with her on earth.

On some level, linking literacy with the devil could be seen as a form of anti-intellectual prejudice. Certainly, well-read medieval scholars such as Roger Bacon and Albertus Magnus were soon after their deaths described as wizards whose works supposedly included tracts on how to use lengthy incantations in foreign languages to raise the devil. In the case of Albertus Magnus, apocryphal works did in fact appear soon after his death that alleged to be the scholar's "magic book" of spells, and these circulated among would-be conjurers into this century. In a culture in which literacy in one's own language, even among wealthy classes, was often the exception rather than the rule, the magical properties imputed to reading and writing may well have been a token of respect rather than envy. The tradition of saying the Christian mass in Latin (the Tridentine liturgy) rather than in the vernacular likewise implied magical properties in the language itself. This implication survives in the stage magician's "hocus pocus," a corruption of the priest's announcement "hoc est corpus" (here is [Christ's] body) at the moment of transubstantiation, the climax of the Mass.

Like the legend, a fetish is a way of capturing something uncanny and making of it an object that can be owned and used for personal good. The term *fetish* was originally a West African pidgin term used by Portuguese merchants to refer to amulets and power objects they found being used in the cultures with which they traded. It was a logical one to adopt, as it previously had been used to refer to the veneration of saints' body parts among Catholics (Pietz 1987; Ellen 1988: 214). The word, however, is cognate with *feitiçaria,* a Portuguese term for sorcery or witchcraft, itself related to other widespread European terms for evil magic, such as the Spanish *hechiceiria* and the German *hexerie* (Pietz 1987: 24, 34). Ultimately, *feitiço* derives from the Latin root *facere,* "to make"—but in a special intensive form, *facticius,* derived from Roman commercial parlance, signifying "man-made" as opposed to goods created (*factum*) through purely natural processes. Hence, it often signified a synthetic form of a valuable natural product, and often implied a counterfeit or intentionally deceptive substitute for it. Early Christian theology appropriated this commercial term, with its pejorative connotation, to refer to Pagan artifacts and, by extension, religious practices, which were seen as counterfeits of the True Faith (Pietz 1987: 24–31).[2]

Significantly, the term often showed up in the early days of Christianity, alluding to practices that were also characterized as "superstitious" or "vain observances." Open opposition to Christian doctrines and worship of other deities were readily labeled as "idolatry" and quickly outlawed in Christian jurisprudence. But "superstition" (originally a term referring to excessive devotion to religious rites) and what St. Augustine alluded to as "the thousands of inane [popular] customs"[3] that were practiced in his time provided a "hard case" for ecclesiastical law. The making and wearing of amulets and ligatures—whether they used explicitly Christian symbols or looked back to older traditions of worship, such as the wearing of the Shema as a protective amulet—fell into a gray area that, like the witchcraft practices discussed in the previous chapter, might be overlooked by authorities at some times and at other times be explicitly outlawed as heretical or sacrilegious.[4] By 1385, Portuguese legal codes had specifically outlawed the production and use of *obre de feitiços,* a vague term covering any kind of magical object. However, Pietz observes, the suppression of witchcraft never became a "burning issue" in that country (1987: 34–35).

Nominally outlawed, the *obre de feitiços* was nonetheless a common object, both childish and trivial in the eyes of authorities. It was for
this reason that the term came readily to hand to refer to artifacts seen as
valuable by West Africans but as "trifles" to the European traders, who
nonetheless eagerly provided them in exchange for gold and other com-
modities. Pietz argues that "fetish" gained its primary significance for
modern thinkers by "naming" a previously undefined intercultural space,
opened up by the emerging commerce between cultures so radically different as to be "mutually incomprehensible" (1987: 24).

The Jewish Qabbalah and Anti-Semitic Crusades

It should be no surprise that the most influential European fetish tradition grew out of Christians' problematic relationship with Judaism. In
that culture, an extensive and influential tradition did indeed associate
books, letters, and the act of writing with a form of practical magic. This
tradition derived from the Qabbalah, an esoteric, highly intellectual form
of Jewish mysticism dating from the twelfth century.[5] In its earliest appearances, "Qabbalah" literally means "oral tradition" and refers to the
mass of religious lore passed on from teacher to pupil without being
committed to written form. In early Talmudic writing, thus, a *qabbalah*
was a teaching attributed to a noted rabbi, not recorded in written manu-
scripts like the Talmud, but maintained orally by the schools that derived from him. In its earliest form, then, the concept of the Qabbalah
was similar to that of folklore, in that it was composed of beliefs and
practices maintained by small groups of Jews outside of the official institutions of the religion as expressed in Scripture and other devotional
writings.
    When it emerged as a formal movement during the fourteenth cen-
tury with written tracts of its own, qabbalism took a variety of forms.
The crucial element, however, was its concept of the symbolic nature of
creation. At the beginning, qabbalists reasoned, God was all-present and
infinite, and thus had to withdraw, or limit Himself voluntarily, to make
room for a nondivine world. God performed this by means of a series of
emanations, divine sparks overflowing and becoming trapped in the
matter of the created world. These emanations include semidivine spir-

its created by God to perform the tasks of maintaining the world, but they also permeate all of visible creation. Hints of the nature and will of God therefore can be found in the most trivial details of natural phenomena.

The enlightened qabbalist was therefore able to enter into a more mystical and direct understanding of God by learning to recognize and decipher these divine sparks through systems of symbolic equations. The most widespread of these symbol sets was organized in terms of ten mystical concepts, understood in terms of ten words used by God to create the world, but usually referred to as "*sefirot*," literally, "ciphers" or "numbers." In Hebrew, as in most European writing systems, letters were used also as numerals until the Arabic system of writing numbers was adopted in the twelfth century. Individual letters in Biblical passages thus could be seen as symbolically significant, and the Qabbalah generated an increasingly complex pattern of links between these hidden revelations in Scripture and equally mystical hints of God's nature in physical nature and historical events.

The Tree of Life, a symbolic means of organizing the *sefirot* into a hierarchy, helped novices to visualize the ten divine emanations governing the world and their perceived interrelationships. Beginning in the thirteenth century, more than 150 commentaries added detailed sets of symbolic links among numbers, letters, animals, plants, and planets. For the more speculative thinkers, this symbolic system was a means of meditating on God's will expressed in creation, and the Tree of Life implied an ideal path for achieving a mystical contact with divinity. The Hasidic movement of the eighteenth century sprang from qabbalism, and its mystical influence is still present in Jewish religious thought. Modern Jewish theologians such as Martin Buber have continued the development of this religious philosophy.

One especially popular direction in qabbalism was its emphasis on theurgy, or the performance of rituals to restructure the divine nature of the world. By performing the Mosaic commandments with the proper intentions, this tenet held, practitioners could work to heal the lost harmony in creation by extracting divine sparks from the material world and opening up channels by which divine power could be transmitted to this world. This was not quite the same as magic, qabbalism historian Moshe Idel notes. "The Qabbalah used biblical commandments to effect its goals rather than magical devices; and whereas magic is chiefly directed toward attaining material results needed by certain persons, qabbalistic activity was primarily intended to restore the divine harmony, and only secondarily to ensure the abundance of the supernatural efflux in this world" (1988: 121).

But this distinction was never clear-cut, even among Jewish communities. Some qabbalistic communities received instructions from angelic messengers who spoke through members in a trance state; others received answers to difficult questions through automatic writing; still others practiced a form of transcendental meditation brought on by reciting divine names. One late-fifteenth-century qabbalist advocated a form of ceremonial magic intended to hasten the arrival of the messianic aeon. Among yeshiva students, even more dramatic practices prevailed: in Germany, starting in the sixteenth century, a form of table-tapping (a predecessor of the Ouija board) was combined with the singing of psalms and the recitation of divine names. Mainstream qabbalistic teachers did not deny that manipulation of the sacred names could produce such results, but they consistently warned against experimenting with such practices. Gershom Scholem sums up the official position: "only the most perfectly virtuous individuals are permitted to perform them, and even then never for their private advantage, but only in times of emergency and public need. Whoever else seeks to perform such acts does so at his own grave physical and spiritual peril" (1971: 632–37). Such warnings were often disregarded among the ranks of the common people, and the philosophical "theoretical Qabbalah" was, at an early period, paralleled by an extensive literature of "practical Qabbalah," which harmonized theology with Semitic folk practices of divination and magical protection.

In particular, this body of philosophy was used to organize and justify a widespread Jewish tradition of using written amulets to protect oneself, one's children, and one's property. In this folk tradition, the various holy names and titles given to God in scripture, and indeed the Hebrew letters from which they were formed, were held to possess magical powers. The act of pronouncing them in the proper context could ward off supernatural threats; carrying an object inscribed with holy words would have the same effect. A typical amulet might contain one of the magical names of God—often the tetragrammaton, or "YHWH," the mystical, unpronounceable name of the deity. The charm might feature parts of biblical texts in Hebrew script, particularly from the Psalms, each of which was held to have specific magical powers. Also included might be the names or symbols of the angels associated with natural and social situations relevant to the task of the charm (Hsia 1988: 7–8). For such purposes and others, qabbalistic writings generated lists of divine names, or *shemot* (singular *shem*). Scholem notes: "The *shem ha-garsi* was invoked in the study of Talmud or any rabbinic text (*girsa*); the *shem ha-doresh* was invoked by the preacher (*darshan*). There was a 'name of the sword' (*shem ha-herev*), and a 'name of ogdoad' [or angelic spirit] (*shem ha-sheminiyut*), and a 'name of the wing' (*shem ha-kanaf*)." Some of these lists, Scholem notes, were not above including "The Paraclete (or Holy Spirit) Jesus," though terming him "son of Pandera" (the Roman soldier held to be Jesus' illegitimate father in anti-Christian propaganda) (1971: 638).

It is not surprising to find such lists of divine names circulating among Christians soon after 1500, when a series of works appeared in Italy and Germany, claiming to offer outlines of the Qabbalah. Some of these translations, produced by converts to Christianity, were intentionally distorted to maintain the secrecy of qabbalistic concepts. Others, such as Heinrich Cornelius Agrippa's *De occulta philosophia* and the widely circulated *Clavicula Solomonis,* were plainly spurious. Nevertheless, a vast number of popular imitations were published, claiming to provide a guide to Jewish magic and tracing their heritage to the magical feats performed in Egypt by Moses that were thence passed down secretly from rabbi to rabbi in a sorcerer's underground. There was a certain legitimacy to this literature, however: often, they were founded in the actual "practical Qabbalah," with its emphasis on pronouncing or writing divine names for magical purposes.

The most widespread treatise of this sort circulating among non-Jews was the *Shemhamforash,* an exposition of the secret significance of the divine names and their use in practical magic. The title (also given as *Schemhamporas* and even *Semiphoras*) is likely a corruption of the genuine qabbalist concept of the *shem hammephorash,* or the distinctive excellent name. This was the divine name YHWH, also known as the tetragrammaton or four-letter name, because it was held too sacred for laypersons to pronounce and so was normally communicated in writing using the four consonants alone (*Encyc. Brittanica,* 11th ed., 26:670). The *shem hammephorash* was indeed used widely in Jewish folklore for amulets and magical formulae. But the treatise to which it gave its name mingled Christian and Jewish concepts—and even averred that the tetragrammaton had now been replaced by a "pentagrammaton," namely, JESUS. "Without the name of Jesus the old Hebrew cabalists can accomplish nothing in the present day" (*Sixth and Seventh Books* [n.d.]: 127, 131). For Christians, the variant spellings "Cabala" and "cabalist" from this point on signified a secretive "inner circle" of conspirators, who acknowledged the divinity of Jesus but maliciously chose not to honor it. Their alternative method of divine magic was thus consciously anti-Christian and therefore satanic by its very nature. The adjective "cabalistic" also applied to any set of mysterious names, words, or symbols that had sinister magical significance within this clique.

The extraordinary interest in ceremonial magic at this time may well have reflected Protestant theologians' repudiation of the Catholic Church's rituals and the move toward presenting the Bible and the normal liturgy in the vernacular, thus eliminating the "hocus pocus" that many cultures had become used to. Prevented from using Christian fetishes, such cultures turned, in growing numbers, to Jews who were willing to support a modest trade in magical amulets and incantations. Village pastors, seeking a neutral vocabulary for the kinds of magical incantations that were part of their routine, increasingly turned to clandestine editions of prayers and rituals in garbled Hebrew. Martin Luther, twenty years after the start of the Reformation, was angered to visit churches in Saxony in 1543 and find dozens of such magical books owned and used by rural ministers (Hsia 1988: 135).

The Blood Libel

This renewed interest in Jewish folk magic was, for many communities, a curse rather than a blessing. For several centuries, Jews had been accused of the Blood Libel: the ritual murder of Christian children. Such a charge may owe something to an ancient piece of anti-Jewish propaganda dating to the desecration of the Temple in Jerusalem by forces under Greek ruler Antiochus IV Epiphanes. When the Greeks entered the Temple, according to rumor, they found a Greek being fattened up for sacrifice (Dundes 1991: 7).

The Blood Libel was also directed at Christians. A particularly detailed version is preserved in Minucius Felix's work *Octavius* (1931 [ca. 200]), in which a pagan orator complains of Christianity as a fast-growing "religion of lust" whose members "recognize one another by secret signs and marks." To join, one must drive a knife into what appears to be a loaf of dough; in fact, a live baby has been placed inside, and so the initiate murders the child. At this point, "the blood—oh horrible—they lap up greedily; the limbs they tear to pieces eagerly; and over the victim they make league and covenant, and by complicity in guilt pledge themselves to mutual silence." After the cannibalistic feast, the group, parents and children, brothers and sisters, sit down to a sumptuous feast. At the end of this, the lights are extinguished, "and in the shameless dark lustful embraces are indiscriminately exchanged," heedless of whether one is committing incest or not (337, 339). Indeed, according to Minucius Felix's contemporary, the Christian apologist Tertullian, rumor held that members seeking to enter the new cult *had* to bring their blood relatives and commit incest with them during the initiation (1931: 45). Minucius Felix's pagan gives what presumably was the standard reaction among non-Christians: "were there not some foundation of truth, shrewd rumour would not impute gross and unmentionable forms of vice" (337)—in other words, widespread belief implies truth. Tertullian asked for the facts: if Christian meetings were constantly being raided by the authorities, then where was the evidence for this cannibalism and these incestuous orgies? "Who yet, I ask, came upon a baby wailing, as they say?" he demanded (39).

In fact, the story can be traced back further, always in the form of an unconfirmable rumor attached to various groups who were the subjects of persecution. Catiline, charged with conspiracy against the Roman government in 63 BCE, was said to have sealed his plot by ritually sacrificing a child and eating it with his cohorts. Participants in the Bacchanalia, a religious movement made up of women, actually engaged in sex orgies and human sacrifice, according to the Roman historian Livy. A contemporary source claimed this movement's ultimate goal was "the control of the state" (Cohn 1975: 6, 10–11).

Once the Christian church had established itself as the Roman state religion, it in turn accused rival religions and schismatic sects of similar bizarre ceremonies involving perverse sex and cannibalism. Targets included the Alexandrian sect of the Phibionites (ca. 330) and a dissident group of clerics at the collegiate church of Orleans (1019), who were accused of engaging in ritual orgies and incinerating the children conceived during them; if a child was conceived in this way, it was ritually burned eight days after its birth, and the ashes preserved as a kind of holy sacrament (Cohn 1975: 20–21; Zacharias 1980: 47–48). By the early twelfth century, a similar story had emerged about a heretical sect making a kind of sacramental bread out of baby ashes. Common to all these stories was the claim that, once a believer had committed cannibalism, he or she could then never leave the cult (Zacharias 1980: 49).

From the thirteenth century on, such rites were less and less commonly ascribed to Christian heretics. Now, they were supposedly carried out in "Synagogues of Satan," and Jews were being accused of slaughtering a Christian child to make sacramental Passover bread (Dundes 1991: 100).

The Blood Libel was first used against Jewish communities in the wake of an incident in Norwich, England, when an intense panic occurred after the body of a twelve-year-old boy was found the day before Easter 1144. Rumors circulated that day and during Easter, claiming that the members of the local Jewish community had abducted and ritually murdered the child. No concrete evidence could be found, and the local sheriff ensured that the Jews were not attacked or prosecuted, but a local cleric, Thomas of Monmouth, compiled a saint's life, *The Life and Miracles of St. William of Norwich*, that included graphic details of how the child had been tortured by vindictive Jews (Bennett 2003). By the 1150s, as historian Gavin I. Langmuir found, the belief had spread "that European Jews annually conspired to crucify a Christian boy at Easter or Passover to insult Christ" (1972: 462). Still, though such accusations emerged frequently in England, they rarely resulted in legal action being taken against the Jews thought responsible.

However, in 1255 another intense panic occurred in Lincoln when the badly decomposed body of an eight-year-old boy named Hugh was discovered in a well. At the time, Lincoln had a large and economically powerful Jewish community, and a few days previous, one of its most prominent families had invited Jews from all over England to celebrate a marriage. Rumors circulated widely that little Hugh's body had been mutilated and disemboweled, and John de Lexinton, a powerful Lincoln nobleman and advisor to King Henry III, took charge of the investigation. With the threat of torture and the promise of immunity, de Lexinton induced a local Jew named Copin to make a confession. According to Copin, the Lincoln Jews had kidnapped Hugh and kept him alive until their brethren in other parts of England could gather to witness the ritual murder. Hugh was then crucified as a mockery of Christianity, and his organs were removed "for magical arts or augury" (1972: 464).

As a result, ninety-one Jews were arrested for participating in Hugh's murder, and King Henry III himself came to Lincoln to supervise the legal proceedings. Despite the promise of immunity, de Lexinton had Copin executed immediately (perhaps to prevent him from retracting his confession in public), and on the strength of his testimony, the rest were found guilty and condemned to death. Eighteen were hanged; while Pope Innocent IV, who had denounced the Blood Libel in 1247, pressured King Henry to release the others, the event led to a series of persecutions. Meanwhile, the incident was kept alive in memory by a widely circulating ballad, "Sir Hugh and the Jew's Daughter" (Child 155). This preserves many alleged details from the actual investigation, including the child's ritual mutilation and the disposal of his body in a well. Significantly, it adds witch-scare details to the Blood Libel scenario, making the villain a woman who entices the child into her house to obtain his blood and organs for magical purposes.

> She pu'd the apple frae the tree,
> It was baith red and green;
> She gave it unto little Sir Hugh,
> With that his heart did win.
>
> She wiled him into ae chamber,
> She wiled him into twa,
> She wiled him into the third chamber,
> And that was warst o't a' . . .
>
> And first came out the thick, thick blood,
> And syne came out the thin,
> And syne came out the bonnie heart's blood,
> There was nae mair within.
>
> She laid him on a dressing-table
> She dressed him like a swine'
> Says, Lie ye there, my bonnie Sir Hugh,
> Wi yere apples red and green.
> (Child 1965, 3:246)

Increasingly, from 1500 on, Jews were scapegoated as secret devil-worshippers as well. A fierce anti-Semite, Luther repeatedly accused Jews of ritual sacrifice and called them "the Devil's children." He also attacked the "word magic" with which Jews were associated, though he felt their practices were less damaging than the analogous beliefs that he felt had contaminated the Catholic Church. The pope, he argued,

> has filled the entire world with swindle, magic, idolatry, for he has his special *Schem Hamphoras* . . . [and] enchants water with wanton, mere meaningless words. . . . He also enchants cowls and tonsures and the whole world with mere words or letters, so that they become monks, nuns and priests, who . . . peddle indulgences, worship dead bones, serve the devil, and through their own work deserve heaven, namely the heaven where the devil abbot and pope are in. (Quoted in Hsia 1988: 134–35)

Thus, the height of witch hunting coincided with the growth of Protestantism and, simultaneously, with a wave of attacks on Jews. However, the two crazes rarely coincided in the same community at the same time, perhaps because (as one anti-Semite author noted) "The Jews have no need to ally themselves with the evil spirits by means of the usual pact, like other sorcerers; their Kabbalistic magic arts are already sufficiently the work of Satan" (Trachtenberg 1943: 86). By 1610, however, witch trial testimony at Aix alleged that the two evil conspiracies were working in tandem. "Sometimes [the witches] ate the tender flesh of little children, who had been slain and roasted at some Synagogue, and sometimes babes were brought there, yet alive, whom the witches had kidnapped from their homes if opportunity offered" (quoted in Summers 1956: 144–45).

At the same time, however, the "Christian Kabbalah" attracted a huge following, the magic being perhaps all the more intriguing to a certain class of readers because it was associated with a persecuted culture already linked to moneymaking, child sacrifice, and evil sorcery. R. Po-Chia Hsia, historian of early anti-Semitic movements in Germany, comments, "For the Protestant Reformation it was no longer blood that held the power of magic but the language of the Jews" (1988: 135).

The Jewish Amulet Tradition as "Satanism"

From an early period, Jews were patronized by the Christian community for protective fetishes, but the craft of making such charms was always associated with rumors of sinister magic. In one such story, a charmer provided an amulet for a horse that had proved difficult to tame. After many years of successful use, the curious owner opened the amulet and found a paper that read, in Hebrew characters, "The master of the horse shall belong to the devil so long as the horse stands still when it is struck" (Trachtenberg 1943: 75). Such stories are still current in Germany and elsewhere, though now their targets are Christian cabalists. During his ministry in Toggenburg, Switzerland, Kurt E. Koch encountered many stories about a witch master named Hugentobler who lived in a nearby village. Rumor had it that he had gained his healing power with a blood pact, and that he healed by secretly promising his patients to the devil. In one case, a father told Koch that he had taken his young son, who had been paralyzed by polio, to Hugentobler, who healed him completely with the help of a leather pouch containing a paper with a charm. All seemed well, but at the age of sixteen the boy committed suicide. The father then opened the fetish and found a paper reading, "This soul belongs to the devil" (1962: 72).

Dutch evangelist Corrie ten Boom likewise relates, secondhand, a case of a twelve-year-old being counseled for suicidal thoughts. On questioning, she admitted she had been healed of a persistent illness by being given an amulet to wear around her neck. "The one who gave it to me said it would be dangerous to [open it]," she told the counselor, who nevertheless looked inside and found a little paper. According to the story, the paper read, "I command you, Satan, to keep this body healthy, till you get the soul to hell!" When the fetish was destroyed, the story concludes, the girl fell gravely ill, but was healed by a Christian laying-on of hands (1970: 22).

The story is paralleled by another account that Koch heard from a fellow minister who investigated a "fire blessing" that had been built into a compartment in a barn near Wurzburg. The yellowed sheet of paper allegedly read, "In the name of the Father, Son and Holy Ghost I, Satan, protect this house from lightning and fire. Signed . . . (illegible)." Koch says that analysis of the paper showed that it was about three hundred years old and written "in a mixture of animal and human blood." As in the previous story, when the charm was removed, the owner was supernaturally punished for removing the protection: within three hours the building was reportedly struck by lightning and completely destroyed by fire (1970: 74).

As in the case of reports of evil witches, it is possible that Koch's fire charm was written by a rural sorcerer who invoked the devil for protective purposes. There is external evidence for using blood to write out an amulet: some Oriental Jews did in fact use the blood of circumcision to make charms against disease (Hsia 1988: 9). However, the practice of invoking Satan to control fire may not have necessarily been seen as an act of devil worship. During the witch-hunts, prosecutors often made a fine distinction between a witch and a Christian sorcerer. If the devil was *asked* to carry out an action, witch-hunters considered this a form of prayer and hence devil-worship. Such a practice was condemned as a form of witchcraft. But if a sorcerer *commanded* the devil to do something in his power in the name of the divinity (as implied in the charm above), this could be considered a legitimate act of Christian worship, since it assumed that the devil was subordinate to God and could be forced to act against his will. Indeed, self-identified sorcerers (who were, like cunning-folk, overwhelmingly male) usually escaped prosecution.

On the other hand, given the notoriously difficult *fraktur* script in which existing Germanic fetishes and fire blessings are written, such stories may have been based on creative decipherment. Julius Sachse (1954) has documented a variety of fire charms used by German Americans in Pennsylvania. Some contained what were alleged to be Hebrew characters and symbolic designs such as the well-known Star of David. Some combined pseudo-Jewish elements with Christian symbolism. The *Feuersegen* used by the religious community in Ephrata, Pennsylvania, in the eighteenth century contained the letters A, G, L, A (ostensibly representing the four Hebrew words signifying "The Lord is mighty in eternity"), with the Latin inscription *consumatum est* ("It is finished": Jesus' last words on the cross) and the three crosses normally representing the Trinity. Others may have been more authentically based in Jewish tradition: as early as 1735, "Levi the Jew" was well known in the Philadelphia area for preparing "authentic" amulets, one of which incorporated Hebrew characters and signs of the zodiac into a Star of David.

Whatever the original language, those who copied such charms quickly corrupted them out of recognition. One charm, published in a Pennsylvania German grimoire, read:

I. m. I. K. I. B. I. P. a. x. v. ss. Ss. vas,
I. P. O. unay Lit. Dom. mper vobism
(Hohman 1992: 48)

Another, preserved in a book by a Pennsylvania family that specialized in making protective fetishes, is written in *fraktur* and apparently reads

Dads, Mads, Damads Dado, Mado, Damado
Frum Irum Dade, Made, Damade Hatte Narum Ich.

Another, apparently a charm intended to repel evil, was completely illegible except for the opening "I R" which the family interpreted as an abbreviation for *"Iesus Rex"* or "King Jesus" (Heindel 1976b: 64, 72). It would not take much for a curious customer to open such a fetish, expecting the usual prayer or Bible verse, and suspect that such an inscription was instead a cabalistic invocation of Satan.

Some healers were not above using the language barrier to make satiric comments on the person being healed. The *Facetiae* of Giovanni Francesco Poggio Bracciolini (1968), who was a papal secretary in the early fifteenth century, contain several jocular stories about such cases. In one, an Italian priest sent to Hungary found that his parishioners expected him to heal people suffering from sore eyes, by sprinkling their pupils with holy water while reciting a Bible verse. Suspecting that the source of their sore eyes was too much banqueting, he instead said in Italian (which the Hungarians could not understand), *"Andatemene, che siate morti a gliadi!"* ("Get out of here! May someone kill you with his sword!") (127). In another case (188–89), a group of opportunistic friars offered to make fetishes for peasants afraid of the Plague, with the warning that they could not be opened for at least fifteen days. When the fetishes were opened, it was found they contained a bawdy verse in Italian:

Lady, if you spin and drop your staff,
When you bend over, keep your ass covered.

Examples of similar tricks appear in contemporary examples. One Pennsylvania Dutch source notes that, when he was a child suffering from a minor hurt such as a stubbed toe, his grandmother "charmed" it with an allegedly magical formula that actually amounted to *"Haila, haila hinkledreck. Bis marya frie iss olles veck,"* or, "Heal-it heal-it, chicken shit. Till tomorrow morning all [the pain] will be gone" (Dieffenbach 1976: 45). Another recalled being taken to a healer to have a burned hand charmed. When he laughed at the ritual she performed, the healer informed him that the healing required one more element, and wrote out a paper "in German characters," cautioning the boy not to look at it until he arrived home. It proved to be an instruction to the lad's parents to whip him "so as to teach him in future to respect old age and venerate a gray head" (Sachse 1954: 9).

Letters from Heaven and Chain Letters as Conjuring

An especially lively tradition of fetish-making that developed in Christian cabalism involved the so-called *"Himmelsbrief,"* or "Letter from Heaven." Dating from the 1700s, this began as a handwritten manuscript, but, as printing became widespread, it mainly circulated as a broadside. It claims to be based on a mysterious letter, written in golden ink by Jesus Himself, and dropped down into a church in Germany by the Angel Gabriel. The contents of the letters vary widely: most of them summarize the Ten Commandments, warn against sin, and exhort to virtue in general, uncontroversial terms; some also add prayers and moralistic verses.

These, however, were not the rationale of such a letter: this lay in the instruction to make copies of the document, keeping one in the house or on one's person for good fortune. From the earliest versions on, this instruction was combined with a curse on anyone unwise enough to refuse to make copies. Fogel notes that the earliest German versions also included "cabalistic" symbols and argues that they were a generalized, public form of magical charming. Indeed, he concludes, they maintain "the old heathenism under the garb of Christianity" (1908: 287–89).

The *Himmelsbrief* of St. Germain (before 1724) contains a characteristic threat/promise:

> Write this letter out, one person to another, or get it printed: and no matter if you have committed so many sins as there are grains of sand by the sea, leaves on the trees, or stars in the sky, they shall be forgiven, if you believe and do what this letter teaches and says to you; but those who believe it not shall die. Beware, or you will be punished in eternity, and I shall demand your many sins of you on Judgment Day, and you will have to answer to me for them. Those who have this letter in their houses or carry it with them will not be harmed by lightning and will be protected

from fire and water. If a woman carries this letter, and abides by it, she will bring into the world a healthy baby with a happy future. (Fogel 1908: 290; my translation)

The Magdeburger Himmelsbrief, a later version of this charm that became extraordinarily popular in the Pennsylvania German country, is rather more explicit about cursing those who fail to distribute the letter: "I, Jesus, have written this myself with my own hand; he that opposes it and scandalizes, that man shall have to expect no help from me; whoever hath the letter and does not make it known, he is cursed by the christian church. . . . [But] he that publishes it to mankind, will receive his reward and a joyful departure from this world" (anonymous 19th c. trans. quoted in Westkott 1969/70: 7; cf. Fogel 1908: 306–7). A garbled English translation had already appeared in 1725, which began with a still more dramatic exposition of the benefits of possessing a copy of the letter: "In the name of the Father, the Son, and the Holy Ghost, as Christ stopped at the Mount, sword or guns, shall stop [for?] whoever carries this letter with him! He shall not be damaged through the enemies [sic] guns or weapons, God will give strength! that he may not fear robbers or murderers and guns, pistol, sword and musket [and] shall not be hurt through by the cannon of angel Michael. In the name of the Father, the Son, and the Holy Ghost." This version concludes the section by challenging the reader to try an ostensive experiment to prove the letter's power: "God be with you and whosoever carries this letter with him shall be protected against all danger, and who does not believe in it may copy it and tie it to the neck of a dog and shoot at him he will see this is true" (Fogel 1908: 297).

The tradition remained vital in Germany up through World War II. Corrie ten Boom recorded an encounter with an old man who had such a letter and had actually carried out a similar ostensive trial. "I tied this paper to a dog during a bombardment in Berlin," the man told ten Boom, "and sent the dog into the street. The bombs were falling around him, and not one touched him." Calling a counselor to pray beside her for spiritual protection, ten Boom solemnly told the man, "You have to make a choice between this letter and accepting Jesus. This letter is not from Him, but from the devil" (1970: 21).

The tradition likewise caught on in North America, although increasingly the element emphasized was not so much the letter's protective powers but the magical effects of copying and distributing it. By

1908, Edwin F. Fogel reported two versions circulating in German Pennsylvania, in English. The shorter one read (in full):

> Oh! Lord Jesus Christ, the eternal God, have mercy upon all mankind. Keep us from all sin and take us to be with Thee eternally. This prayer was sent to Bishop Lawrence,[6] recommending that it be sent to nine other persons; it must not be signed; he who will write it for nine days, commencing the day received, distributing it to nine different persons, and sending one each day, will on and after the ninth day experience a great joy.
>
> Oh, Jerusalem, at the feast it was said: he who will write this prayer will be delivered of every calamity. Please do not break the chain and please copy as received, trusting that the blessing of God may rest upon you and on whom sent to by you.[7]

A longer version, not given, contains a more elaborate prayer and also "a curse on all those who refuse to obey the directions indicated in the 'Prayer'" (Fogel 1908: 307).

The contemporary version derived from this tradition maintains the essential elements of the *Himmelsbrief:* an unexceptional religious sentiment followed by directions to copy and distribute it in the form of written, typed, or printed copies. Those who do so are promised some providential good fortune, and those who break the chain are threatened with death or supernatural punishment. However, as Daniel Van Arsdale (1998) observes, twentieth-century chain letters developed in a direction distinct from the *Himmelsbrief* tradition. Compared with the earlier tradition, chain letters are briefer (generally about a hundred words), and, while they usually begin with some similar reference to a prayer or a saint, they tend to replace explicit claims of divine authority with "vague popular superstitions." Moreover, the promise of good fortune to those who copy or possess such a letter gradually becomes the dominant theme, there often being a minimum number of copies that have to be made and a stated period in which they have to be completed. They also tend to include brief narratives of cases in which good or bad luck came as a result of the chain. A 1952 version (Van Arsdale 1998) illustrates the newer form:

> This Prayer has been sent to you and has been around the world four times. The one who breaks it will have bad luck.

The Prayer. Trust in the Lord with all thy heart and lean not on thy own understandance [*sic*] in all thy ways acknowledge him and he will direct thy path.

Please copy this and see what happens in four days after receiving it. Send this copy and four to someone you wish good luck. It must leave in 24 hours. Don't send any money and don't keep this copy. Gen Patton received $1,600 after receiving it. Gen Allen received $1,600 and lost it because he broke the chain. You are to have good luck in 4 days. This is not a joke and you will receive by mail [*sic*].

A 1960s chain letter likewise began with a prayer: "Trust in the Lord with all your might, and always acknowledge Him and He will light your way." But, by this time, the instructions for circulating the letter had been made more rigorous—*twenty* copies were required—reflecting the greater access to photocopy machines. More to the point, the series of brief narratives now put much greater emphasis on people who suffered bad fortune by breaking the chain: "Don Elliott [received] $60,000 but lost it because he broke the chain. While in the Philippines, Com. Mapak lost his life[8] 6 days after receiving this copy. He failed to circulate the prayer" (Dundes and Pagter 1992: 6). In later versions from the 1980s and 1990s, this section has been gradually lengthened (and the "prayer" curtailed even further), so that it now makes up most of the letter:

Joe Elliott received $40,000 and lost it because he broke the chain, while in the Phillipines [*sic*] Gene Walsh lost his life six days after receiving the letter. He had failed to circulate the letter. . . . Carlo Dadditt, an office employee, received the letter and forgot it had to leave his hands within 96 hours. He lost his job. . . . Delan Fairchild received the letter and not believing threw the letter away, nine days later he died. In 1987 the letter was received by a young woman in California, it was very faded and barely readable. She promised herself that she would retype the letter and send it on. But she put it aside to do later. She [was] plagued with various problems including expensive car repairs.

Biologist Richard Dawkins has suggested that such documents constitute "mind viruses" that exploit human instincts to ensure their own survival (see Ellis 2001: 79–80). Van Arsdale tends to agree, saying that chain letters exist in an information environment in which the "fittest" versions continue to circulate, while those that give the recipients less reason to pass them on simply disappear. "They have evolved independent of our real needs and beyond our control," he concludes (1998).

It is certainly plausible that the modern instructions are somehow adaptive for survival, accurately demanding the minimum number of copies needed to maintain the letter's circulation and offering the right mix of promise and warning needed to get at least one of the twenty recipients to pass it on. Still, simply describing the chain letter as an entity largely independent of the persons who circulate it ignores its fetishistic nature. Charismatic theologian Don Basham, an influential antioccult crusader, was actually closer to the truth when he included the modern chain letter among his list of potentially satanic practices. He described it as a means "to psychically compel a person, since the usual rewards for compliance are material wealth or power, and refusal to comply . . . is met with a curse or future bad luck, or even death" (1974: 115). In this case Basham is right: the chain letter is essentially a contagious curse, contained in an amulet-like piece of writing, which can only be removed by passing it on to other people.[9]

The chain letter thus cannot be separated from the older tradition of fetish-making through the use of writing or producing copies to bless and curse. As we have seen, the occult use of language has always involved the promise of good fortune tied up with the secret threat of some supernatural calamity. In the next chapter we will look more closely at "the making of books," of which the Bible correctly says there is no end, and the way in which the fetish practices we have surveyed here are amplified into "Black Bibles."

Chapter Four

Satanic Bibles

Amulets and *Himmelsbrief* documents were not the only items that were fabricated and circulated to gain good fortune. Entire documents existed that claimed to contain magical charms and the instructions for carrying them out. To an extent, these items resembled the list of required textbooks taken by a puzzled Harry Potter to Diagon Alley at the start of his apprenticeship:

> *The Standard Book of Spells (Grade 1)* by Miranda Goshawk
> *Magical Drafts and Potions* by Arsenius Jigger
> *The Dark Forces: A Guide to Self-Protection* by Quentin Trimble
>   (Rowling 1998: 66–67)

Even though these books did not actually exist (though Rowling subsequently fabricated editions of a few of them), information from them is liberally scattered through her books, to the concern of antioccult critics. "Harry Potter learns how to obtain and use witchcraft equipment," Pastor Meyer observes, adding that he "also learns a new vocabulary, including words such as 'Azkaban,' 'Circe,' 'Draco,' 'Erised,' 'Hermes,' and 'Slytherin'; all of which are names of real devils or demons" (Meyer 2000a). One could retort that these names are not in fact used to invoke spirits in the *Harry Potter* books, but are a mixture of place, object, and personal names. "Erised" is in fact "Desire" spelled backwards and comes from the widdershins inscription around the Mirror of Erised in the first *Harry Potter* book (1998: 207–8). Still, Pastor Meyer expresses concern that "By reading these materials, many millions of young people are learning how to work with demon spirits" (2000a).

One may smile, but the authentic spell books of tradition, as surveyed by occultist A.E. Waite in his *Book of Black Magic* (1972 [1898]), had, if anything, even more delicious titles:

The Arbatel of Magic: Isagoge [or "essential instruction"]

True Black Magic, or the Secret of Secrets

The Scarlet Dragon, or the Art of Commanding Celestial, Aerial, and Infernal Spirits

The Praxis Magica Fausti, or Magical Elements of Dr. John Faust, Practitioner of Medicine

The Black Pullet, or the Hen with the Golden Eggs, comprising the Science of Magic Talismans and Rings, the Art of Necromancy and of the Kabbalah

In some cases, these were preserved in manuscript form within families. One such, containing the family charms attributed to Peter Saylor, a legendary healer from near Easton, Pennsylvania, was made by his nephew in 1840 and is now in a university archive (Heindel 1976b: 23). Others, like the *Romanusbüchlein* (the "Gypsy's Little Book"), were published in cheap editions sold by occult specialty houses (see Yoder 1976). Most of these claimed to be collections of *good* magic, with the charms regularly ending with "the three highest names," or the Father, Son, and Holy Spirit. Nevertheless, such works promised to help curious readers learn the names of the celestial (and not-so-celestial) spirits that could be commanded to one's benefit, and to teach how to fabricate and use the paraphernalia needed to contact and control them. To the eyes of the orthodox, such books were never better than diabolical, however benevolent their stated intentions.

Brauch Books and Evil Books

One such was *Der Lange Verborgene Freund* [The Long-Lost Friend], compiled in 1819 by Johann Georg Hohman, a German immigrant who lived near Reading, Pennsylvania. Hohman had previously added to his meager farming income by charming various diseases and selling copies of a *Himmelsbrief*. Aware that publishing an extensive collection of charms was likely to draw attacks from Protestant clergy as a magic book, he included a lengthy defense of his work as a preface:

> Many people say it is right to print and sell such books. But a small number say that it may not be right. I sincerely pity people who have gone so far astray, and I wish that everyone would do

their best to guide them back from their straying. It is true that whoever abuses [*mißbrauchet*] the name of Jesus commits a great sin. But doesn't the 50th Psalm specifically state: "Call on me in need, and I will rescue you, and you shall glorify me"? I say: we commit a grave sin, and even deny ourselves heaven, when we willingly let a neighbor lose an eye, or a leg, or any other limb, if we could have helped with this little book. Such people reject what the Lord commanded: namely, that we should call on him in need.

If we dare not use [*brauchen*] words and the Highest Names, they would not have been revealed to this earth's inhabitants, and the Lord would not come to help, if anyone used [*brauchen*] them. There is no power that can force God to act, if it is not His divine will. (1904: 102–3; my translation)

The term "brauchen" (literally, "to use") became the normal euphemism among the Pennsylvania Germans for charming. "A brauch book is no evil book," one twentieth-century source explained to folklorists. "There is nothing in such a book but prayers and there are some persons who call it a prayer book" (Dorson 1964: 111).

In fact, much of Hohman's book consists of techniques and formulas commonly used by magical healers in the European tradition. A remedy for worms advises the reader to stroke the afflicted person or animal, while repeating a verse:

Mary, God's mother, traversed the land,
Holding three worms close in her hand;
One was white, the other was black, the third was red.

At the end of the ceremony, the charmer was to tell the worms to leave within a set period of time, "but not less than three minutes" (1992: 20). Other items give herbal cures for various illnesses, and one gives ingredients for a fish lure. But one does not need to read far to find other entries that have less to do with healing and more with witchcraft. One describes the making of a wand to use in finding water or valuable ore: on Christmas night, facing east, break off a forked twig while invoking the Highest Names. Then, Hohman instructs, one should strike the ground while saying, "Archangel Gabriel, I conjure thee in the name of God, the Almighty, to tell me, is there any water [or ore] here or not? do tell me!" In response, the instructions say, "that which you desire will appear immediately" (1992: 21).

Hohman's book includes directions for making a variety of self-protective amulets in a number of strange languages. Indeed, the book itself was self-advertised as a fetish, as it ends with the promise, "Whoever carries this book with him is safe from all his enemies, visible or invisible; and whoever has this book with him cannot die without the holy corpse of Jesus Christ, nor drown in any water, nor burn up in any fire, nor can any unjust sentence be passed upon him" (1992: 57). *Der Lange Verborgene Freund,* both in the original German and later in two different English translations, was widely reprinted in a variety of cheap editions. Many of these were pocket-sized editions with black leather covers resembling small Testaments, indicating that many people bought it more as a talisman than as a practical manual for magic. It remains in print, and folklorist Eric Maple records that as recently as the Vietnam War, recruits from the Pennsylvania Dutch country went into battle carrying a copy of this charm collection (1973: 106).

Hohman's collection was influential in the United States, perhaps because Anglo-American culture lacked a strong tradition of the grimoire and ceremonial magic. In European cultures the *Romanusbüchlein* was only one of many published books of magic. In Scandinavia, the *Book of Cyprianus* was the most commonly mentioned spell book; in France and Germany, a number of volumes attributed to Albertus Magnus remain popular. These include *Les admirables Secrets du Grand Albert* (frequently rendered in German as *Ägyptische Geheimnisse* [Egyptian Secrets]); an abbreviated version of this work was circulated as *Le Petit Albert.* Other grimoires that had a wide distribution were *Le Véritable Dragon Rouge/Der Wahrhaftige, Feurige Drache* (the genuine scarlet [or fiery] dragon) and the *Key* [or *Clavicle*] *of Solomon the King.*

These, however, paled in contrast to the *Sixth and Seventh Books of Moses,* the most frequently mentioned compilation of black magic techniques. Ironically, some accounts say it was originally compiled as a defense against an even more evil book, known only as *The Black Bible* (Sebald 1978: 76). By the nineteenth century, however, it had become, in tradition, the satanic parallel to the Scriptures, and mere possession of it was thought to imply a pact with the devil. Like *Der Lange Verborgene Freund,* it went through a variety of cheap editions, many of which resembled "a small Bible or a New Testament," and Koch confiscated and burned many such copies from the mid-1930s on (1962: 131–33). In the

United States, it circulated both in German editions, usually claiming to reprint one from "Stuttgart 1849," and in an English translation that was first published by the New York firm Wehman Brothers in 1880 (González-Wippler 1982; Heindel 1976a: 21–22).

Once owners began to read the contents, both legend and antioccult propaganda agree, they implicitly became committed to the devil, unless a priest or *Braucher* (good charmer) could "read them free." Even if no ill effects were noted at first, Koch observed, ownership of this book led to psychological problems, though many times they did not appear until the person was on the brink of death. At this point, Koch says, three possibilities emerged: Diabolical visitors might tear away the mask of "white magic," and owners die cursing or otherwise signifying their damnation. Owners might try to give away the fatal book before death, by initiating a family member into its mysteries. Or they might renounce the book and ask their family to burn it. Legends illustrating all three situations appear frequently in folklore collections and archives, as in this German American legend from Illinois:

> About ten years ago [1923] a woman out at Liberty was a witch. . . . One day she got real sick and was sick a long time. She sent for the Lutheran preacher. He told her she could not get well or die until she would give up a witchcraft book she had. She said she wanted her son to have the book so he could bewitch. . . . The preacher told her she could not die in peace until she gave him the book. At last she reached under her pillow and got the book out and gave it to him. The preacher went and put it in the cookstove to burn; and while it was burning, this old witch died. (Hyatt 1965: no. 15878)

However, such deathbed legends appear mainly in witch masters' propagandistic legends *about* witchcraft. When we turn to the more objective traditions preserved within families that possessed and used such books, it turns out that *reading* the book was optional. As with Hohman's volume, many editions of the *Sixth and Seventh Books of Moses* contained an assurance that owners would be protected from harm and able to command the devil so long as the book was in their possession. An example of this is provided by Richard Shaner, who learned that his Aunt Annie, a reputed witch, had owned a copy of the book. After her death, he convinced his uncle to show it to him:

He laughed and took me upstairs to his bedroom. In a special dower chest where he kept his most treasured possessions was the dread book as well as one by Albertus Magnus. I must admit that I was disappointed for the red cloth-bound books did not appear to be older than about sixty years and were in English. Knowing that my uncle read English very poorly and that most Pennsylvania Dutch read German I did not consider that the books were used much at all. (1972: 41)

What did this book contain that gave it such a sinister reputation? Clearly, both the legends and indeed some of the editions themselves diverted people from looking too closely at its contents. Koch pointedly refuses to characterize its contents, saying only that it explains how to contact Satan. Informants in Franconia were often so vague about it that they most often referred to it simply as the *Sixth Book of Moses*, while German Americans most often called it the *Seventh Book*. Most other legendary accounts are so vague that at least two American folklorists wondered if it existed at all (Wukasch 1991: 48). Some editions of the book obviously capitalized on its reputed diabolical nature: one "Philadelphia" German edition contained black seals to the right of the title page with the imprint of a skull and crossbones; presumably these had to be broken before one could begin to see what was in the book and so provided a guard against the owner "reading himself fast" in the book (Shaner 1972: 42).

In fact, the core of both German and American editions of the *Sixth and Seventh Books* is an anthology of woodcuts, supposedly traced from an old manuscript, illustrating conjuring amulets and protective talismans. These are purported to have been drawn "from the Mosaic books of the Cabala and the Talmud." The introduction to the *Sixth Book,* for instance, claims that the following tables and seals were revealed to Moses on Mount Sinai and communicated secretly to Aaron and Joshua, and thence via their descendants to King Solomon, who used them to command spirits to collect his legendary wealth. The preface also notes that the material, though "the highest mystery," was discovered in 330 by the Roman emperor Constantine and given to Pope Sylvester, who had it translated but ordered that it never be made public, under threat of excommunication. In 1520, however, a copy came into the hands of the Holy Roman emperor Charles V,[1] who "highly recommended" it and allowed it to be published (*Sixth and Seventh Books* [n.d.]: 6).

What follows are seven "secret seals" to be used with accompanying conjurations to achieve various practical results. Two of these, much like the ceremony in Hohman's book for locating water or ore, bring hidden treasures to the surface of the earth. Others promise help in gaining fortune or healing sickness. Perhaps to save money, these woodcuts were printed in negative impressions, producing the "white letters on a black background" described both by folk tradition and *Jay's Journal* (figure 1). The incantations are composed of a bewildering combination of German, Latin, and garbled Hebrew words and phrases. The theology is also confusing: apparently Jewish phrases and concepts freely mingle with explicitly Christian references. The conjuration accompanying one seal is typical:

Fig. 1. Magical seals from *The Sixth and Seventh Books of Moses.*

I, N. N., a servant of God, desire, call upon and conjure thee, Spirit Phuel, by the Holy Messengers and all the Disciples of the Lord, by the four Holy Evangelists and the three Holy Men of God and by the most terrible and most holy words Abriel, Fibriel, Sada, Saday, Sarabo, Laragola, Lavaterium, Laroyol, Zay, Sagin, Labir, Lya, Adeo, Deus, Alon, Abay, Laos, Pieus, Ehos, Mibi, Uini, Mora, Zorad, and by those holy words, that thou come and appear before me, N. N., in a beautiful human form, and bring me what I desire. (This the conjuror must name.) (8)

The *Sixth Book* goes on to recommend a number of spirits who could also be conjured with the same seal, but, as before, the ritual seems optional, since making and carrying the seal on one's person is enough to bring one "great fortune and blessing." Hence, as with the *Himmelsbrief* and its chain-letter descendants, the act of copying the seal is the heart of the tradition, not the act of conjuration.

The *Seventh Book* is similar, providing negative-image woodcuts of twelve magical "tables" to be carried on one's person to achieve results such as good luck in play, victory in lawsuits, and success in finding buried treasure. These, also, are accompanied by brief incantations summoning spirits. The rest of the volume consists of a diverse collection of items:

- A lengthy essay on "The Magic of the Israelites," discussing the role of conjuration and exorcism in both Old and New Testaments
- Additional woodcuts of charms in Hebrew script from "the magical Kabala"
- A set of instructions on how to conjure, attributed to the legendary Dr. Faust of Wittenberg
- Magical seals and instructions for raising spirits such as Mephistopheles
- Instructions on how to use the "Schemhamphoras," or sacred names of God
- A pseudo-cabalistic treatise on how to use each of the Biblical psalms for magical or self-protective purposes
- A miscellany of magical cures and superstitions supposedly drawn from the Talmud

Fig. 2. Magical pentagram from *The Sixth and Seventh Books of Moses.*

Koch notes that the contents of the editions he examined "vary widely" (1962: 132; 1978: 203), but the one connecting link is that the book purports to be a compilation of Jewish magic. Will-Erich Peuckert (1957) has shown that the contents do contain some genuine information derived from the Talmud and Qabbalah; this is, however, freely mingled with material from Christian grimoires (especially from *Le Véritable Dragon Rouge*) and from German (non-Jewish) folklore. Examination of the contents by rabbis showed the allegedly Hebraic inscriptions to be garbled and the description of magic practices fraudulent (Sebald 1978: 90, 96). The *Sixth and Seventh Books,* therefore, fall into a long and unsavory German tradition of equating a garbled version of Judaic mysticism with devil-worship (see Trachtenburg 1943: 76–87).

The book remains vital in rural Germanic cultures. In the 1950s, Planet-Verlag, an occult publisher in North Germany, printed and sold 9,000 copies. In 1956, a coalition of antioccult authorities, including Koch and antisuperstition crusader Johann Kruse, sued the publisher, claim-

ing that some of the spells included might be taken as encouraging occult murders. Although folklorist Will-Erich Peuckert testified for the
defense, a lower court in fact found Planet-Verlag guilty of "harmful
publication" and imposed heavy fines (Sebald 1978: 94–95). In Pennsylvania, after Richard Shaner admitted in 1960 that his family had owned
a copy of the book, he and the Pennsylvania Folklore Society were flooded
by requests from residents for help against jealous neighbors (1961: 62–
63). Cheap reprints of the Wehman Brothers publication remain readily
available, and Hans Sebald notes that they are popular among African
American occultists as well as with those of German ancestry (1978: 95).

What lies behind the continuing popularity of this volume, then?
Is it a reflection of anti-Semitic prejudices, muted but not destroyed in
the wake of horror over the Holocaust? The relationship of the book to
its possessors is much more complex: while rejecting as evil the tradition
from which the book came, rural Christian cultures nevertheless circulate and use it because they find some of its rituals and talismans useful
for certain purposes. In fact, the book's power may be enhanced by the
superficially Judaic trappings, which make the contents seem far more
diabolical than a list of charms made in the name of the Christian Trinity. For Protestant audiences, the claim that the volume is secretly owned
by the Vatican Library is further proof both of its evil nature and of the
need to own it oneself for self-protection.

Significantly, a survey of the spells included in the *Sixth and Seventh Books* shows that many are medicinal and self-protective charms
similar to those found in "white" magical volumes. Many of the practices
that Koch claimed to have located in the *Sixth and Seventh Books* are in
fact rituals found in the folk medicine of many countries, as in this case:
"A bishop in northern Germany told me about the following custom
found in his diocese. In order to remove warts the men sprinkle themselves with some water used in the washing of a female corpse. Women
do the same with the water used in washing a male corpse. While they
are doing this they repeat a spell found in the 6th and 7th Book of Moses.
The warts do in fact disappear" (1970: 122).[2] Only a minority of the
books' spells are "hexes" that promise harm to another person; nevertheless, these are the ones stressed in accounts describing actual use of
the volume. Whatever the actual contents of the *Sixth and Seventh Books*,
then, the important thing for the people using it was that its scope extended beyond the implicit limits given to the folk healer and into an
active sphere of folk magic. Here, practitioners could not only react to

the threat of misfortune but initiate actions intended to punish the source of this misfortune. This active role, as before, mirrors that of the crusaders who were themselves trying to neutralize the threat of occult books.

Spellbinding: The Conjurer as Psychic Cop

One role made possible by ownership of the *Sixth and Seventh Books* was that of a kind of supernatural court of appeal for any dispute that could not be settled in normal ways. We have noted already that witchcraft, even though feared, was in some cases a valid alternative to calling in institutional authorities such as priests or police. Particularly in cases in which both theft and complex family or clan ties were involved, bringing in outside authorities might be seen as embarrassing. But if reliance on *Braucher*s proved insufficient to punish or deter theft, grimoires like the *Sixth and Seventh Books* included a scattering of rituals threatening severe supernatural penalties. Thus, the possessor of this volume had the extra-legal power, potentially, to "throw the book" at a person or family who had committed some crime.

We have seen that antioccult lore warns that anyone who began to read in magic books would become frozen or "read fast." This is paralleled in witchcraft traditions themselves by the belief that a witch or sorcerer could punish those who crossed him by "spellbinding" them— that is, by fixing them in their places. Koch relates a story about a cunning-folk who used such power to ensure that all of his customers would pay him. "Anyone who after a consultation does not voluntarily offer to pay his five or ten francs finds himself unable at the station to board the passenger train.... The railway officials know of the situation and laughingly tell such passengers, 'First take your five francs to [the cunning-folk,] then you can get on'" (1972: 143; cf. 1962: 82).

Koch concedes that he had this story secondhand from three Swiss friends, so he could not confirm its literal truth. As with ostensive witches, though, it is possible that the charmer encouraged circulation of the tale as a way of ensuring that visitors leave him payment before heading for the railway station. Like most cunning-folk, the Swiss charmer could not directly charge for his cures; however, many such persons expected that patients would voluntarily leave something, either in cash or barter. One Pennsylvania healer in fact commented that payment made the healing more effective: "They have to give ya a little bit, something to throw that [disease] away from them. . . . They gotta lay it down someplace and you don't touch it until they're gone" (Westcott 1969/70: 8). Barbara Reimensnyder likewise noted a widespread belief that if one did not pay a healer, or gave only a small amount, the treatment would not work (1989: 49). The tradition, whether or not it has a basis in posthypnotic suggestion, provides a safeguard against casual patients taking advantage of cunning-folk by choosing not to leave any reward.

This ability to immobilize someone was attributed to many "white" witches who were able to use "spell-fixing" as a way of preventing or punishing theft (e.g. Hyatt 1965: nos. 16112–23; Reimensnyder 1989: 103). One such was the legendary cunning-folk Peter Saylor, from the Easton, Pennsylvania area: "he butchered a hog and, not having sufficient time to properly dress it and take it into the smokehouse, he left it hanging outside from a tree limb, protecting it with a 'charmed circle' which he drew on the ground around the tree. Next morning a thief was found transfixed within the circle, unable to move. The doctor administered a severe reprimand and sent him on his way" (Heindel 1976b: 22). A British "cunning man" from Ipswich was said to have charmed a thief from a distance "so that he wandered around the scene of his crimes like a blind man and was unable to make his escape" (Maple 1964: 159).

Germanic folk magic provides several elaborate charms "to fix a thief." Typically, these were recited while walking around in a circle, to which the thief was supposed to be drawn during the night. Most of these begin in an apparently Christian context, as in this nineteenth-century North German example:

> Mother Mary was journeying over the land,
> she had her beloved child by the hand.
> Then came the thieves and would steal.
> Then spake she to St. Peter: "Bind!"
> St. Peter said: "I have bound
> with iron bands, with God's hands."

A repetitive incantation follows that binds the thief to "stand as a stock, and look staring as a goat" until he or she counts "all the grass that grows on the earth," "the stars which stand in heaven," and "the sand that lies on the sea's ground," a magical formula also used in the *Himmelsbrief* to describe the number of sins forgiven if one copies the text. Then the incantation ends on a surprising note.

The heaven I give thee for thy hut,
and the earth for shoes to thy feet.
Amen! in the devil's name.[3]
(Thorpe [his trans.] 1851: 3:178–79)

Similar diabolical spells were preserved in *Albertus Magnus; or Egyptian Secrets,* another spell book widely published in Pennsylvania Dutch country. One very elaborate conjuration, headed *To Compel a Thief to Return Stolen Property,* includes this passage:

Asteroth, God in Gods and of God, the thief who robbed N.N.,
that thief, be it male or female, bring hither to me in my N.N.
house with the articles stolen. Beelzebub be bound, Lucifer be
bound, Satan be bound with the rays which emanate from the
holy countenance of God . . . Moloch, Lucifer, Asteroth Pemeoth
Forni gator Anector, Somiator, sleep ye not, awake, the strong
hero Holaha, the powerful Eaton, the mighty Tetragrammaton;
Athe, Alpha et Omega, compel ye that the thief may return the
stolen articles into the house of N.N., and that the thief shall have
neither rest nor peace through sand and land, through sea or air,
on mountain or rock, thou accursed devil, lead the thief back
into my house with all the stolen goods (n.d.: 79–80).

Even Hohman's "white magic" spell book contains several "spell-binding" spells, including a version of the verse above. This lacks the appeal to the devil's name, but it and others include common black magic elements. One requires that three coffin nails "greased with the grease from an executed criminal or other sinful person" be ritually pounded into a pear tree, while reciting an incantation that states that the nails are spiritually entering the thief's brain, lungs and liver, and feet (1992: 45–46). A third method of binding thieves involves reciting a charm while turning a wagon wheel backwards, to draw the guilty party to the scene of his crime. Hohman published a "Christian" version (1992: 53–54), but a similar ritual was included in the *Shemhamforash* section of the *Sixth and Seventh Books of Moses:*

if a man has committed murder, theft, or any other act which his
conscience condemns . . . his conscience will then give him no
rest until he returns what he has stolen, or until he has suffered

the punishment due to his crime. Therefore, in the name of the Father, Son and Holy Spirit, take three small pieces of wood from the door-sill over which the thief passed in leaving the place where he committed the theft, place them within a wagon-wheel, and then through the hub of the wheel say the following words: "I pray thee, thou Holy Trinity, that thou mayest cause A, who stole from me B, a, C, to have no rest or peace until he again restores me that which he has stolen." Turn the wheel round three times and replace it again on the wagon.[4] (1970: 133)

Dr. E. Grumbine of Lebanon County, Pennsylvania, records an account of a fellow veterinarian who performed this ritual, asking his son to help him turn the wheel. "The son must have laughed in his sleeves while going through the performances," Grumbine notes, "for he himself was the thief!" (1905: 272).

From the Arcan Bible of Moses.

Fig. 3. The Shemhamforash from *The Sixth and Seventh Books of Moses*

Such traditions use the supernatural power of "spell-fixing" as an analogue to the way in which police officers literally "arrest" malefactors and, if possible, make them return the stolen property to the owners. Just as the healer and witch were both seen as rivals to priests, then, the sorcerer often functioned as a kind of "psychic cop" called in to deal unofficially with crimes. Robert Muchembled, among other historians of the witch trials, has suggested that the emerging legal establishment had as much to do with defining devil worship as a social problem as did theologians. He sees prosecutors' emphasis on stamping out such occult practices as an episode "in the conquest of the West European countryside by the forces of law and order . . . the advance of public authority against particularism, against the rural custom of settling disputes between man and man with the least possible recourse to outside tribunals" (Muchembled 1990: 139). If the possessor of a fetish, whether an amulet or a grimoire, thereby appropriated some kind of quasi-legal powers, we see one additional reason why law enforcement communities, from an early period, saw such practices as an unusual threat to their legitimacy. Over and above any crimes that these writings might incite, then, successful magic makes law and order itself dispensable. Marlowe's Doctor Faustus puts the principle well:

> Emperors and kings
> Are but obeyed in their several provinces,
> Nor can they raise the wind or rend the clouds;
> But [the wizard's] dominion that exceeds in this
> Stretcheth as far as doth the mind of man.
> A sound magician is a demigod. . . .
> (I.i.57–62)

Good ethnographic descriptions of such supernatural "police work" are, however, uncommon. Sebald does give a detailed account of a clan feud between families he calls the "Meddlers" and the "Fruitgrowers," in which the black book played a prominent role (1978: 104–8). Both families, apparently, were prone to using witchcraft in times of need, but a season in which the Meddlers experienced more trouble than usual with their livestock called for special action. The Meddlers suspected their Fruitgrower neighbors, who had also been in the annoying habit of reaping grass from the Meddler side of their boundary line, of placing a hex. The family first called in a Christian-oriented healer, who, after performing a ritual to neutralize the hex, told them that the first person to try to borrow something from them would be identified as the guilty party. This, not surprisingly, proved to be one of the Fruitgrowers, so the matriarch of the Meddler family decided to take the initiative.

She knew that one of her distant relatives owned a copy of the *Sixth and Seventh Books of Moses,* and that it contained a spell to punish a thief by making his or her animals sicken. Given the circumstances, this seemed an appropriate supernatural penalty for the Fruitgrowers, who were seen as guilty both of stealing the grass and of afflicting the Meddlers' livestock. Which spell was used (and whether it is contained in the editions consulted) is unclear, but it presumably is the same as one used by another Franconian witch to punish a thief, which warns the user not to "commence in God's name, but in the name of three devils" (Sebald 1978: 118).

Sebald comments that, while the family copy of the black book was never shown to nonrelatives, nevertheless "its possession was as secret in a village of approximately two dozen peasant families as a house on fire" (91). Likewise, the Meddlers' use of the book was barely concealed; indeed, Sebald found numerous variants of the account in local tradition, most of which exaggerated the Meddler matriarch's involvement in black magic. The spell, according to family history, made its point: the thief from the Fruitgrower family did indeed come to the Meddlers to admit her theft and ask forgiveness, in return for lifting the hex. Afterwards, the copy of the *Sixth and Seventh Books* was returned to the original owners. Despite this resolution, the incident had long-reaching consequences: the two families continued their petty feuding, and the Meddlers eventually quarreled with the relatives who had loaned them the book. Tradition attributed a string of personal misfortunes to their use of the grimoire, and eventually the family homestead passed into the hands of outsiders, an unusual event in the area.

Much of Sebald's information came from villagers hostile to the participants, so we need to interpret it cautiously. It is clear, though, that the Meddlers' motives for using the *Sixth and Seventh Books* were desire to protect themselves against the rival family's use of magic and to punish them for a petty but chronic form of theft. Their use of an antitheft spell took the place of legal actions that might have been unsuccessful and certainly would have been expensive and embarrassing. However, taking this step subjected them to a form of scapegoating that outlasted their actual use or possession of the dread book.

The same, obviously, is true on the establishment side: it is far easier for law enforcement agents to warn others not to study occult texts, and so hide their ignorance of what they contain, than it is for them to begin a study of occult texts. Still, the psychological dangers of becoming educated in the lore of magic may be exaggerated, but probably do exist. Kurt E. Koch warned his readers not to use his antioccult counseling techniques without caution. He noted that one Christian doctor who had begun to use his *Christian Counseling and Occultism* in his practice was soon after found wandering in a forest, insane. He died shortly, purportedly a victim of psychic attack from demons (1973: 150; Koch and Lechler 1970: 87). Perhaps both sides are conceding that contact with such practices can "read persons fast." One may not become "arrested" on the spot, but one may find that it is easier to become a "psychic cop" than to stop being one.

To sum up, lore about the *Sixth and Seventh Books of Moses* pointed to its pseudo-cabalistic contents to portray it as a Jewish devil-book. To this extent, reactions to the book were based on anti-Semitic ideas, but the focus was not on its ownership and use by Jews. Rather, cunning-folk who were Christian-oriented used it as part of their own tradition of charming in the name of the Trinity. Its use, therefore, was grounded in a narrow threshold between acceptance of Christianity as a personal religion and skepticism about the moral and civil authorities whose job it was to enforce Christian tradition as an established code of morality.

Use of a grimoire such as the *Sixth and Seventh Books* allowed one to skirt the fringes of establishment religion: Jews were assumed by their enemies not to be bound by the Christian duty to love one's neighbor; hence their magic was more flexible in dealing with cases in which anger and desire for revenge were more appropriate than meek forgiveness. Still, many of the allegedly Jewish incantations did, after all, mention Christian figures and implied the validity of Jesus as the Son of God, so users were not directly renouncing their salvation, as many of the libels suggested. Hence, the popular conception of such a book opened up personal space to retain social powers, in supernatural form, which in their literal forms now had to be surrendered to authority figures.

We can see use of diabolical magic, then, as an effort to retain personal independence in the face of growing religious and civil authoritarianism. One folk aspect of this might be the belief that the mainstream tradition of charming in the name of the Trinity was, in some cases, not strong enough. But even in the absence of a charming tradition, Koch tells us, German adolescents often picked up the book as a token of their rebellion against establishment religion.

> At a youth conference a 17-year-old lad came to an evangelistic meeting with a New Testament in his left pocket and, bound in similar format, the 6th. and 7th. Book of Moses in his right. . . . We looked through the magic book and found that the lad had bound himself to the devil by putting his signature underneath a picture of Lucifer. We then burned the book. The parents, who did not know that the lad had this magic book, made a typical answer to our inquiry. They said that the lad suffered from strange fits of mania, and possessed in general a strange, dark, restless character. They simply could not make him out. (1972: 155)

Anton La Vey's Satanic Bible: a Folkloristic Analysis

In the United States, this darkly rebellious class of adolescent proved precisely the audience for Anton Szandor LaVey's *Satanic Bible*. Originally published in 1969 in the wake of publicity over his San Francisco "Church of Satan," much of the book consists of LaVey's self-assertive philosophy and critique of organized religions. Claiming to be an ex-police photographer, LaVey said he had become disenchanted with the doctrines of Christianity, which did not fit the grim realities of life, and in fact seemed to outlaw everything that individuals enjoyed doing. The first sections of the *Satanic Bible* argue these points at length, stating that people should preach what they practice, making their appetites their gods, rather than unsuccessfully trying to practice what religious authorities preach. Much of this philosophy, objective readers have found, derives from long-standing doctrines of free-thinking, influential in American thought, that advise readers to take nothing for granted, even in allegedly inspired scriptures or doctrines, but to challenge and test all things. LaVey, like the American deists, accepts the notion of a life after death, arguing that if the ego has remained vital through life, "it is this ego which will refuse to die, even after the expiration of the flesh which housed it" (94). Likewise, he states orthodox reasons to discourage suicide (94–95) and outlaw human or animal sacrifice (89).

The book remains central to the American occult scene. In surveying 140 self-identified satanists, James R. Lewis (2002) found that, even after LaVey's death, it remains "the single most influential document shaping the contemporary Satanist movement." A fifth of those surveyed specifically mentioned their reading of the *Satanic Bible* as the single most influential factor in their joining the movement, and a number volunteered "conversion" stories featuring it. "After being told my choices in clothing, music, art, poetry, etc. were Satanic," one commented, "I decided to buy *The Satanic Bible* to see if it was as bad as [my step-father] made it out to be." While Lewis found that most of his respondents had become involved in the satanic movement as teenagers, he was nevertheless surprised by the seriousness with which his respondents took their religious choice, even though two-thirds had sampled at least one other occult tradition (usually Neo-Paganism).

While it may, as Lewis suggests, be naive to assume that the popularity of the book is merely due to a reaction against mainstream Christianity, clearly the core doctrine appeals to a personality that is not satisfied with following "school rules" set up for the masses, but instinctively experiments and finds one's own rules through experience. Nevertheless, *The Satanic Bible* would not have generated the notoriety it commands, among both cult crusaders and questioning adolescents, had it not been for LaVey's adroit use of the grimoire tradition. The book was cobbled together quickly in response to a publisher's interest in exploiting rising fascination with the occult, spurred by popular press reports about the Wiccan revival and movies such as *Rosemary's Baby* (in which LaVey himself played Satan). Gathering a variety of mimeographed handouts prepared for early converts, LaVey found that he simply did not have enough copy to meet the publisher's guidelines, so he expanded what had begun as a series of polemic essays about religion by adding magickal-*looking* materials. In an introduction, LaVey condemns previous magic books as "sanctimonious fraud-guilt-ridden ramblings and exoteric gibberish" (21). Nevertheless, the format of his book indicates his awareness and appropriation of material from these sources, particularly the *Sixth and Seventh Books of Moses.*

This can be seen in the cover of the popular paperback edition, which contains the title—white writing on a black background—above a cabalistic sign printed in a lurid red, in which five Hebrew letters surround the five points of a star. LaVey explains this as a symbol of "Baphomet" or the carnal nature of humanity, and adds, "The Hebraic figures around the outer circle of the symbol which stem from the magical teachings of the Kabala, spell out 'Leviathan,' the serpent of the watery abyss, and identified with Satan. These figures correspond to the five points of the inverted star." LaVey's figure, while drawing on Masonic and anti-Masonic lore (which we will examine later), corresponds exactly to one of the more elaborate of the woodcuts in the *Sixth and Seventh Books*, where it is described as a protective symbol within which the conjurer stands to summon spirits (figure 2). Like LaVey's symbol, it incorporates Hebraic letters, and the rituals which follow it include an invocation of Leviathan, here described as a monster of hell.

LaVey also adapts the *Sixth and Seventh Books*' emphasis on lists of names as a conjuring device. His "Satanic Ritual" prescribes the reading of a list of "infernal names" drawn from the cabalistic tradition, to which the names of "evil" spirits from other cultures have been added. (Coyote, the mythic trickster figure in many Native American cultures, is included, for instance, as an "American Indian devil.") This parallels the instructions given in the earlier grimoire to raise spirits by reciting a list of angelic or divine names. Indeed, the earlier book's emphasis on the "Shemhamforash," or seals containing the divine names of God, resurfaces quaintly in LaVey's instruction that, after each prayer to Satan, the participants say both "Hail, Satan!" and "Shemhamforash!"

LaVey concludes his book with nineteen "keys" in a magical language purporting to be "Enochian" and derived from the crystal-gazing experiments of the Elizabethan mage John Dee. One of the brief keys reads, "Ilasa! tabaanu li-El pereta, casaremanu upaahi cahisa *dareji; das* oado caosaji oresacore: das omaxa monasaçi Baeouibe od emetajisa Iaidix. Zodacare od Sodameranu! Odo cicale Qaa. Sodoreje lape sodiredo Noco Mada, hoathahe Saitan!" (245). Similarly, much of the *Sixth and Seventh Books* consists of phonetically transcribed invocations in "Hebrew" that, like LaVey's keys, resembles the "completely unknown language" of the legendary *Black Bible*. The "citation" (or invocation) of Mephistopheles reads, "Messias, Adonaij, Weforus, Xathor, Yxewe, Soraweijs, Yxaron, Wegharh, Sljahor, Weghaij, Wesoron, Xoxijwe, Zijwonwawetho, Regthoswatho, Zebaoth, Adonaji, Zijwetho, Aglaij, Wijzathe, Zadaij, Zijebo Xosthoy, Athlato, Zsewey, Zyxyzet, Ysche, Sarswwu, Zyzyrn, Dewononhathbo, Xyxewem, Syzwe, Theos, Yschaos, Worsonbefogosy, Gefgowe, Hegor, Quaratho, Zywe, Messias, Abarabi, Mephistophiles" (103). LaVey prints his Enochian keys with a "Satanically correct" translation, but comments, "the meaning of the words, combined with the quality of the words, unites to create a pattern of sound which can cause tremendous reaction in the atmosphere" (155). He follows in this respect the compiler of the *Sixth and Seventh Books,* who sometimes included translation of the "Hebrew," but stressed that the mystical language itself creates the effect. "The Citation-Formulas contained in this book must only be pronounced in the Hebrew language, and in no other. In any other language they have no power whatever, and the Master can never be sure of his cause. For all these words and forms were thus pronounced by the Great Spirit and have power only in the Hebrew Language" (67).

Thus, the *Satanic Bible* continues, in detail and spirit, the fetish tradition that appropriates nominally Jewish ideas and symbols to communicate the idea of evil magic. Despite the deistic philosophy of the polemic essays (which LaVey demands, optimistically, that readers read and understand before proceeding to the rituals), much of the book remains essentially a cabalistic grimoire. Like the *Sixth and Seventh Books of Moses,* it stresses the essentially magical properties of language. Further, by using an *unknown* language to embody its rituals, LaVey requires his followers to purchase and read aloud from his book, in much the same way that grimoire compilers stressed both the unintelligibility of their charms and the need to reproduce them with precision. Only by fabricating a written or printed document and commodifying it could this be done.

This aspect of LaVey's book, much more than the self-assertive philosophy he advocates, made it an appropriate item for rebellious youth to purchase. A black book superficially resembling a small Testament, offering directions on how to cast spells that harm people who deserve punishment, and containing long stretches of an unintelligible language, the volume embodies a tradition of beliefs about what a "Black Bible" *ought* to be like. Its continuing popularity among the age and class most disenchanted with religious and legal institutions likewise reflects a centuries-old conflict between the individual-based social code of marginalized cultures and the growing authority of law and order. The number of persons who read the volume carefully and carry out the rituals in the vein that LaVey intended is doubtless much smaller than those who simply own the book. Nevertheless, as Robert Hicks reports, many religious and law-enforcement experts sincerely believe that the book itself contains satanic power, and that "body-snatching demons arise from the printed page" (1991: 55). In much the same way, Pastor Meyer claims that, when *Harry Potter and the Goblet of Fire* was placed on sale at midnight on July 8, 2000, "These books were taken into homes everywhere with a real evil spirit following each copy to curse those homes" (2000a). For many people, critics and adherents both, simply having a book about witchcraft in one's possession is magic and social protest enough.

Chapter Five

(Why Is a Lucky Rabbit's Foot Lucky?

Harry Potter begins his practical career as a wizard by visiting a shop labeled "Ollivanders: Makers of Fine Wands since 382 B.C." There the proprietor offers him a series of wands, until he finds one that is exactly right. "Every Ollivander wand has a core of a powerful magical substance," he explains to the young wizard. "We use unicorn hairs, phoenix tail feathers, and the heartstrings of dragons. No two Ollivander wands are the same, just as no two unicorns, dragons, or phoenixes are quite the same" (1998: 83–84). Mr. Ollivander is emphasizing a fact central to many fetish traditions: it is necessary to use a substance from a living being as the "core" of the magical object. While the feather that forms the essential core of Harry's wand was given voluntarily by the phoenix that grew it, in most actual traditions, the core of the fetish must be taken by force.

This leads to a seemingly simple question with a surprisingly complex answer: what made the muggle practice of carrying a rabbit's foot—a dried body part from a living animal—so popular in the twentieth century? The practice, like that of chain letters, has been so widespread that, paradoxically, little has been done actually to document the tradition. On an American commercial postcard, copyrighted 1909, the rabbit's foot was included as part of an array of immediately recognizable lucky objects, along with a horseshoe to hang on one's door, a bunch of four-leafed clovers, and a wishbone. The other three have a long history in Anglo-American folklore,[1] and one might assume that belief in the rabbit's foot was, likewise, of long standing. Yet, surprisingly, it is not recorded as common in Great Britain or North America until the beginning of the twentieth century.[2]

If we examine the making and carrying of a rabbit's foot as a modern example of a fetish, then we see that it is more than a good-luck token. It is an object specially constructed to carry *social* power. The making, commodifying, and possessing of rabbits' feet need to be seen in the context of a broader belief-language, and the act understood against a background of many other analogous practices. This is why we will need to discuss the rabbit's foot custom in the context of *human* body parts and their symbolic replacements.

We will look first, though, at the documentable history of the rabbit's foot tradition in the United States, finding its roots not in primitive nature worship but in the politically subversive tradition of African-American *conjure*. As such, it expresses in a culturally ambiguous way many core beliefs found in both Anglo-American and African-American folklore. We will look at three closely related traditions of fetish that collectively weave a tapestry of meaning for the rabbit's foot tradition: one focusing on graveyard artifacts, one focusing on the body parts of animals, and, finally, one focusing on human body parts. These underlying traditions repeatedly concretize (or territorialize) social tensions in a reified way that allows the maker and user of the rabbit's foot to act directly on these tensions. The rabbit's foot can then be seen as one of many traditions arising from the ambiguous social and political relationship between Black and White cultures in the mid-twentieth century.

The Background of the Rabbit's Foot Belief

Initially, it seems like we have good documentation for this belief, as American folklorists recorded it frequently during the twentieth century. However, most statements are vague and generalized: "To keep a rabbit's foot brings good luck" (Hand 1962–64: no. 5789), or "A rabbit's foot is a charm against harm" (Hand 1962–64: no. 5792), or "Sometimes a rabbit foot is used as a watch-charm for luck" (Hyatt 1965: 80, no. 2030). Harry Hyatt's comprehensive collection of beliefs in Adams County, Illinois, recorded fifteen versions, all but one expressed in a single sentence. Most of these agreed that the rabbit's foot should be carried on one's person, but they differed widely in detail: around the neck, in a left hip pocket, on a watch chain, in a small bag, in one's pocketbook, and so on. The benefit of carrying one was generally unspecified, though one source said it was to ensure that one would "never be without money," and another indicated a simple ritual in case "you think you are going to get into trouble." How one obtains the rabbit's foot is even more uncertain: one said that, to be lucky, the bearer should *personally* kill the rabbit, while another said it should be "caught by a Negro after midnight in a Negro cemetery" (1965: 80, nos. 2022–36).

This vagueness suggests that the rabbit's foot, unlike the other luck charms, was a recent borrowing, with little sense of its background, from another culture. In fact, as the last belief suggests, the rabbit's foot fetish had its immediate origins in an African American magical tradition, and early collections of black folklore are specific on how the amulet was to be obtained and used. Newbell Niles Puckett summarized several such beliefs collected as early as the 1880s, and noted that jewelry stores in black sections of New Orleans were then doing a brisk sale in rabbit's-foot charms. To be effective, some informants stated, the rabbit had to be shot at night in a graveyard as part of a prescribed ritual. One item bought by Puckett in New Orleans came with the certification that it was "the left hind foot of a graveyard rabbit killed in the full of the moon by a red-headed, cross-eyed nigger at 12 o'clock at night, riding a white mule" (1926: 475). Such descriptions appear to have been standard in the commodified form of this fetish. A 1908 British account reports rabbits' feet imported from America being advertised as "the left hind foot of a rabbit killed in a country churchyard at midnight, during the dark of the moon, on Friday the 13th of the month, by a cross-eyed, left-handed, red-headed bow-legged Negro riding a white horse" (Simpson and Roud 2000: 289).

Such descriptions are almost catalogs of "backwards" elements. The *left hind* limb is exactly opposite the *upper right* limb, the one that normally would be associated with status and luck. A body part from the rear of the animal and on the left (or "sinister") side would normally be taken as ill-omened, doubly so if the person killing the rabbit was also left-handed. Persons with red hair and physical deformities such as crossed eyes and bowed legs were normally thought to be unlucky or sinister (a persistent folk tradition holds that Judas, the betrayer of Jesus, was a redhead). Likewise, an albino mule or horse was thought to be bad luck, though one could turn the luck to good by spitting. Bringing all these together into the ritual act of killing the rabbit in a graveyard precisely at midnight—the witching hour—and at a powerful phase of the moon effectively historicizes the fetish, as a way of representing all these folk beliefs in concrete form.

While other collected versions[3] disagree about exactly when the rabbit must be killed, all indicate that the rabbit's foot historicizes an especially uncanny or evil time: the *dark* of the moon; a Friday; a *rainy* Friday; a Friday the Thirteenth. Some versions specify that the rabbit must be shot with a silver bullet, the usual means of harming a supernatural being, such as a witch traveling in the form of an animal. Rabbits were a common shape for an evil witch to take. So we could interpret the historical event implied and represented by the rabbit's foot as a vigil intended to catch a witch-revenant in an evil place at an evil time. The foot of a rabbit shot in a graveyard with a silver bullet at the witching hour would thus be a symbolic substitute for a body part of a witch who was ritually murdered at such a time. Alternatively, it could be—literally or symbolically—the physical remains of a powerful person's revenant, caught outside its grave and magically prevented from walking again.

To be sure, this belief was diluted as it passed from African American tradition into mainstream European lore. Even in its original context, there might well have been a jocular element to the complex instructions given to make the rabbit's foot truly effective. Harry M. Hyatt, whose *Hoodoo—Conjuration—Witchcraft—Rootwork* volumes are an encyclopedic survey of African American magical practices, initially disparaged the rabbit's foot belief, saying, "I suspect that [the superstition] was largely developed by comedians." He claimed that he could find little about the graveyard rabbit, "except that he lives or runs through a graveyard and has a lucky left-hind foot" (1970–74, 4:3375, no. 7862). Puckett, too, tended to disparage the belief as facetious. He commented ironically that if *all* the talismans sold were what they said they were, "the peace of many a rustic graveyard must have been broken by the midnight roar of artillery to supply the huge numbers of rabbit's feet these New Orleans jewelers have" (1926: 475).

Nevertheless, Hyatt collected a number of detailed and serious accounts from his informants on how to turn a rabbit's foot into a powerful fetish. A root doctor from Savannah, for instance, told Hyatt that, to hold power, a rabbit's foot should be taken from an animal that was still living. A person planning to open up an illegal whisky joint, the doctor said, should cut off the foot and then immediately soak it in "Heart's Cologne."[4] "De next day," he said, "don' care whut man yo' know, law or no law, yo' go on, go out there, say, 'Ah think ah'll open up a likkah joint.'" Carrying the rabbit's foot fetish, in short, gave one social power over white law enforcement agents, and, in the root doctor's words, let the bearer say, "Yo' know ah'm de law" (1970–74: 4387, no. 12715).[5] One key to understanding this version is the emphasis on taking the body part from a *living* animal. The same point was stressed by another of Hyatt's informants: "Yo' wants luck, wants re'l good luck, say yo' go ahead an' yo' ketch chew a rabbit an' yo' cut his foot off—cut off his front left foots whilst he's 'live, don't kill dis rabbit" (1970–74: 198, no. 601).

The subsequent popularity of this practice does not show that all of those who carried rabbits' feet did so because they believed that a symbolic substitute for a witch's bone protected the bearer from supernatural harm. Some did so, and Hyatt acknowledged that this interpretation was current among his informants even as he disparaged it, saying, "*Of course* [the graveyard rabbit] can be a witch in disguise, but so can a pig or a dog and other animals" (1970–74: 4: 3375, no. 7862; emphasis added). But there were more fundamental reasons for the sudden cross-cultural popularity of the custom, and analyzing it as a fetish helps us see what might have made it attractive. In the early expressions of the belief, we find the following elements:

1. The rabbit's foot's power is tied to its alleged fabrication as part of a unique historical event that combines a number of common folk beliefs (date, location, physical properties of the hunter, etc.).
2. The rabbit's foot is a body part, taken from a living animal (in some cases killed during the ritual, in others, allowed to remain alive but mutilated), that continues to hold part of the animal's charisma.
3. The preparation, commodification, and eventual ownership of this body part all imply ability to manipulate others socially.

In fact, we do find many of these same elements lying explicitly behind a range of similar fetish beliefs in both Anglo- and African-American sources.

Gravesite Fetishes

The experiences of Diana Hume George and Malcolm A. Nelson in studying gravestone art led them to an understanding of the way in which such markers become invested with fetishistic meaning. The material of the marker itself, they note, is prosaic, even when it is partially prepared and displayed for sale. When it is finally purchased, inscribed, and ritually placed in proximity with a dead body, however, it displaces the survivors' reaction to the impermanence of the deceased person's life. A fetish, they argue, is a physical object that gains deep symbolic power, "a meaning so powerful that it is often a deep fear transmuted and euphemized into hope, the power of evil propitiated and familiarized into potential good." Fetishizing the gravestone thus gives survivors symbolic power over the threat of death, as the stable substance symbolically replaces the invisibly decaying body of the person buried underneath. Paradoxically, George and Nelson note, gravestones in time also decay, and this deterioration all the more closely associates the substance of the grave marker with the moldering human body it was intended to replace (1982: 140–41). The fetish becomes ambiguous, potentially frightening as well as comforting, particularly when the person memorialized had lived an eccentric life or suffered a violent death.

If we look at such objects as territorialized surrogates for the physical remains of deceased human beings, then taking home a tombstone, or even a part of a tombstone, is a thinly disguised form of appropriating a human body part and, by extension, a part of the deceased person's charisma. This piece of stone, therefore, is a kind of bone with supernatural powers, and those who possess it are assumed to be using its power to manipulate society in some potentially dangerous way. George and Nelson note that even their collection of gravestone rubbings,[6] which they proudly display on the walls of their house, made some visitors "profoundly and clearly uncomfortable," even though the rubbings were yet another degree removed from the human corpse commemorated. They continue, "The questions asked by new visitors sometimes indicate that, although they had thought us to be normal folks, there is now considerable doubt. Many people have said we must be 'morbid'; a few have said that rubbing gravestones strikes them as 'ghoulish.'[7] . . . It is probably not coincidence that in our tiny rural town, our old farmhouse has come to be known as haunted, to the degree that several teenage friends of our teenager will not stay overnight here" (1982: 139). More seriously, they report that when they found an old grave marker abandoned in a trash heap, restored it, and placed it on their mantelpiece, a number of neighbors inferred from this act that they were "criminals of the worst order" (1982: 140). Clearly, such reactions reflect a deeply felt belief that graveyard artifacts, even when no longer used, retain some of the properties of the once-living persons with which they were ritually connected.

Appropriation of such artifacts, at best, was irreligious; at worst, it could imply some kind of evil intent, and certainly grave-tampering has often been associated with alleged satanic cults (Ellis 2000: 202ff).

Similar beliefs remain common in Anglo-American adolescents' "legend-tripping" rituals, discussed in the next chapter. One common type of legend-trip involves a cemetery being identified as the resting place of a witch or community of witches, and teens proving their bravery by vandalizing the cemetery. The decrepit graveyard of St. Joseph's [Roman] Catholic Church of Buck Mountain, Pennsylvania, has been known to several generations of teens as the cursed "Weatherly Cemetery," burial ground of a community of witches and wizards. Stories are quite variable. Some say that a building nearby is a "devil-worshipper's church," or that an altar behind the cemetery is used for animal sacrifice. Others focus on a mysterious "caretaker" who wanders the area in a red or black robe, firing a shotgun at those who disturb the peace. Still others add taboos: if one curses three times inside the cemetery, a supernatural penalty will follow. No two accounts of visits are the same; instead, we find free-floating adolescent horror motifs, such as balls of fire, trees that contain the face of witches, dense clouds of fog that disable cars, white wolves, grim reapers, and a phantom "black hearse" that appears and disappears behind cars on their way to and from the site.

One element, though, that continues to cause concern is the stealing of grave markers. One self-collected account of the Weatherly Cemetery tradition reveals that many gravestones have been stolen. "But the vandals who have stolen the tombstones did not keep them very long, for these people are open to many dangers. Usually after close encounters with severe auto wrecks while leaving the cemetery the tombstone is usually returned that very hour. If the thief is lucky enough to make it home the visions he is supposed to witness during that night's sleep will have him returning it before sun up" (PSUHFA: Bruno 1988).

A few firsthand accounts of participating in such acts or near-acts of desecration exist in folklore archives. One gravestone robbery illustrates the way in which violation of the taboo, ironically, becomes a badge of achievement.

We went out [to Weatherly Cemetery], and we got a little more adventurous. We walked around, and it's, like I said, it's a decrepit cemetery. . . . Well, there's broken pieces of stone all over the place, and one of my friends decided to pick one up and take it along. Bad move, big-time bad move. He picked up the piece of stone and started walking with it. All of a sudden, we heard rattling, we heard someone moving very quickly through the grass. *Oooooo.*

I was scared . . . and we heard somebody yell, "PUT THAT DOWN!" No, no flashlight turned on this guy or anything like that, we just decided to start running. [My friend] decided to hold on to this piece of stone, and he's running with this piece of stone: "Wait up, guys, I can't catch up with you guys, wait up!" So we started running. I tripped and fell a few times, I was like— "Holy shit, I'm gonna die, I'm gonna die!" The thing that scared the hell out of me was a gunshot in the air.

Whoa!

Yes. And from that time on I haven't returned to Weatherly Cemetery.

And the stone? Has he still got it?

He got the stone, and still has it, and nothing bad has happened to him, but he has said that a lot of strange things has happened to him. . . . he says that he's gonna get rid of it one of these days, that's it's doing strange things to him, and all that sort of stuff.

(PSUHFA, Gryn 1989)

The experiences that teens have during such rites may not have significant impact on their worldview. In fact, they may not seriously believe that such stones are really associated with witchcraft. But such adolescent rituals do reproduce serious beliefs held by others.

Certainly, this would apply to African American beliefs collected by Hyatt concerning the magical powers of "graveyard dirt," especially from an evil person's grave.[8] One simple version reports that "some people say you go to the graveyard and get some dirt from a <u>sinner-man's grave</u> and bring it home, and put that in a box and put a hole in the top and bury that underneath the house, and nothing will come there to hurt you" (1970–74: 450, no. 1318). A more elaborate version collected in Brunswick, Georgia, stresses the ritual through which graveyard dirt is fetishized in order to appropriate the deceased person's power. Simply to protect oneself from evil, this version begins, one should go precisely at midnight to the grave of a person who had "died good." "When yo' go dere yo' have prayer, see. After yo' have prayer, yo' always de—yo' talk to dem jes' lak ah'm talkin' to yo', 'Ah am takin' dis dirt from yore grave for yo' tuh take care of me. Yo' know, when yo' wus livin' yo' always believed in things that were right. Things is goin' wrong wit me an' now ah <u>want chew to drive away all evil spirits</u> an' <u>bring good things toward me</u>.' However, the same source added, "<u>if yo' wanta do hard wit dat *graveyard dirt*, yo' goes to a sinner grave.</u> Yo' go dere to a sinner grave; <u>yo' don't have tuh pray wit a sinner.</u> Yo' go dere an' git dat dirt, yo' go dere an' cuss 'em. Yo' cuss 'em jes' like he did—jes' de life dat he lived. Yo' go to his grave an' git it an' act jes' lak ah'm tellin' yo.' Yo' say, '<u>Yo' know yo' raised hell an' made things go jes' yore way. An' now, ah'm comin' heah tuh git dis dirt from yo' tuh make things go mah way—jes' lak yo' did when yo' wus livin'</u>'" (1970–74: 448, no. 1308).

Any physical artifact from a graveyard might be seen as equivalent to a body part from a buried skeleton. Another of Hyatt's informants in fact connected the graveyard dirt tradition with the rabbit's foot: one must collect dirt from "de head of a sinner's grave"—not just from the surface, but from deeper down, where the earth became "marshy." "An' den dey would put it in a bag an' git whut dey call a rabbit foot an' put in dere with it," this source continued, "an' dat would cause to bring good luck" (no. 12718, 1970–74: 4388).

Indeed, some sources reported that to be really effective, the rabbit's foot should come from an animal shot on or near the grave of an evil person. Puckett observed that one famous rabbit's foot given Grover Cleveland when he was running for president in 1884 was said to have been killed "on the grave of Jesse James, the famous outlaw," who had been assassinated only two years previously. The idea was, Puckett continued, "that the more wicked the person who is dead the more effective the charm associated with his remains" (1926: 475). In this case, the rabbit's foot was a thinly disguised substitute for the truly effective charm, which would be a body part from Jesse James's own fresh corpse. So belief in the power of a rabbit's foot drew initially from beliefs that the remains of a witch or an evil person retained charisma similar to that held by the relics of saints and holy people.

Animal Body Parts as Fetishes

Why a *rabbit's* foot, then? A number of animals have been associated with witchcraft for many years, among them the black dog, deer, rat, bat, pig, hedgehog, owl, crow, toad, and bug. Of these, certainly the most common in Anglo-American lore were the black cat and the rabbit, both of which inspired fetishistic beliefs. African American magical traditions frequently refer to a certain bone from a black cat that provides the bearer with magical powers, including invisibility, luck in gambling and getting work, and curing abilities.[9] Significantly, many of the rituals used to produce the specific bone that holds the charm stress that the black cat, like the rabbit in the beliefs referenced above, should be captured and then boiled while still alive. Another informant made a similar recommendation about a paw cut from a black cat: "yo' kin go in any bank, any place, anywhere, git anything yo' wanta git,' long as dat cat still stirring. But when dat cat dies, dat kills de foot" (1970–74: 95, no. 320).

A common legend type describes how a neighborhood witch is detected through encountering her in her animal shape. The animal is injured, and later on the witch exhibits the same injury in her human form.[10] In a Welsh legend, two witches were said to run an inn and steal from travelers during the night by changing into cats. One man kept watch and slashed at a cat when he saw it creeping toward his purse. "In the morning," the legend concluded, "the elder sister tried to hide herself, but the traveler insisted on seeing her and saw her right hand bandaged" (Winstanley and Rose 1926: 166).

Another common legend relates how a man cuts off the paw (or part of a paw) of a cat that is worrying him. The paw turns into a woman's hand (or finger), and the witch is subsequently identified by the missing hand. Found in Ireland and northern England, this story became very popular in the United States, particularly among revivalists, in the "Jack Tale" form narrated by Jane Gentry and her daughter Maud Long.[11] But the story was also current in African American communities. In one version, collected by Elsie Clews Parson in South Carolina, the hero is a fearless preacher who agreed to spend the night in a haunted house. As he sat reading the Bible, this version goes, "a cat jumped on the table with a pair of eye-glasses on, and slapped over a bottle of ink. The man took the hatchet and cut off its middle toe, and found a ring on it." The witch is detected by the missing finger and killed, and the preacher wins the house as a reward (1921: 9–10).[12]

Similar motifs of witches in rabbit form circulated in England. A Lincolnshire informant recalled in the 1930s "that it was our sport o' Sundays, us lads, ter get tergether an' look for owld Nancy [a woman reputed to be a neighborhood witch] an' chase 'er, for she used ter use a

White Rabbit ter go about in; but she allus bettered us an' got away, but rare fun we 'ad wi' th' owld gal, though!" One local story held that a local gamekeeper, who had prosecuted two of the witch's sons for poaching, was punished by being led on a fruitless chase by the white rabbit. "It was no use 'im shootin' at 'er 'cos 'is shot was only lead," the informant explained, "but if 'e'd 'ad *siller* shot now, t'would 'ave been a different matter—'e could 'a gotten 'er wi' *that*, they say" (Rudkin 1934: 257–58). We recall that some of the rabbit's foot beliefs specified that the animal should be shot with a silver bullet, a motif that suggests that the belief is a concretization of legends like the above.

Sometimes the rabbit is indeed wounded by those who are wise enough to shoot at the animal with a silver bullet. In one such case, reported from Aberystwyth, Wales, the rabbit disappears when the shot rings out, but at the same moment an old woman in the marketplace screams and falls to the ground; bystanders find her wounded and bleeding profusely (Winstanley and Rose 1926: 166). The Lincolnshire "owld Nancy," too, is exposed when she becomes too careless with a neighbor whom she allegedly enjoyed harassing: "'E was 'edgin' [trimming a hedge] one day, an' there was this 'ere white rabbit, a-skitterin' about in an' out of the 'edge, an' 'e knowed it was th' owld woman tryin' ter vex 'im. 'E tried chasin' 'er away, but she cum back; then 'e gets waxey [angry], an' 'eaves 'is 'edge-knife at 'er, an' cotched 'er on the toe wi' it, an' do you know, *th' owld woman was lame for weeks!*" (Rudkin 1934: 258). Similar stories travelled to the United States. An informant from rural North Carolina had heard a story of a man whose car had broken down, who went to the home of a woman alleged to be a witch in order to use the phone. When he came to the door, he spotted in a corner, much to his astonishment, "a blue-eyed rabbit about three or four feet high . . . with human features." The animal disappeared, and soon the witch, as a beautiful young lady, answered the door. The story ends like the British versions given above: one day the woman is found dead at home from a gunshot wound, and a local farmer recalls that he had recently used "a load of silver" to shoot a strange creature disturbing his livestock (Johnson 1974: 115).

Versions like this suggest that even though Hyatt was dubious about the seriousness of the rabbit's foot charm, both Anglos and blacks considered it a metonym for complex folk narratives. These narratives, in addition, could be quite different in import. The Anglo stories suggest that the witch-rabbit is a threat to society who deserves to be wounded, mutilated, or killed. By contrast, in the African tradition, B'rer Rabbit often plays a trickster role in fables, where he manages to elude or even conquer more powerful animals like lions, foxes, and alligators through his cleverness. John W. Roberts cautions against seeing B'rer Rabbit as being a simple hero, since in many narratives he appears as "a thief and malicious liar who manipulate[s] others to achieve his goals." Rather, he argues, the rabbit functioned as a symbol of how "cleverness, guile, and wit" were appropriate reactions to certain social situations in which slaves (and their twentieth-century descendents) saw themselves as powerless in the face of Anglo hegemony (1989: 37–38).

One area in which this impotence was particularly visible, Roberts notes, was the realm of law, where white policemen and sheriffs frequently enforced regulations against victimless crimes such as gambling and moonshining in an inequitable way that in fact upheld white interests. For this reason, figures such as B'rer Rabbit and, later, bad-man heroes such as Stagolee and Railroad Bill were seen as heroic precisely because they resisted a legal code that the black community saw as intrinsically corrupt. This helps us see why, in the versions collected by Hyatt, the fetish-makers saw this tradition as a way of empowering individuals to say "Yo' know ah'm de law" and imitate the badman's way of making "things go mah way."

The rabbit's foot in black lore held a significance that was analogous, but not identical, to the role of the rabbit in white tradition. Instead of seeing the rabbit as an uncanny creature, associated with evil, whose power is destroyed by injuring its paw, the African American magical tradition stressed its role in subverting conventional power structures. For blacks, the fetish was usually an object intended for some specific practical end and not simply a general luck token or protection against undefined evil (see Puckett 1926: 259 ff.). And if we see this tradition against the broader context of using objects associated with the graves of known badmen, we then see the rabbit's foot as part of a broader agenda of black folk magic: the use of power objects to help the bearer resist a status quo viewed as ethically bankrupt.

Human Body Parts as Fetishes

If, indeed, graveyard artifacts and certain animal body parts were symbolic substitutes for *human* body parts, then we would expect to find traditions involving fetishistic use of the latter. And, in fact, we find such traditions spanning Anglo- and African American culture back to the slavery period. An especially common tradition involved the ritual use of hair in keepsakes intended to memorialize a dead person. Pamela A. Miller (1982) has documented the extraordinary popularity of "hair jewelry" during the mid-nineteenth century. Saving a lock of hair from a family member, particularly a mother or dying child, was a widespread custom, and Miller shows that while there was an individual side to this practice, it was also highly commodified. Lockets were specially designed to hold and display a lock of hair, along with a miniature portrait of the dear departed. By 1860, an active industry had sprung up of weaving display objects like pins and earrings from quantities of preserved hair.[13]

But hair was a potentially dangerous power object in many traditions of folk belief, and a lock of hair is often mentioned in many folk traditions as a fetishistic extension of the living person's charisma. Human hair was one of the commonest ingredients in *mojos* or *conjure bags* used in African American magical traditions to cast a spell on an enemy (Hand 1962–64, no. 5543; cf. nos. 5536, 5546, 5548–49, 5563). A number of other beliefs concern the preservation of hair from a deceased person, one such noting, significantly, that if you put a lock of a dead person's hair in a special place, "you will always know where his spirit is. If you remove the hair, you will be haunted" (Hand 1962–64, no. 5719). This implies that some human essence survives death and is preserved in the lock of hair. Conversely, saving a *living* person's hair was sometimes felt to be unwise, as such persons were then apt to die young (Opie and Tatem 1985: 185). Miller, surveying Anglo-American folk beliefs about hair, likewise concludes that such objects reflect a conviction that the dead person's spirit survives death and is in some way expressed in a power object containing his or her hair. Indeed, she notes, a common belief holds that the hair of a corpse continues to grow even after it is buried (1982: 90).

Such an ambiguous object thus could be manipulated to control or use the person's charisma for magical purposes. Such a belief, explicitly connecting both the Anglo-American sentimental and the African American conjure traditions, was in fact used by the American author Harriet Beecher Stowe in her best-selling novel *Uncle Tom's Cabin* (1852). A famous sentimental set piece in the novel focuses on Little Eva, a sentimental "dying child," who ritually cuts off locks of her hair before her death, so that her relatives and the slaves she loved most could continue to feel her influence. This practice would have been familiar enough to

Stowe's high-Victorian white audience, but the author's research had also made her familiar with the African American beliefs that paralleled it. Uncle Tom, a nominally Christianized slave, nevertheless follows African American conjure customs by keeping his lock of Eva's hair in a mojo bag hung around his neck, along with a silver dollar.[14] Stowe makes her awareness of this tradition clear when Uncle Tom is sold to the evil plantation owner Simon Legree, and one of the overseers confiscates the pouch and brings it to his master.

> "What's that, you dog?" said Legree.
> "It's a witch thing, Mas'r!"
> "A what?"
> "Something that niggers gets from witches. Keeps 'em from feelin' when they's flogged. He had it tied round his neck with a black string."
> Legree, like most godless and cruel men, was superstitious. He took the paper and opened it uneasily.
> There dropped out of it a silver dollar, and a long, shining curl of fair hair,—hair which, *like a living thing,* twined itself round Legree's fingers.
> "Damnation!" he screamed, in sudden passion, stamping on the floor, and pulling furiously at the hair, *as if it burned him.*
> (1998: 402; emphasis added)

The sinister motif of the hair curling around Legree's fingers reflects a complex synthesis of two traditions, white and black. Anglo-American sentimental folksong, as I have argued elsewhere, focused on female heroes such as dying children and aged mothers who were represented as fragile and passive. In fact, through a subtle form of spiritual warfare (which I termed "vindictive forgiveness"), these sentimental figures could exert considerable power over their male counterparts (Ellis 1978).

Stowe makes it clear that such a spiritual conflict is present in this scene by having Legree recall his benevolent mother's unsuccessful attempts to reform him. Having rejected her in order to carouse with drunken companions, he remembers, he received a letter reporting that she had died, blessing and forgiving her son with her dying breath. Contained in the letter was a lock of her "long, curling hair," which, like Little Eva's, fell from the envelope and wrapped itself around his fingers. The motif of the twining hair is not unique to Anglo-American sentimentality,

as conjure lore also contains the belief that "little coils of hair," strategi-
cally placed, have the power to entrap unwary persons and give the conjurer power over them (Hand 1962–64, no. 5536). Stowe comments, in
one of her most Gothic moments:

> There is a dread, unhallowed necromancy of evil, that turns
> things sweetest and holiest to phantoms of horror and affright.
> That pale, loving mother,—her dying prayers, her forgiving
> life,—wrought in that demoniac heart of sin only as a damning
> sentence, bringing with it a fearful looking for a judgment and
> fiery indignation. . . . often, in the deep night, whose solemn
> stillness arraigns the bad soul in forced communion with herself,
> he had seen that pale mother rising by his bedside, and felt the
> soft twining of that hair around his fingers, till the cold sweat
> would roll down his face, and he would spring from his bed in
> horror. (1998: 403–4)

Stowe's immensely popular novel both incorporated and dissemi-
nated this fetishistic belief. Stowe's own term for this belief—necromancy—literally means using a body part from a dead person to work
magic. More than a hundred years after the publication of Stowe's novel,
a rash of grave disturbances, first in Great Britain, then in the United
States, led many law enforcement agents to believe that necromancy was
once again being practiced by occultists (see Ellis 2000: 210 ff.). In 1972,
journalist Dave Balsiger had noted an increase in "grave robberies by
occultists and Satan worshipers who use skulls and bones in their ceremonies." He claimed such bones could be charged on a credit card
through a phone order to "one of those underground occult distributors
who operate from a secret warehouse supply through a post office box
number and clean up on millions of dollars every year." But neither he
nor the supposed ex-satanic high priest Mike Warnke explained how
they were used (Warnke 1972: 189).

In the 1980s, many rural panics resulted when authorities suggested
that graveyard desecrations had "ritual significance," and police publications asserted that a collection of human bones was a sure sign that the
owner was an advanced practitioner of satanism.[15] In some cases, the
"ritual" was imaginary. Hicks cites one instance in which a group of high-
school students was arrested while digging into graves. They confessed
that, after a drinking party, they had decided to go digging for "Civil War

or Indian artifacts." But other recent cases clearly do involve ritual elements. In a 1988 Myrtle Beach affair, four youths admitted breaking open a burial vault and, when arrested, gave police "some books on Satanism," claiming that the vandalism was "preparation for a Satanic worship ceremony" (Hicks 1991: 284–85). Official concern seems justified: a certain number of teens do in fact desecrate graves and disturb corpses in a manner related to ritual magic.

Why were bones thought to be needed for satanic rites? A 1987 law enforcement publication speculated that cult members felt human remains "supposedly contain the magical potency of the victim" (Raschke 1990: 73–74). This would make sense if the bones came from an individual specially killed by the cult, or a relative. Indeed, Balsiger notes that one grave desecrated was that of the mother of the Florida Highway Patrol's chief. Although neither Warnke nor Balsiger claim this, such a theft might be interpreted as a magical means of gaining control over the police under the chief's control, thus protecting the cult from detection. But, most often, the graves disturbed seem to be randomly chosen. Standard Anglo-American collections of folk beliefs do not include many descriptions of necromancy: the few instances recorded come from African American informants. Most of these are general and do not involve any ritual. One North Carolina record notes that when an Indian mound was dug up, "all the Negro workers took a metacarpal bone for good luck" (Hand 1962–64: no. 5785). The same informant called such a human bone "a proof against conjure." In his note to this belief, Wayland Hand commented that "the use of *human* bones must be considered exceptional" (1962–64: no. 5564). However, a more detailed look at African American lore shows that Hand's impression was faulty, for black conjure lore does frequently refer to human bones used as fetishes.

Hyatt found several informants who provided detailed accounts of using such objects as fetishes to gain power over other people. One informant emphasized that the bone could not be random, but should belong to a person who had been "very, very, very evil . . . yo' could take dat bone wit chew home [from the cemetery]. Yo' put it an' bury it undah dere back steps unbeknownst tuh [one's enemies] . . . It'll worry dem tuh de grave" (1970–74: 3409).[16] Another of Hyatt's informants said that the most powerful bone to obtain was from the wrist of an "evil person . . . all dose fellahs had police records, bad. Dey got kilt, dey died bad. Dey had tuh hold 'em down . . . Done are people dat yo' know [about], yo' know where day grave, buried at, an' yo go tuh dat most pahticlah [particular] grave an' git dat bone." The bone was then put into a small pot and boiled "tuh keep a certain pressure on 'im. Den yo' . . . say, "Ah demand yo' wit *controllin' powah* tuh go ovah an' do such-an-such a thing. Go ovah an' kill such-an'-such a one.' An' yo' [the spirit] must do so" (1970–74: 3418–19, no. 8054). Even so, another informant, a moonshiner anxious to avoid interference from white police, suggested that randomly collected toe bones had power enough to protect his moonshine still against law officers. As a result, if police came to arrest him, their spirits would keep them away. "Dey cain't never git in dere," he told Hyatt, "dey's always scared out. An' evah time dey pull out dey pistol an' go tuh shoot, dey'll lose it or sompin, dey cain't shoot" (1970–74: 3417, no. 8052).

The most common practice seems to have been to "dress" or ritually fetishize the bone in some way by bringing it in contact with other power objects and substances, to provide luck in gambling. A New Orleans informant said that a small bone would be carried in a bag with steel dust and red beans; another, that it should be anointed with "Heart's Cologne"; yet another, that a "gambling hand" could be made of four metacarpal bones placed in a bag with a lodestone and six gold-eyed needles (1970–74: 3408, 3414, nos. 8025–26, 8043). As before, however, informants differed on which bone was preferred: some specified that a certain finger of the hand was the only powerful one, but they differed as to the left or right hand, and many sources specified leg or toe bones. In general, though, it seems that any conveniently small human bone could be used to gain luck in gambling or protection from the law.

How did this hoodoo belief cross the color line, either as a model for teenage acts of desecration or as a law enforcement interpretation of vandalism as "ritual"? There seems to be no direct link, but it is significant that the rabbit's foot belief became popular on both sides of the color line at a time when using human body parts as fetishes appeared frequently in legend and occasionally in practice. As ancient as the use of gravesite artifacts is the custom of preserving body parts from defeated enemies as trophies of reaffirmed hegemony. We recall that the Israelite founder-king David is said to have displayed his superiority over the rival Philistines by carrying away a hundred foreskins from slain soldiers.[17] And during the American Civil War, a persistent rumor held that Confederate soldiers carried away some of the bones of their fallen antagonists as fetish objects. Nathaniel Hawthorne, a connoisseur of legends with a touch of the grotesque, recorded the claim in a journal that he kept. After noting that the rebels had abandoned many of the material spoils that they had won in battle, such as hats and bayonets, he added that "their peculiar taste inclines them to prefer the immediate and personal memorials of their slain foemen, such, for instance, as ornaments neatly carved out of a brave man's bones, to hang a lady's watch-chain, or a skull to hold their whiskey and water, and to be passed from lip to lip of man and maiden at their social and family gatherings" (1985: 1–2). Of course, this might have been an unfounded atrocity story similar to many circulated in time of war to fire hatred against the other side. A persistent rumor circulating during World War I was that German soldiers occupying Belgium had cut off the right hands of as many as four thousand children, allegedly to prevent them from ever taking up arms against the Fatherland (Gide 1951, II:91–92). But Anglo participants in the campaigns against Native American tribes in the following decades were impressed enough by the latter's practice of preserving scalps of their opponents that they themselves made collections of body parts from the tribes they massacred. Rumor had it that some soldiers also mutilated the corpses of both male and female opponents and tanned the private parts as souvenirs (Connell 1984: 176–79). Still more recently, veterans from the Vietnam conflict alleged that some of their colleagues removed ears from Viet Cong casualties and preserved them as fetishes (Pearson 1990).

This tradition seems initially to have little in common with what we have learned about the roots of the rabbit's foot tradition, but in fact both traditions helped concretize ways of dealing with an Other's power over one's own culture. The conjurers interviewed by Hyatt described using human bones, as they had done with animal parts and graveyard dirt, to gain access to the dead person's power and use it purposefully in practical matters such as gaining luck in gambling or evading the law. Although soldiers may have felt that possessing a body part from an enemy conferred some kind of protection in battle, these acts seem primarily to have territorialized a moment that symbolized power already gained over the Other. In short, while the African American fetish tradition was a means of empowering a group that otherwise possessed little power over the Other, the Anglo-American tradition of mutilating dead enemies was a means of reinforcing its hegemony over the Other.

Certainly this explains why fetishizing human body parts played a central role in the nearly five thousand documented cases of lynchings of African Americans by whites. Trudier Harris shows that such mutilations comprised a ritual expulsion of evil, in which rumors of blacks attacking whites—particularly white women or children—provoked community action. Removal of body parts was nearly obligatory in the rite, and graphic photographs of such lynchings were often reprinted as souvenirs for people wanting to possess at least a visual memento of such memorable historical events. Lynching reached a peak around 1900, and such rites became increasingly rare as the century progressed, due to popular outcry and increasingly strict enforcement of antilynching laws. But Ronald Baker has shown that precise details of one such event were accurately preserved in oral history more than seventy years later. One of his informants said, "I heard some people in Terre Haute still have the fingers and toes," adding, "One of the guys that worked at my father's mine showed me one of the guy's thumbs" (1988: 324).

Body Parts and Intercultural Space

The rabbit's foot was lucky because it served as a metonym for a ritual event in which an animal's body part is acquired as a substitute for a human body part. It is a sign of its power as fetish that, in spite of its original context in African American folk magic, it was quickly adopted by Anglo-Americans. True, its significance to most whites appears to have been only vaguely understood, as indicated by the brevity of most collected versions of white folk beliefs regarding the rabbit's foot. But it was assimilated into white culture at the very moment when lynchings were rapidly becoming more and more politically risky. This suggests that the first generations of whites who adopted the custom, aware of its black origins, found that appropriating and reinterpreting a black fetish for their own purposes was a culturally acceptable way of maintaining their hegemony. It marked the first of many borrowings from blacks, in which cultural products often disparaged as trivial or disreputable (like jazz and rhythm and blues) became a means of communication between two initially estranged societies. Although it had a different place in each culture's context, the core belief was the same in both: possession of a body part expressed or conferred the ability to manipulate Others. And, far from being trivial, its emergence and popularity in the early twentieth century coincided with the most difficult period of American race relations.

So we see that the rabbit's foot custom fits into a nexus of practices present in Anglo-American and African American culture in the late nine-teenth and early twentieth centuries. A body part from an animal con-nected with witchcraft was further contextualized as a graveyard artifact, which made it a socially acceptable substitute for a fetish literally made from a gravesite or, more dangerously, from a human bone. We note that the early records agree that rabbits' feet tended to be produced for a market in large quantities rather than being personally made by the us-ers. Such a marketplace context placed yet another protective layer be-tween the production of the fetish through (allegedly) committing a series of cultural and the person who (actually) purchased and used of it. The commodification of the rabbit's foot tradition was central to its popu-larity, since its *claim* to be a graveyard fetish was balanced against the *fact* that it was physically impossible for all the fetishes sold to have come from rabbits that had really been shot in rural graveyards. For this very reason, Hyatt's disparaging remark that the belief "was largely developed by comedians" has some point, as the practice penetrated American cul-ture far more effectively because the owner could on some level laugh at the practice while simultaneously engaging in it. Purchasing a rabbit's foot from a middleman (who likewise was not directly involved in its fabrication) meant that the owner could neither attest to its origin—in a magical ritual suggesting the symbolic appropriation of a human body part—nor completely discount it.

The fetish originally was a means of acquiring enough charisma to challenge a power structure. The ability to amputate or remove a body part demonstrates one's ability to appropriate the vital power of an Other. Similarly, the fetish at the heart of Harry Potter's wand is eventually bal-anced by the grimmer fetish process at the conclusion of *Harry Potter and the Cauldron of Fire*. Here, his evil counterpart Voldemort regains physical form as part of a ritual that demands a body part from both a supporter and an adversary, in this case Harry himself. By appropriating part of his substance, Voldemort is able to absorb some of the power he gave up in his first, unsuccessful attempt on Harry's life, and carry on his quest to overturn the power structure of wizards that he despises. In real life, the rabbit's foot, whatever else it may represent, is taken from an animal that for both Europeans and African Americans represented a challenge to hegemony. The rabbit's foot belief, however simple it may have appeared to many of those who practiced it, connects to a complex body of folk beliefs and practices dealing with body parts and symbolic substitutes that concretize and territorialize the power of the Other.

Anglo-American tradition might have seen it as a metonym for the potential of a witch or ethnic newcomer to threaten the traditional power structure, while for African Americans it may have been a means of challenging a white-dominated legal system.

But for both, the principle was the same: social power resided in being able to take and carry such a fetish. Possessing a fetish that embodies the essence of Others—whether tricksters, badmen, witches, or the body politic—reduces the power that they hold (or threaten to hold) over the one who holds the fetish.

And that's why a lucky rabbit's foot is lucky.

Chapter Six

Visits to Forbidden Graveyards

"First years should note that the forest on the grounds is forbidden to all pupils," Professor Dumbledore tells the incoming class at Hogwarts, adding, "And a few of our older students would do well to remember that as well." "The forest's full of dangerous beasts, everyone knows that," Percy, the prefect of Gryffindor, explains to Harry Potter (1998: 127). Naturally, as the books progress, we find that this rule is observed rather flexibly, with Harry and his friends repeatedly entering the forest on one mission or another. True, the woods are dangerous, but they are also a place where those who enter learn things, about the spiritual world they inhabit and about themselves.

In much the same way, legend-tripping rituals define certain spots as uncanny, the locus of dangerous beasts and evil spirits. In this common Anglo-American practice, young people travel in groups, sometimes on foot, more often by automobile, to a place that is "forbidden to all" by the legends they know. They perform rituals intended to invoke supernatural beings, which often include acts of vandalism. A common legend-trip location is a graveyard held to be the resting place of a witch or community of witches; teens prove their bravery by damaging such cemeteries.

"Bloody Mary's Grave," near North Vernon, Indiana, is a typical example. The core story varies from teller to teller—Mary is said to have been a woman who died a tragic death, or committed suicide, or threw her baby in the river, or was otherwise mistreated—but the activity it sets up is fairly consistent: listeners are told that if they go to her grave site at midnight, stomp on her grave, and curse her, she will punish the intruders, usually by making them bleed. One source explained: "whenever anybody goes down there, if they get out of the car and walk around

112

her grave and start yelling at her and cussing at her that when they get back in their cars they'll have blood somewhere on their bodies. The vines are supposed to grow up around your ankles and hold you there until Bloody Mary can get out of her grave and get you" (Ray 1976: 176). Another "Bloody Mary" visitor recalled:

> *When you went there did you go at nighttime?*
> Uh huh. We made it a point to be there.
> *Did you go with anyone else?*
> Oh yes! That was the thing. You're supposed to have a gang go with you. It's no fun unless there's more than one.
> *What did you do when you got there?*
> We cursed at her.
> *What kind of things did you yell?*
> Well, obscenities, anything . . . "G___ d___ you Bloody Mary!" or "F___ you Bloody Mary, come on out." . . . Anything that would provoke a person like that. And really people are more afraid than you'd think. (Ray 1976: 180–81)

One adolescent said his group had been challenged by the police, who accused them of uprooting gravestones and throwing them into the river. This was not mere harassment: an accompanying photograph in *Indiana Folklore* showed a toppled and broken stone that might well have been "Mary's," or another grave marker in the same cemetery (Ray 1976: 181,186).

"Friend-of-a-friend" stories tell how the spirit of the witch cast a curse on the desecrators, who later came to harm, often on the very night. But firsthand stories told by those who actually defied the curse of the witch's grave involve no more than near misses or minor fender-benders and strange feelings, all of which give the vandal status by showing that he is bold enough to summon the supernatural. Nevertheless, such adolescent rituals, just like the practice of carrying a rabbit's foot, do reproduce serious witchcraft beliefs, and in both traditions an artifact from a cemetery is held to appropriate the evil charisma of those buried there. As a result, young people's ritual visits to cemeteries have often sparked serious concern over the rise of interest in the occult. The series of grave desecrations that occurred at the British village of Clophill, beginning in 1963, was influential in creating widespread concern over alleged "witchcraft" and "Satanic cult" activity in that country (see Ellis 2000: 210ff.), and grave-tampering was a common trigger of rumor-panics in the United States during the 1980s.

There is some justification for this concern. Such a ritual is "satanic," at least in the sense in which Anton LaVey defined the term: it deliberately outrages a dominant culture's mores. Adolescent legend-trips, like African American badman traditions, are essentially means of subverting a set of moral norms that the participants intend to challenge. However, a survey of accounts of legend-trips collected by local historians and folklorists shows that there is nothing especially new about this kind of activity. Certainly, the ritual dates to medieval times; late-classical records show similar kinds of rituals already provoking official censure; and the way in which Neolithic monuments repeatedly appear in accounts suggests that the tradition is older still.

Legend-Tripping and Its History

Ritual visits to uncanny places in the United States have been termed *legend-tripping* by folklorists who have studied the contemporary practice intensively since the late 1960s. As previously discussed, the legend-trip involves a set of cautionary legends that both warn of the danger of a site, and then function as a dare to visit the very place and carry out the ritual that leads to danger. The number of youngsters involved in this activity is unknown; however, surveys suggest that a significant proportion—between 14 percent and 28 percent—of American adolescents participate in legend-tripping in some way. Most will engage in one or two ritual visits out of curiosity, but several folklorists have noted the role of small groups of "experts" in publicizing and perpetuating the tradition (Ellis 1996: 169, cf. Ellis 2001: 186ff.).

The dynamics of legend-tripping remain relatively unclear, since folklorists often have focused most of their attention on the narrative texts or legends produced by the trips. The extreme variability of these legends itself suggests that the trip, not the legend, is the most important thing in the tradition. The stories alone thus cannot be understood without setting them into the context of this more complex folk tradition of deviant play. By emphasizing a certain place's eeriness, they provide a mood of anticipation that is necessary to the trip. Such legends may explain why the place is haunted to begin with, and they may reinforce the threat by expressing some taboo against performing some kind of ritual.

A secondary, "add-on" set of legends may provide examples of teens who visited the place earlier and incurred some supernatural misfortune. As folklorist Gary Hall (1980) has observed, the function of narratives here is to "cultivate an atmosphere of fear" that makes the trip itself an exciting event. Kenneth A. Thigpen (1971) calls this the most crucial stage: the orally narrated legend serves to enhance "the receptive psychological state of all involved, so that they will be more likely to perceive the 'supernatural' occurrence" when they travel to the site. Stories about tragic sequels to dumb suppers and mirror-gazing rituals serve to heighten the tension essential to the vigil that follows. Similarly, legends about teens who violated supernatural taboos and suffered the penalty do not discourage the rite that follows; in fact, like the Hogwarts house rules so frequently cited and as frequently disregarded, they function as a *dare* to see which of the participants are adult enough to risk contact with the supernatural.

The ritual climaxes in a tense vigil at the spooky site, as participants wait for *something* to happen that they can interpret as a response to their actions. As Thigpen says, participants try "to merge the supernatural realm described in the first part with reality." At the allegedly cursed site, they dare each other to break the taboo and put themselves under the power of the supernatural. Such ritual actions may involve no more than stopping the car and turning off the engine (many haunts have the power to prevent cars from starting again). But often the ritual involves complex acts intended to invoke the supernatural, such as walking around tombstones, blinking car lights, or sitting on cursed stones. This action, then, is a form of ostension, in that it literally enacts the first part of the cautionary narrative in order to make the second part occur as a "sign." This, too, is a way of performing the legend, as Thigpen observes: "Whether the words of the legend are spoken or not, the awareness of all present centers on its message." Whatever happens in this charged atmosphere, then, is likely to be interpreted as extraordinary.

After having challenged the powers of the place, the group retreats to discuss members' perceptions of the experience. Any unusual event then can be interpreted as a brush with the supernatural and become the core of a personal experience story that will then be passed around among the teens' peers. Such stories, Thigpen concludes, "may also be told as memorates to the uninitiated and thus be added to the basic legend complex to be told as the first part of the performance" (1971: 205). Hence the experience may enrich the reputation of the site by becoming the basis of a new "add-on" legend. Such a firsthand story was related by another North Vernon legend-tripper: "I don't know if it's from Bloody Mary or what, but one individual hid behind a tree and then as we were, it was real dark and we were scared to death and we were stomping [on the graves] and cussing and everything and we thought—I guess we were kind of hoping it would come true. One guy jumped out from behind the tree at us and a girl fell on a rose bush or something and cut herself. We don't know if Bloody Mary caused that or not but someone did bleed from it, because of that rose bush" (Ray 1976: 178).

It is, however, impossible to distinguish such legend-focused behavior from other kinds of activity that form part of the trip, such as illegal drinking and marijuana smoking. After surveying 218 accounts of Ohio legend-trips, I concluded that trying to experience the supernatural was like such recreational drug use "in that both are 'trips'—deliberate escapes into altered states of being where conventional laws do not operate" (2001: 189). Similarly, committing outrageous pranks, such as impersonating the legendary threat to frighten others, was a regular and accepted part of the tradition.

Finally, sexual experimentation appears frequently as part of the tradition. Many times, the haunted places are simultaneously used as lovers' lanes, and the legends are told by young men to their dates "on the exact spot where they happened." Assuring a girlfriend that they are becoming intimate in a supernaturally dangerous place at first seems incongruous. Yet, most versions comment that the legends in fact have a paradoxical effect: many girls use them as an excuse to snuggle up closer to their boyfriends. Thus, the legend-trip may have an aphrodisiac function as well (Dégh 1971: 65–66; Ellis, 2001: 189).

Such Dionysian elements in ritual visits to supernatural places are not just reflections of American teenagers' lifestyles, but can be traced back several centuries in European records. British legend-trips have not been collected as intensively as in the United States, where the teenage automobile culture may well have revitalized a tradition of visits originally made on foot and known only within a small radius. Still, we find many of the same dynamics in scattered press reports of ritual visits. A 1963 item in the *Tonbridge Free Press* (which I found while researching the graveyard desecrations in nearby Clophill) cites teens in the village of Saltwood, near Hythe (Kent), as saying that some kind of supernatural being was appearing at "Slaybrook Corner, said to be the scene of a bloody battle centuries ago." One narrative held that the revenant was that of a certain William Tournay Tournay [*sic*], the eccentric owner of an estate that supposedly stood where the local secondary school was later built. When he died, he was buried on an island in the middle of a lake, wrapped in the skin of his favorite horse and with his dog next to him, since he hated women.

Significantly, the ghost appeared only to villagers under twenty-one, and mostly when they were taking girlfriends for a walk. The specific experiences vary widely, as one would expect from the firsthand stories that grow up around legend-trips. One witness saw "a red light and then this eerie, bat-like figure"; another saw "this red light, like a red ball of fire" that coalesced into a figure with "webbed feet and no head. It was carrying a red lantern. We just ran."[1] The one common factor, though, was that the girlfriend invariably said she was terrified. The context, however, of appearances during couples' walks through the countryside, suggests that Slaybrook Corner was something of a lovers' lane, and that the stories functioned much as did the American stories: as a way of encouraging intimacy. It would not have been out of place, either, for other local youths to arrange elaborate pranks for unwary couples coming down the path.

Around 1860, local priests were unsuccessfully trying to abolish "pagan merrymaking" at "The Druids' Cemetery," an ancient set of stone rows in Brittany (Burl 1985: 33). Ritual visits to British "holy wells" often included elements of drinking and antisocial activities. An eyewitness to the rites at one Irish site commented, "it seems more like the celebration of the orgies of Bacchus, than the memory of a pious saint, from the drunken quarrels and obscenities practised on these occasions" (Bord 1986: 76). At the time of the witch trials, authorities in many areas were forced to control or abolish sometimes raucous parties at such "pagan" sites. Historian Robert Muchembled, surveying seventeenth-century court records, found many such official edicts against dancing and partying at remote locations late at night (1990: 149–50).

Tale 155 of the *Gesta Romanorum*, a fifteenth-century German collection of sermon illustrations, begins with a detailed description of Wandlebury Mound, the remains of a Neolithic fort near Cambridge, England. The *Gesta* alludes in turn to the legend-rich thirteenth-century work *Otia Imperialia*, by Gervase of Tilbury (1150?-1235?), which claimed that if anyone rode his horse up the mound by moonlight and announced, "Let my adversary appear!" then he would immediately be confronted by a mysterious black knight, who would engage him in single combat.

"About this fact," the account says, "I can tell an actual happening, well-known to many, which those who lived there and nearby told to me." This legend told of a young man who overheard a series of cautionary stories about visits to the place (in a fashion analogous to teens sharing stories about modern legend-trip sites). He was "not satisfied by the report" and decided to test for himself whether it was true or not. He went to the place, performed the ritual, and claimed to have defeated the phantom knight; but, like the teens visiting Bloody Mary's grave, when he returned and undressed, he found his leg covered with blood from a wound inflicted during the battle (Oesterley 1980: 534 [my translations]; cf. *Gesta Romanorum* 1891: 300). Interestingly, Wandlebury Mound is still considered to be an uncanny site: in the summer of 2001, two crop circles, mysterious phenomena interpreted by many psychic investigators as the result of uncanny forces, appeared in fields alongside the site. One had a diameter of precisely 666 feet (supposedly revealing its diabolical origins) and appeared to be governed by a "death energy." One investigator found that, like the medieval legend-trippers, he could not stay inside the crop circle for long, as he was "repeatedly attacked by a massive bumble bee" (Newman 2001). A website gave detailed instructions to other interested parties on how to locate and visit these crop circles (now, alas, destroyed by harvesting).[2]

Other medieval records show that when churches were built in or beside such Neolithic monuments, youths were not above merrymaking there. One of the most popular cautionary legends of medieval times held that a group of young people who had gathered to sing and dance in the churchyard of Kolbeck were cursed by the priest and forced to dance without stop for an entire year (Grimm 1981: 1, 96–97, 388–89). A number of ancient sites in England and France are linked to a similar legend: they are the petrified bodies of young people who fell afoul of God or the devil by dancing after midnight into the Sabbath (Burl 1976: 84). In fact, priests' complaints about youths using churchyards for dancing and merrymaking are found as far back as the fourth century, when the church father Basilius fiercely denounced "shameless women" who used the graveyards as a meeting place for revels: "They have attracted to themselves the young men's wantonness and danced before the town at the graves of the martyrs, turning the holy places into a stage to display their shamelessness. They have desecrated the air with their lecherous songs and desecrated with their impure feet the earth. They have gathered together a swarm of young men to watch them, whores that they are, and mad—greater madness were not possible. Could I be silent about all this? How can I berate it as it deserves?" Likewise, St. Augustine records that authorities had to suppress youngsters who were in the habit of visiting the martyr Cyprian's[3] grave: "All night they sang these impious songs, and as they sang, they danced" (Zacharias 1980: 37–38).

Living Rocks

One belief central to many such visits is that a stone or grave marker is a living extension of the supernatural. We find on both continents the belief that certain monuments have lifelike abilities to move or punish desecrators. This belief is quite likely ancient: in England and in Brittany, a number of stone formations—natural and artificial—are said to be able to spin around, travel, or dance at certain moments (Bord 1978: 144–51). One such is the Cheesewring (Bodmin Moor, Cornwall), a natural formation of boulders stacked one on top of the other. Whenever a cock crows, the top boulder spins three times. The Tingle Stone, a Neolithic monument near Avening (Gloucestershire), supposedly dashes around the field when a nearby clock strikes midnight.

Some of these beliefs are jocular: there are no farms near the Cheesewring, and many accounts stress that the stone must *hear* the clock strike or the cock crow—a patent impossibility. One such belief makes this explicit: the Pyrford Stone (Sussex) turns when it hears the clock in the nearby church chime midnight—but villagers know the church has never *had* a chiming clock. We could consider such beliefs as random leg-pulling, similar to the British belief that the notoriously crooked Chesterfield steeple became twisted when a bride and groom who were both virgins got married there, and will untwist if ever such an event happens again (Addy 1973: 60). But the steeple remains twisted to this day, because one or both parties always test the waters before going to church.

The author recalls being instructed with an ironic wink how to tell if my date was a virgin: take her to the Lawn at the center of the University of Virginia and walk with her up towards the Rotunda at the stroke of midnight. Halfway, we would come abreast of two statues, one of Jefferson seated, the other of Washington standing. If my date was truly chaste, as we came alongside them, Jefferson would stand and Washington would sit. As with the British belief, the legend is in fact a sexist comment that all women are secretly promiscuous. Many similar college legends cast doubt on women's virtue by claiming that certain statues will roar, wave, tip their hats, or otherwise become animate whenever a virgin walks past; since this never happens, all women must be potentially available (Dorson 1959: 254–55; Bronner 1990: 179–85). An outsider might take such statements out of context and assume that American college students "believe" that statues have magical properties to come alive on certain occasions; conversely, we cannot assume that every legend of dancing or walking stones was told to be taken seriously.

Still, many Neolithic sites gained a reputation for being "uncanny" (or incomprehensible) in some way. A common motif holds that the stones at Stonehenge or other complex monuments cannot be counted; or, if they are counted, the person doing so will raise the devil, contract a fatal illness, or go insane. The first surveyor of the extensive Neolithic site at Stanton Drew (Avon), John Wood, recorded in 1750 the belief that "No one . . . was ever able to reckon the Number of these metamorphosed Stones, or to take a Draught of them, tho' several have attempted to do both, and proceeded until they were either struck dead upon the Spot, or with such an illness as soon carried them off." And, in fact, violent storms did break out just at the start of the initial archeological measurements of both Stanton Drew and Stonehenge (Michell 1977: 12). It is still half-seriously believed by archaeologists that whenever an old burial monument is excavated, a thunderstorm will begin within minutes or hours (Williamson and Bellamy, 1983: 124).[4]

As we have seen before, the concept of counting something or reducing it to quantified measurements was equal to the act of "naming" in European traditions, since numerals and letters were identical until Renaissance times. Thus, the act of counting stones or other objects in an uncanny site was an effort to gain control over the supernatural spirit of the site, an act that, if not done correctly, could be dangerous. Folklorist Jacqueline Simpson (1969) has documented a large and active body of lore about the Sussex beauty spot Chanctonbury Ring. This site, a grove planted in the 1700s inside an ancient hill fort, has since the beginning of the century supported several beliefs: one is that the number of trees growing inside the ring could never be counted properly, as "there is some sort of spell on them." If one ever did do so, the ghosts of Julius Caesar and his invading armies would be raised (128). Nevertheless, archaeologists note that visitors to stone circles continue to leave chalk marks, indicating that the ritual of counting is still being performed—so the belief functions not so much as a warning as a dare.

Scattered but consistent records show that, in addition to hosting groups of drunken merrymakers, such monuments were thought to be propitious places for fornication. In Brittany, newlyweds would come after dark to Kerloas, the tallest prehistoric monument still standing in the region. According to archaeologist Aubrey Burl, they would "strip and, one on each side of the stone, rub themselves . . . in the hope of having sons." By the last century, this rite had been euphemized to a daylight visit by the couple, who would try to stretch their arms around the shaft (1985: 64). Couples who make love on the ground inside the Cerne Abbas giant, a gigantic human figure with a prominent erect phallus, carved out of the turf in Dorset, are believed to be sure to conceive.

In this respect, we find many striking parallels between the folklore of prehistoric sites and contemporary American high school and college ritual play. A distant cousin of this body of lore may be preserved at American college campuses that set aside special spots—oftentimes stones—where women "officially become coeds" by kissing their dates (Bronner 1990: 185–86). "Spoofer's Stone" at the University of Arkansas is one such site, being allegedly the place where couples left notes after the college forbade "all intercourse between boys and girls." Another tradition instructed couples at Purdue University to kiss under the arch of the clock tower of Heavilon Hall. At the first stroke of midnight, however, the two were instructed to race across the mall to founder John Purdue's grave "and commence more serious business before the last chimes strike" (Dorson 1959: 258). This tradition is similar to the athletic tradition of racing around the quadrangle of Trinity College, Cambridge, while midnight chimes sound,[5] a considerable but barely possible feat (Menefee 1985: 1, 15). But at Purdue, the two sites are nearby, so racing from one to the other while the clock strikes midnight not only is possible, but would leave the participants enough energy to go on to "more serious business" (presumably fornication) after such a race.[6]

One seemingly trivial college custom may in fact be related to the old custom of counting stone monuments. At Cedar Crest College, students claimed that a dating couple could win a wish by silently counting the steps behind the former president's home. If they arrived at the same number and sealed it with a kiss, the wish would come true (Bronner 1990: 186). Interestingly, a much older Breton tradition told dating couples to go to the prehistoric monument at Essé at the time of the new moon. The girl would go around the site clockwise and her date would go the other way, each counting the stones; if their sums agreed "within a count of two," they would marry happily (Burl 1985: 85). These rituals resemble each other too closely to be simply coincidental, especially since their point in common is the same counting ritual that we have found widely distributed regarding Neolithic monuments in Great Britain.

Finally, the ritual visits often include some element of retaining part of the stone's magic in the form of a charm. The association of fetishism with death sites or megalithic monuments (usually understood as burial sites, regardless of the original use) is ancient. Some of these traditions did not involve harming the monument. In the twelfth century, Geoffrey of Monmouth said that visitors poured water over the rocks at Stonehenge, then carried it home to pour into baths as a healing charm. As early as the eighth century, the Venerable Bede mentioned a number of such practices connected with the Christian king Oswald. Dust from the spot where he fell in battle was collected for its supposed healing powers, and, Bede comments, "This practice became so popular that, as the earth was gradually removed, a pit was left in which a man could stand" (III.9). These early Christian beliefs paralleled those attached to prehistoric monuments. Visitors to the King Stone at the British Neolithic Rollright monument "used continually to be chipping off pieces, so that formerly the stone was bigger than it is now," according to one antiquary (Bord 1978: 32). A now-modest Neolithic standing stone near Penvern, Brittany, was said to heal the ills of those who rubbed against it. "Alternatively, a piece of the stone could be dropped into a potion and drunk," an archaeologist notes, adding, "The worn-down side of the stone testifies to the popularity of this practice" (Burl 1985: 43). If we recall that the King Stone is, according to one legend, the petrified remains of a prehistoric king who was turned to stone by witchcraft, then it would make sense that removal of a part of the stone territorialized part of this legendary figure's powers.

Such practices could be seen as mere souvenir hunting, but, more likely, these pieces were thought to have fetishistic value. If we look at such objects as fetishes—that is, as quasi-animate extensions of supernatural power—then one aspect of the ritual may hinge on taking home a chip or splinter or packet of dust or jug of water that appropriates part of this power. A piece of stone, therefore, is a kind of bone with supernatural powers. This is particularly clear in cases like the King Stone just mentioned. We recall that the rabbit's foot killed on Jesse James's grave was seen as equivalent to a bone from his buried skeleton.

But another aspect of the ritual relies on it being a ritual defiance of the supernatural, which is not far from ritual defiance of mainstream religion, which is not far from the spirit of satanism. Going around the Chanctonbury Ring a certain number of times, according to a still-active tradition, will cause the devil to appear to you. Accounts vary widely about when, how, and how many times one should do so. The earliest says that you should go there on a moonless night and walk seven times around without stopping; many others specify midnight, and many indicate the pagan holy day of Beltane, or Midsummer's Eve. Most versions also stress that you should *run,* and one even says that you should run *backwards,* though this is probably facetious, as the grove is by no means small (as I learned by walking around it just once). Nevertheless, Simpson reports that already by the late 1960s, a number of local people took such traditions seriously enough that they assumed that satanists did use the ring as a place for cult ceremonies. Thirty years later, an elaborate local tradition had grown up about an evil cult linked both to the Chanctonbury traditions and to a range of local animal mutilations and unexplained deaths (Simpson 1994).

There may well have been an adolescent circle behind these stories. A porter at the local railway station confirmed that he had seen "a strange light and heard weird noises" when he passed Slaybrook Corner at night. This might have been supernatural; more likely it showed that the site was a gathering spot for adolescents wishing to party in privacy. Many American traditions have a similar double nature: while for some the uncanny spot is dangerous to pass, for others it is a perfect place for a party around a bonfire. The two may coincide when merrymakers, aware that couples are likely to come past to test their courage, arrange some kind of "apparition" to enact the legend—an act of ostension which may in turn lead adults to believe that some kind of witchcraft is being practiced there. As with Chanctonbury, local "experts" were quick to assume that satanists were somehow mixed up with the Slaybrook Corner stories. The local rector told the press, "I've heard rumours that a black magic circle meets secretly in the village. . . . I am making my own investigations. This is the evil sort of thing they would do."[7]

In sum, a legend-trip to a graveyard (particularly one that involves drunken partying or fornication) is a ritual act that presupposes a supernatural threat that is meant to be defied. It often involves the social creation of a fetish—a bone, stone, or other artifact—that is a physical manifestation of the site's supernatural power. And its practitioners have always been the young men and women whom crusaders assume are most likely to dabble in antireligious behavior. We turn now to the specific dynamics that might encourage legend-trippers to destroy monuments and even open graves.

Defying the Witch: Rites of Rebellion

One common type of legend-trip defines a certain cemetery as the resting place of a witch or community of witches, and encourages teens to prove their bravery by damaging the cemetery. This may be expressed in relatively benign form, such as the "Bloody Mary" ritual that demanded only that trippers stamp on her grave and curse her out loud. But even there, vandalism clearly had taken place (Ray 1976: 181, 186). In other cases, vandalism is specifically mentioned in the legend and hence encouraged as a test of the tripper's bravery. But, as I noted in a previous study of this ritual, to say that breaking a witch's tombstone satisfies a test of manhood evades the question: why focus the rite on vandalism in the first place? Perhaps the answer, as I suggested, is "that the legend-trip is more than an initiation into the supernatural; it functions . . . as a 'ritual of rebellion.' The trip is the significant thing to the adolescent, and the legend serves mainly as an excuse to escape adult supervision, commit anti-social acts, and experiment illicitly with drugs and sex. Both legend and trip are ways of saying 'screw you' to adult law and order" (2001: 188). Hence the ritual curses spoken on Bloody Mary's grave are directed not so much at a witch—a person who embodies an ideology counter to conventional society—but at a representative of adult morality. Legend-trips create a play-like situation that gives participants an excuse to indulge in deviant play behavior that explicitly "gives the finger" to Bloody Mary and other bogies, but the actions themselves—drug use, vandalism, and sex—in fact defy adult figures and adult morality.

Sociologist Ikuya Sato (1988), studying adolescent motorcycle gangs, has made a similar observation about the activities of adolescent gangs: they tend to engage in play rather than ritual. Play creates a context in which participants can define their acts in terms of an alternative reality that contains comic caricatures of adults and allows them to enact improvised dramas, "street corner myths," as he calls them, in which they express their independence. As I argued, "the couples continue to make out in spite of the threats. The illicit nature of the sexual adventure is the key: authority figures such as parents, teachers, and other chaperones are united in trying to keep the sexes apart, thus essentially castrating them until the age of socially-recognized maturity. It is thus significant that the maniac or other threat is often identified with older, parental figures. . . . these legends project social warnings against sex onto marginal figures like ghosts and lunatics whom the participants can defy in good conscience" (2001: 189).

This element distinguishes legend-trips from the more serious fetish practices carried out by representatives of the community's everyday life. These latter function by taking an object defined as belonging to an evil, deviant force, such as the rabbit's foot, and using it to counter another form of mischief. The legend-trip, by contrast, temporarily inverts normal social mores by temporarily identifying the social norm with the evil figure who deserves to be defied. This ritual thus works by naming everyday morality "witchcraft," and the teens' illegal response its "exorcism."

If the antiworld drama thus created encourages teens to curse adult morality, then the act is not far from cursing God in a symbolic way. Indeed, these American traditions of ritual cursing have much in common with the lore of the "Deity Stone," part of an ancient stone circle near Penmaenmawr (Gwynedd). According to a Welsh tradition first published in 1909, this physical representation of God would bend its head down and strike anyone committing blasphemy in its presence. Here is one account, which sounds much like the cautionary legends that set up contemporary American legend-trips:

> A man from South Wales played cards with some friends beside this stone on a Sunday, and when the men returned to the village with cuts about their heads, the people knew the Deity Stone had smitten them, though they would not admit having had punishment. A notorious blasphemer who came from Merionethshire laughed to scorn the story of this stone. One night he went to the Druid's Circle alone and at a very late hour, and shouted words of blasphemy so loud that his voice could be heard ringing down the Green Gorge. People shuddered as they heard him. The sounds ceased, and the listeners ran away in sheer fright. In the morning the blasphemer's corpse was found in a terribly battered condition at the base of the Deity Stone. (Quoted in Bord 1978: 158)

Similar dynamics—cautionary legends setting up ritual acts of blasphemy—have informed American legend-trips for many years. In the previous chapter, we discussed how a cemetery near Weatherly, Pennsylvania, was the subject of legends that dared teens to fetishize its tombstones. Similarly, the isolated Mount Olive Cemetery north of Butler, Ohio, has been known since early in the century as the location of "Mary Jane's Grave." The site most often pointed out as hers, at the foot of a huge pine tree, is the resting place of one Mary Jane Hendrickson, who died on 3 March 1898 of natural causes. Since 1910, however, local youths have been told that she was an evil witch who was hanged on that tree, the sap of which supposedly formed a natural cross the next day. Alternatively, she was executed on the town square of nearby Mansfield and buried as far out in the woods as possible to keep her spirit from returning. Another stone reputed to be Mary Jane's, though, bears the inscription, "Not dead but sleepth" [*sic*], suggesting to some that in fact she became a kind of vampire, who simply rested in her grave until she was provoked into action. Teens warn that she will avenge any harm done to her grave site, and a common cautionary legend tells of a group of youths who defied the curse:

> The legend goes that somebodies, I can't remember whose now, but these three guys went down there one night, and they were real bold. They were from my high school. Now this is true. This really happened to them, but these three guys went down there, and you know it was always fun, you'd go at night and get drunk or whatever or you'd go down to drink or just go to get scared, whatever. So anyway, the place is scary, definitely scary, because you drive forever and go down this steep hill, to the end of this dirt road and there's the graveyard. But, the three guys went down there and two of them decided they were going to piss on her grave. So they did and the third one, he chickened out, he wouldn't do it. So they pissed on the grave and all of a sudden, up in the window of the house, this shadow came into the window. There was a light on in one window. It was this old woman and she started screaming. OK, so they got paranoid and they left. They jumped in their car and they took off. On the drive back, they had a wreck and two of them got killed.
> *Which two?*
> The two that pissed on the grave got killed, and the third kid,

he's the one who told the story. They went to my high school when it first opened, like early '60s. Anyway these two guys got killed. (OSUFA, Heck 1981)

Alternatively, as the car was leaving "it just seemed like someone took hold of the wheel and drove them into a ditch" (OSUFA, Pfizenmayer 1989), or "a white wolf jumped out in front of the car and they run into a tree" (OSUFA, Mitsch 1978).

Likewise, Stepp Cemetery outside of Bloomington, Indiana, has inspired a cycle of beliefs and legends, many focusing on a carved stump in the middle of the cemetery that teens believe holds a curse. One version, heard in a fraternity, explains:

Some of the "actives" in the fraternity had been daring some of us pledges to do some things that they hadn't had the nerve to do themselves. The subject centered around various acts against sororities and the University. Suddenly, one of the active's eyes lit up and he exclaimed that he knew something that none of us would do. He began his tale concerning "The Death Chair." He told us that forty years ago a woman in the area of the Morgan-Monroe State Forest had a child that was hit by a car and killed. She buried her child in a cemetery located in the State Forest. This woman also had the tree next to her child's grave cut down and had the stump shaped into a chair so that she might sit in it and guard her child against any strangers that entered the cemetery. When she was not in the chair it is said she had put a curse on it to protect the grave. It is said that if anyone sits in the chair or even touches it when she is not in it, that person will die one year to the day that he touched the chair.

Everyone in the room laughed off the legend when it was related to us but I am sure each person felt more seriously about it than anyone let on. (Clements and Lightfoot 1972: 97, 99)

In fact, reactions to the "dare" incorporated in this story vary widely. One version, collected from a young male, comments:

. . . and that, like, they always said that if anyone ever sat in that stump, that chair . . . I mean I never sat in it, of course . . . I'm a believer.

I've sat in it.

Oh, . . . I wouldn't even touch it. I wouldn't even go four feet away from it. . . . But [this guy] he, he apparently . . . I forget the girl . . . I knew who she was, but I don't remember who she was . . . she was in high school. . . . Anyway, he'd had a fight with his girl friend and he went out there and sat in the stump-chair . . . and he died in a car crash that night on his way back to town. . . . Now, whether he just drove his car off the road, you know, or whether that had anything to do with it, I don't know. But he died that night coming back from Stepp's. (Clements and Lightfoot 1972: 114)

But another male informant said, "I have sat in the chair many times, as Stepp Cemetery is a favorite out-of-the-way place to take your beer or whatever mindbenders if you are under the legal age or similar circumstances. It is also a very popular place for teenagers to go with their dates to park. So if there is a curse on the chair, I have absorbed more than my share of them" [*sic*] (Clements and Lightfoot 1972: 100). In all three cases, the legends clearly did not warn teens away but made the sites all the more popular as places for partying and parking with girlfriends—and all three cemeteries have in fact been extensively vandalized. As we turn to participants' own comments on such activities, we at last gain an inside perspective on ritual desecration of graveyards.

The Self-Healing Gravestone

Another link we can document between contemporary legend-trips and lore about prehistoric monuments is the warning that if stones at such sites are removed, they will mysteriously return of their own accord (Bord 1972: 160; Bord 1978: 191ff.). One of the Rollright Stones (Oxfordshire) was taken from its place to be used as a bridge, according to tradition, and a team of horses was used to haul it downstream. But it proved unsatisfactory, as it shifted every night—so it was returned, with *one* horse being enough to pull it back uphill to its original site. The Thigh Stone on the island of Anglesey, Wales, was able to return by itself: in the time of Henry I, it is said, a local earl had it chained to a larger stone and thrown into the sea, but the next morning it was back in its original place. Those who tamper with such stones are often punished with injury or death. Another curious person tried to remove the Thigh Stone, but had his own thigh turn putrid. And tradition holds that a Cornwall farmer once tried to drag away an ancient monument to use as an animal's watering trough:

> For a long time it resisted the efforts of the oxen, but at length they succeeded in starting it, and dragged it slowly up the hill-side to where the wain was standing. Here, however, it burst away from the chains which held it, and, rolling back again to the well, made a sharp turn and regained its old position, where it has remained ever since. Nor will any one again attempt removal, seeing that the farmer, who was previously well-to-do in the world, never prospered from that day forward. Some people say, indeed, that retribution overtook him on the spot, the oxen falling dead, and the owner being struck lame and speechless. (Bord 1978: 194)

A similar cautionary legend is told about the Stone Couch, a seat made from discarded construction materials on a road between Weatherly and Eckley, Pennsylvania. Like the Warlock Seat, those who sit on it (some variants specify three times in the light of a full moon) will die mysteriously. One version continues:

> . . . I heard that some kid, he had a pick-up truck, right? (*Uh-huh.*) And he went over to the Stone Couch and he had this—I don't know if it was a chain or rope—but he tied it around the couch. He moved it out, he only moved it a couple feet or so, you know how it's away from the road?
> *Yeah. Was it onto the road he moved it?*
> No, he just moved it closer to the road. 'Cause it's about two feet back. (*Uh-huh.*) So he went home then and on the way home he was in an accident. His friends went up the next day and the couch [had] moved back to where it was. (PSUHFA: Watkins, 1989)

In fact, several American legend-trips include the belief that markers have the power to return to their original places if moved. Similar stories could be collected in many parts of the country: Ian Frazier, in a journalistic narrative of his travel through the Great Plains, notes in pass-

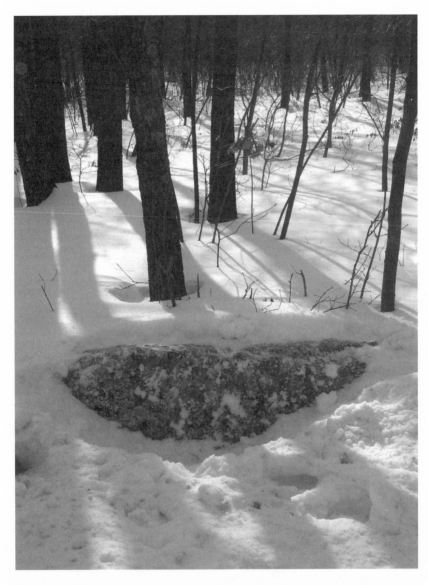

Fig. 4. The Stone Couch in east central Pennsylvania, between Weatherly and Eckley. Courtesy of the author.

ing "Devil Butte" near McLaughlin, South Dakota, and records the tradition that "High-school kids go up there and try to arrange these white rocks to spell out their initials, but by morning the rocks always rearrange themselves into the shape of a devil's head" (1989: 52). One Mansfield male remarked that every so often Mary Jane's tombstone turns up missing, but it always seems to return, adding, "Hey, that stone has been thrown in the lake twice." At Stepp Cemetery, the Warlock Seat likewise has the magical power to restore itself. One teen recalled, "My cousin, I don't know if he heard or he was out there when this guy did it, but he supposedly pulled up the stump and moved it one night. . . . And uh, they went back the next night and it was back in the same place and it didn't look like it had ever been moved. And there was no chain marks on it where they used a chain to pull it up. And there was no chain marks on it" (Hettinger 1982). Another Bloomington teen recalled a similar event.

> . . . I took a chunk of the chair, a piece of the wood about like this [holds hands about a foot apart] and about two inches wide, and I locked it up. Put it in a strongbox and locked it up. I brung it home and I was laid off December fourth, 1981, and unlocked the strongbox, opened it up and it was gone. She [the witch of the cemetery] had followed me . . . and tooken back her chunk of chair.
>
> *Did you go back out there to see if it was back in place?*
>
> Yes, it was back in place. We even chopped chunks of it out and we locked up chunks of it, uh, in Morgan Monroe [State Park] Forestry's safe out there. And they opened it up and the pieces were gone. (Hettinger 1982)

Stated this way, such traditions do not seem to encourage stealing grave markers for occult reasons; in fact, if these stones are, somehow, living extensions of supernatural force, this might be a good reason for not desecrating graveyards. But such a literalist approach ignores the ways in which such beliefs can act as dares, to see if stones actually do have the power to return or punish those who move them.

It is therefore significant that both ancient and contemporary sites show repeated vandalism. Archaeologists have attributed some of the earlier damage to efforts by the new Christian establishment "to reduce or eliminate the survival of pagan idolatry" (Grinsell 1976: 14). But still other sites were destroyed in relatively modern times by less official parties who believed that they would locate some kind of treasure underneath them. Yet others appear to have been obliterated by owners who wanted to discourage visitors. One such was the Isle of Skye farmer who found his grain constantly trampled by people visiting the Bowing Stone on his property in order to walk three times around it. Similarly, owners of houses or trees that become sites of modern legend-trips often find that the only way to stop groups of youngsters from coming there is to demolish them.

Feelings that such ancient stones should not be disturbed remain surprisingly strong in Great Britain. An interesting flap occurred in 1944 at the village of Great Leighs (Essex) when, during the war effort, a local road was widened by bulldozing aside a two-ton boulder that residents called the "Witch's Stone." Allegedly, it lay over the body of an old woman convicted in a seventeenth-century witch trial and buried there with a stake through her heart to keep her from returning. Alternatively, it marked the site where she had been burned at the stake, the stone being placed over the ashes from the fire.[8] Such beliefs may well have been invented, but residents still blamed the stone's dislodging for a large number of mysterious accidents that occurred immediately afterward, and they were not appeased until the boulder was returned to its original location during an improvised midnight ceremony (Cooper 1944; Price 1945: 301–2; Valiente 1973: 352–54). Other communities could be even more insistent: archaeologist Leslie V. Grinsell notes that in the Orkney Islands, neighbors ostracized the man who moved an allegedly sacred stone in the nineteenth century, and in fact attempted to burn his house down (1976: 64).

Given the prevalence of cautionary legends imposing supernatural penalties, it seems likely that damage to these sites was caused during unofficial tests of manhood among youths reacting against a firmly held belief that such sites were holy. On the other hand, during the 1600s one resident of the village adjoining the great Neolithic complex of Avebury gained renown as the "stone-killer," repeatedly defying the curse attached to the megaliths by toppling and smashing them. An earlier skeptic apparently paid the price: when one toppled stone was restored in recent times, a skeleton was found crushed beneath it; coins found with the body dated this event to the early fourteenth century (Bord 1972: 17; Grinsell 1976: 14).

A somewhat more graphic description of a visit to Mary Jane's Grave also includes the exaggerated "brave male" and "scared female" roles that contribute to the simultaneous feelings of fear and "fun":

> The first time I was ever there, this good buddy of mine took the girl I was dating, the girl he was dating, and a whole bunch of other girls there. All their friends, you know. We got in his car. It was a little Opel Kadette station wagon and had people just packed in there. A bunch of girls, you know, we're going to Mary Jane's Grave, telling them the story, getting them paranoid as hell, they're screaming, you know, they're having a good old time.
>
> So we're driving down there and we stop and we park. The girl I was dating was a real wimp, so she was like hanging on to me, screaming, and I'm loving it, you know, this is great.
>
> And we walked to the grave, and Curt pulls out a shovel and goes, "Hey, let's dig it up." I said, "Well, O.K., O.K." And this girl goes, "No! You guys are crazy!!" And we're going, "Yeah, come on, let's just start diggin.'"

But they chose not to, at least on this occasion. Instead, they visited a nearby "old witch's house." When they got to where they could see the house, the informant recalled, "These girls are nuts, I mean, they're losin' it, they screamin', we're lovin' it, you know, we're havin' fun" (OSUFA, Heck, 1981).

Fig. 5. Mary Jane's Grave in Butler, Ohio. Courtesy of the author.

Ikuya Sato warns, however, that when participants are not fully committed to adult norms, their activities may lead to a "corruption of play." Deeply involved in a group situation, participants may violate so-cial rules beyond the point of no return, leading to real criminal actions with serious consequences (1988: 203–5). This kind of boldness, how-ever, can extend the drama-like scenario of defying the witch into crimi-nal acts of vandalism and even grave-robbing, as in the infamous Highgate Cemetery vandalisms (Ellis 2000: 201ff.).

At Stepp Cemetery, legend-trippers fell afoul of the law in this way as early as 1966, when three adolescent males were arrested for leaving the body of a German Shepherd dog near the mysterious "lady in black's" grave. The dog was killed when the cruising teens accidentally ran over it. After unsuccessfully trying to locate its owner, the youths told police, they decided to take it to the cemetery, where they hung its body from a tree to frighten other visitors. Rumors spread quickly about the "sacri-ficed" dog, and when police arrived the following night, they found a crowd of teens around the hanged dog, allegedly waiting for the "witch" to appear.

Police discounted its significance as a prank in bad taste, but the hanged dog quickly became a standard item in Stepp Cemetery legends. In versions collected after this case, the witch was said to go after, kill, and hang dogs (primarily German Shepherds) to provide a mysterious dog of her own supernatural company. She now appeared in legend as-sociated with "white wolves" who (as in the Mary Jane lore) appear to motorists and try to wreck their cars. The Stepp Cemetery witch's pref-erence for killing and mutilating German Shepherds, in fact, is a striking predecessor of a rumor that gained currency among anticult investiga-tors some twenty years later: that is, that satanic cults collected and ritu-ally sacrificed this particular breed of dogs (Terry 1987: 162).

Overall, we find most of the elements of crusaders' accounts of cemetery desecrations present in adolescents' legend-trips. This is not to say that *all* vandals are involved in legend-trips, or that all legend-trippers desecrate cemeteries. But the atmosphere of antisocial "fun" set up by this ritual activity clearly extends to gravestone smashing and removal, grave-disturbing, and something close to animal sacrifice. The rite of legend-tripping is much better documented and attested in the years before the present satanism scare than any occult tradition involving grave-robbing. Further, as we shall see, legend-tripping actually appro-priates official definitions of such acts as "satanism," so that, paradoxically, efforts to stem such activities may instead heighten the "black magic" elements that teens include.

Ironically, then, one result of such warnings was to introduce devil-worship themes into adolescents' legend-trip traditions, or to further develop previously vague "devil" motifs. One such tradition focused on a barn on a remote road outside of Tontogany, Ohio, eleven miles south of the Toledo suburb of Maumee. In the light of the full moon, spectators were supposed to be able to see the face of the devil. During the 1960s, the legend consisted of little more than this; but, by the late 1970s, elements of satanism had become a commonplace in Toledo-area legend-trips, and many freely incorporated official beliefs in secret cults that met in cemeteries and held weird ceremonies (see Ellis 1991: 288).

So, in 1985, Maumee teens had joined the legend of the barn with the devil's face to one of a cemetery near Tontogany where a "cult sacrifice victim" was supposed to be buried. When he was found, he was "all mutilated and his body organs were missing," the legend went, and the word "revenge" was found written in his blood beside the body. This was interpreted to be a message from the deceased, so the cautionary legend warned teens that his spirit would take revenge on anyone touching his tombstone. Informants described the ritual this set up: those willing to accept the dare would hug the tombstone, and others created a panic by shouting, "The guy's coming!" A mad rush to the car ended the visit, but add-on legends told of one participant who broke his leg the next day when he fell down the steps of his school "as if someone had pushed him real hard from behind."

More interestingly, when word of this legend-trip came to parents, a small panic broke out, with adults calling each other to exchange concerns that their children were "taking a chance." This and other legend-trip rumors eventually set up an official inquiry, during which the county sheriff announced that cults were indeed at work and probably had committed human sacrifices. His official response, paradoxically, was to dig for bones at a site he had identified as a cult cemetery. Shortly before Midsummer's Eve, 1985, an isolated vacant lot popular as a teen parking spot was excavated: hundreds of animal bones were found (not surprisingly, since a previous resident had used it as a pig farm), along with a number of artifacts that were widely displayed as tokens of victory over the cult.

Interpretation of these artifacts varied. One inventory, published in *Penthouse,* included "a headless doll with a small pentagram ornament, an eight-inch dagger with blood on it, pots of tempera paint, a crucifix mounted upside down, and several large crosses" (Norris and Potter 1986: 50). Other observers, including an archaeologist called in by police, were far more skeptical about the value of any of these items as evidence. And no human remains were found. But the "Toledo Dig," as it came to be called, was a huge success as a media show, and the artifacts found were regularly cited as hard evidence for cult activity (Ellis 1991: 287–91; Victor 1992: 20). This makes sense from the folk traditions we have previously seen: anything taken from a "witch's grave," whether human bones or symbolic substitutes, has value as a fetish against the same kind of evil power. To antioccult crusaders, then, the articles found in the Midsummer Eve Toledo Dig were, therefore, similar in value to the mummified foot of a rabbit shot at midnight on an evil person's grave.

Adolescents were less respectful. One legend-tripper commented that the dig was an "enormous snowball that has gotten out of hand." To his peers, the Tontogany ritual was a "means of escape from the everyday doldrum," because "they like to believe in the supernatural and the thrill of getting away with something they aren't supposed to just encourages them on." Adults, by contrast, "are out to get rid of the harm and the problem the legend provides"; in their sight, the adolescents' legend "becomes a threat to their world" (OSUFA, Weekley 1989). And such a message, transmitted to youths, simply reaffirms the value of the tradition as a rite of rebellion.

The Legend-Trip—Ritual or "Fun"?

Legend-tripping is, in short, a trial of passage that tests adolescents' bravery by creating an imaginative supernatural threat, then inviting them to defy it. It is certainly "pagan," in that it celebrates typically adolescent joys of life and sex. But it is not distinctively "cult-oriented" in the sense that crusaders have indicated, since it does not indoctrinate participants into any set ideology. Rather, like other forms of play-like deviance, it simply inverts existing cultural norms. Although Eric Maple saw authentic occult rituals behind cemetery vandalisms, he still refused to conclude from this that there was an actual resurgence of satanic cult activity. He commented, "the newspapers, by persistently featuring the activities of Satanists, and radio and television, by popularizing the activities of modern witches, have succeeded in bringing to the surface many emotionally-charged concepts which have not troubled mankind for generations. It is notable that the incidence of churchyard vandalism rises and falls with the publicity it receives" (1966: 177). For youths, the more attention given "satanic" desecrations, the more status one might gain by carrying them out in real life. Hence official attention given such events may "network" such rituals far more effectively than any underground "cult" conduit. Similarity of graveyard rituals nationwide may simply reflect common themes in media warnings against satanism. Ironically, Anton LaVey's comments in the *Satanic Bible* are exactly apropos: "Any ceremony considered a black mass must effectively shock and outrage, as this seems to be the measure of its success. . . . If the Satanist wishes to create a ritual to blaspheme an accepted institution . . . he is careful to choose one that is now in vogue to parody. Thus, he is truly stepping on a sacred cow (1969: 101).[9] This principle, it seems, is true regardless of when the ritual was performed. In a community where ancient monuments were revered, rebels would circulate legends and beliefs describing their magical powers and then gain status by attacking these same sites. In a Christianized culture, the same dynamics would lead to legends about churches and cemeteries and to ritual vandalisms. And, as LaVey's principle suggests, in a setting where older "pagan" ideas are being revived as part of "earth mysteries," the dynamics of desecration would switch back to alleged Neolithic sites. It is thus instructive that ley-hunter Tom Graves records that the Rollright Stones, now the focus of a series of New Age "stone energy" experiments, have already been desecrated by vandals who left the remains of a mutilated puppy there (1986: 121).

The goal of such visits, as many accounts make clear, is "having fun," not working any form of magic. Central is the creation of an alternative definition of reality, in which participants could *act* as if they were confronting supernatural evil. As one visitor to Mary Jane's Grave concluded, "in the night time it's like you're tripping all the way down all the time[;] whether you're straight, stoned, drunken or what it's just real spooky" (OSUFA, Mitsch 1978). The oral narratives of the legend-trip thus cannot be distinguished from the actions that they motivate, much as warnings given a character in a fairy tale cannot be understood by themselves, as they are plot elements setting up what happens when the character ignores them.

Studying cautionary legends alone misses the real focus of the legend-trip, which generates excitement with an alternative, play-like redefinition of reality in terms of a supernatural "dare." Teens need not believe that they are visiting a real witch's grave or putting themselves in real danger. By means of the legend-trip, they temporarily escape what they perceive as a restrictive, adult-oriented, everyday world. One teenage girl who participated in a legend-trip to a "warlock's" grave near Dover, Ohio, commented, "I am convinced that there is a basic need in people to be placed in terrifying positions where your life is in jeopardy. Very little in Dover serves as a threat, yet up on Ridge Road you can always find a full moon and a warlock. You get your adrenaline flowing on a boring evening, rush back home after a close brush with death, and somehow Dover doesn't seem so stagnant" (quoted in Ellis 2001: 190). Another legend-tripper, a young male who had become an expert on Mary Jane's Grave, similarly commented:

> In essence folklore of the supernatural legend genre becomes an intellectual playground for adults or in some instances it may simultaneously become an actual physical playground for the adult expression of adventure and creativity; even though physical destruction of property may occur, a creative and imaginary scene is played out and anxiety is released. . . . In this sacred place it is even permitted to turn dogs into fierce wolves and dead people into social taboos or spirits which are begging you to defy them. I ask you, what other dimension in our society permits this kind of creativity? The writer perhaps or the movie producer even but not the assembly line worker or the sales clerk or even shop keeper. Folklore is one of the few refuges set aside for the non-professional imagination, to create without limitation by the laws of physics.
>
> Without any hesitation, I hold the boring, dull, gray, or spiritless capitalistic technique of mass production to be the causal agent behind the great need for the human mind to express itself in this increasingly popular outlet for creativity (OSUFA, Mitsch, 1978).

The problem is that this "playground" is in fact partly intellectual and partly physical: "creativity" aimed against stagnation and adult regimentation leads to actual acts of vandalism. Calling the witch out of the mirror also flirts with the fringes of reality: the successful ritual draws the participants into an imaginative world in which the supernatural threat is made just barely "real." The ensuing retreat closes off such contact and its consequences. But the legend-trip, in Sato's sense, is prone to corruption of play: even when participants define their actions in terms of a supernatural plot that they recognize as fictitious, they in fact cross over the boundaries of imagination into real life. Hence, in pursuing the logic of the plot that the teens have generated, they may well commit acts with consequences for themselves and their community that do not vanish once the "game" is completed. When group dynamics force participants beyond this boundary, serious consequences can result. As Erik Erikson put it: "in adolescence . . . the grown-up body, the matured genital equipment, and a perceptive mentality permit actions on the borderline of mere playfulness and utterly serious reality, of passing prank and irreversible deed, of daring pretense and final commitment. In negotiating these borderlines together, young people may be able to share transient conflicts which might otherwise force each individual to improvise his own neurosis or delinquency, but they obviously also can lead each other into permanent involvements out of line with their self-image, their conscience—and with the law" (1970: 15).

Folklorist Michael Licht (1974) has described a range of car games that also play at the fringes of outright deviance. Driving duels such as "chicken" allegedly test one's courage by having two cars drive directly at each other; the "loser" is the one who first swerves. Of course, as Licht notes, the only game in which both participants "win" is one in which they do crash head-on, potentially fatally. The legend-trip, I have argued, "is a way of playing chicken with adolescent anxieties" (2001: 197). It is easy to see how groups of teens could become so intensely involved that they would feel challenged not only to deface or vandalize tombs but even to open graves and remove bones as "souvenirs" of their bravery.

This aspect of legend-tripping provokes—and should provoke—the most anxiety. Ritual visits to graveyards regularly lead to illegal acts. Official concern over such activities is justified: active legend-tripping can have a devastating effect on old, historically valuable sites. All the sites named in these traditions, British and American, have suffered repeated smashing and toppling. Mary Jane's gravestone is the most completely damaged marker in the churchyard. The Warlock Seat in Stepp Cemetery, despite its reputation for self-healing, was little more than splinters when I saw it in 1982. And grave markers grow few and fewer in Weatherly.

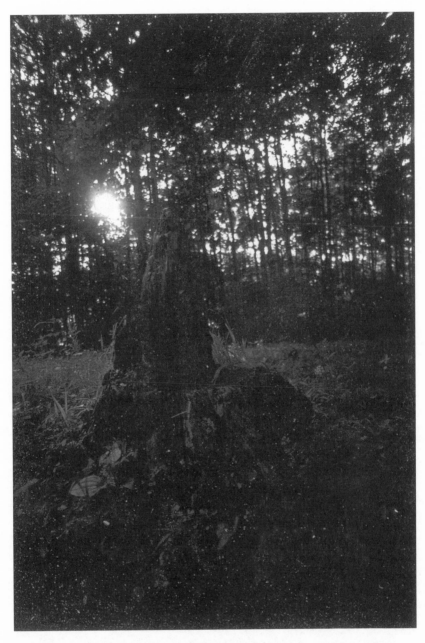

Fig. 6. The Warlock's Seat at Stepp Cemetery. Courtesy of the author.

Besides, such activities may not always end with petty vandalism. Richard Kasso, leader of one drug-focused "satanic" gang in the Long Island community of Northport, was indicted for stealing a skull and left hand from a grave. Reportedly, he believed that both were necessary for "Satanic death rituals." While awaiting trial, he quarreled with another gang member over a drug theft and murdered him during an improvised devil-worship ceremony. Even if no underground ideology coordinates such "satanic" activities, they remind us that adolescents' occult play begins as a rite of rebellion, but through corruption of play can lead to the commission of serious crimes.

So to call graveyard visits "just" play is as naive as to assert that participants are seriously practicing witchcraft or satanism. A realistic view of such activities must acknowledge their psychological benefits, affirming the importance of adult everyday norms even as they invert them. It should recognize that these activities are universal, practically unavoidable elements in adolescent life. But it must also concede that these rites walk the fringes of genuine antisocial behavior, and that, when play becomes reality, the results may damage both the sites visited and the teens who visit. In visiting the forbidden forest, Harry Potter learns that there are sometimes good reasons to violate rules set up by adults. But he also learns (as do many legend-trippers) that there are dangers out there in the world, as well as responsibility to be taken for choosing to defy them.

Chapter Seven

Table-Setting and Mirror-Gazing

The folk practices underlying authentic records of folk magic and witch-craft were often feared and denounced by religious and secular leaders, even at times when they were tolerated. Nevertheless, the decision to practice folk magic was more often tolerated if the person was mature, and most often when the practitioner was male as well. Indeed, the common stereotype portrays witches and wizards alike as senior citizens, with wrinkled and wizened faces like those of Richard Harris and Dame Maggie Smith (Professors Dumbledore and McGonagall in the movies). Even when cunning-folk and wise women were tolerated, though, such practices were not as respectable when they were carried out by curious adolescents, and a common legend type cautions that youngsters' dabbling in ritual magic may prove disastrous.

The story type of the naive "sorcerer's apprentice" teaches that incomplete knowledge is a dangerous thing. One British legend, "The Schoolmaster of Bury," describes how a group of boys at a grammar school repeat the Lord's Prayer backwards to raise the devil—but, having summoned him, find they cannot send him away. Their schoolmaster has to take charge and command the devil to count the letters in the church Bible. The evil one departs, leaving a telltale crack in the floor of the grammar school to remind future students of the story (Briggs 1971: B.1.135–36).

Such warnings are still current in the propaganda of contemporary antioccult crusaders, who hold that children and teenagers are the group most at risk of being seduced into satanism. One Christian video, titled *Harry Potter: Witchcraft Repackaged*, describes the hero of Rowling's books as "a modern sorcerer's apprentice." According to a positive re-

142

view of the documentary, "The video plainly points out [that] 'all his teachers are practicing occultists, and tutor their students in the dark arts and curse casting.' Many of the Harry Potter web sites are hyper linked with sites that contain occult information. Our children are learning how to cast spells and mix potions. Their imaginations dream of having the same power that Harry has" (Downs 2001). The difficulty, according to some fundamentalists, is that once this imagination is encouraged, and young people are induced to dabble in occult crafts that they do not have the experience or maturity to master, they can get themselves into serious magical trouble, just like the grammar school children in the legend. "I don't think people fully realize what they're dealing with," the manager of a Christian book company commented at the 2000 meeting of the Christian Booksellers Association, adding, "I think anyone who knows anything about spiritual warfare knows those books can open the door to spiritual bondage." A fellow Christian backed her up, saying, "And I think it's worse that children are the target.... It opens the doors for young minds. You put sorcery in, what do you expect to get out?" (James 2001).

According to a four-tier behavioral model frequently circulated by antioccult crusaders, youths first become ensnared by evil by engaging in what seems to be a simple occult game, and remain in bondage unless more knowledgeable adults (like the Schoolmaster of Bury) intervene. Unless this happens, they proceed to the second tier, in which they improvise some kind of "self-styled" satanic rituals, which frequently include sex and drug use. Third, they are drawn by satanic recruiters into organized covens. Finally, they participate in a Black Mass, which may include human sacrifice or cannibalism. After this point, it is difficult or even impossible to leave the cult except through suicide (see Hicks 1991: 32ff.). However, adults who have gained some knowledge of spiritual warfare may intervene, banish the influence of the cult (or, indeed, of the devil himself), and return the teen to safety.

The logic of this model has been criticized by debunkers of the Satanism Scare, but it does incorporate a motif that can be traced well back in Anglo-American culture: the wide range of occult play activities engaged in by adolescents, both in historical times and today. We should not be quick to dismiss such rituals' significance simply because many teens assert that they are "only games." Games, as folklorists have noted, are transcriptions of serious, real-life concerns, and their play-like elements often allow these concerns to be expressed more directly than they would be in passing conversation. This is particularly the case in considering young women's ritualistic games. As we have seen, adult witchcraft often incorporated serious elements of protest against male domination in the religious and social world. Women who adopted the witch's role could gain and wield considerably more power than they could by conforming to "good" images of femininity. We can expect similar elements of protest against conventional female role models in these forms of play, and perhaps in a more visible form.

Witchcraft and Occult Play

In 1616, in the midst of the witch hysteria in Great Britain, the Rev. Alexander Roberts laid out some of the reasons why females were more prone to be seduced by the occult than males. First, he argued, they "are by nature credulous, wanting experience, and therfore more easily deceived." Second, they are overly curious "to know such things as be not fitting and covenient." Third, they are more impressionable and thus more easily influenced by the devil. Fourth, they fall more easily, as did Eve in the Garden of Eden. But most importantly, Rev. Roberts stressed,

> this sex, when it conceiveth wrath or hatred against any, is unplacable, possessed with unsatiable desire of revenge, and transported with appetite to right (as they thinke) the wrongs offered unto them: and when their power herein answereth not their will, and are meditating with themselves how to effect their mischievous projects and designes, the Divell taketh the occasion, who knoweth in what manner to content exulcerated mindes, windeth himselfe into their hearts, offereth to teach them the meanes by which they may bring to passe that rancor which was nourished in their breasts, and offereth his helpe and furtherance herein. (1971: 41–42)

Collections of folk beliefs and rituals do in fact contain disproportionate numbers of items reflecting practices by groups of young women in social settings. As early as the 1690s, Cotton Mather complained that Puritan Massachusetts was beset by a plague of "little sorceries," including palmistry, "conjuration with sieves and keys, and peas, and nails, and horseshoes," and other like rituals (quoted in Boyer and Nissenbaum

1974: 1). The Puritans were concerned by the mutual relationship between witchcraft legends and the practices of "white witches" who specialized in countering evil hexes and punishing the culprits. Even these allegedly godly wise women, Increase Mather argued, had "fellowship with that hellish covenant" that linked black witches and the devil, for, indeed, such acts could have no power "but by vertue of a compact with the devil" (quoted in Dorson 1973: 33).

Others seem to allude to practices common among young women speculating about their future husbands. *Mother Bunch's Closet*, a 1760 pamphlet containing a number of magical practices, advises young girls to "Seek a green peascod, in which there are full nine peas; which done, either write or cause to be written, on a small slip of paper, these words, 'Come in my dear, and do not fear.' Which writing you must enclose within the aforeseaid peascod, and lay it under the door, then mind the next person who comes in" (Opie and Tatem 1989: 302). The same ritual was still current in the Sheffield, England, area at the turn of the last century (Addy 1973: 83) and was still being practiced in the Ozark Mountains fifty years later (Randolph 1947: 175).

The sieve-and-keys ritual was well known in England as an early form of divination with the help of an object held between two persons. In *The Discoverie of Witchcraft* (1584), Reginald Scot explained that those practicing it would "Sticke a paire of sheeres in the rind of a sive, and let two persons set the top of each of their forefingers upon the upper part of the sheeres, holding it with the sive up from the ground steddilie, and aske Peter and Paule whether A. B. or C. hath stolne the thing lost, and at the nomination of the guiltie person, the sive will turne round" (Opie and Tatem 1989: 356). While often used to detect a thief, it could also be used to divine the name of one's future husband. Often, after a prayer, Bible verse, or invocation of the Three High Names, the participants then would go through a list of likely names. At the correct one, the sieve would move, working much like the planchette of a modern Ouija board (Henderson 1866: 196–97).

Folklore collections from England and the United States contain many such rites practiced by young women speculating about their future husbands. Some seem only playful, such as the practice of writing boys' names on slips of paper and placing them under one's pillow: the one the girl pulls out in the morning is her intended. Others appear to have strong connections with pagan religion, such as the custom of rising before dawn on the First of May (the old pagan holiday of Beltane or

Walpurgisnacht), going to a spring, and breaking an egg into a cup; her husband's face, or some token of his identity, is said to appear in the cup. A similar tradition allegedly was practiced by the "afflicted girls" at the center of the Salem Witch Panic, as Increase Mather, in 1684, had warned against "The foolish Sorcery of those Women that put the white of an Egg into a Glass of Water, that so they may be able to divine of what Occupation their future Husbands shall be. It were much better to remain ignorant than thus to consult with the Devil" (quoted in Opie and Tatem 1989: 135).

Many explanations—religious, psychosexual, economic, and feminist—have been presented for the development of the witch-hunt that followed. It is clear that its trigger was hysteria among a group of adolescent girls practicing some form of supernatural divination. The witch-hunt that followed may have been directed by male authorities, but it was focused on "the afflicted girls," who, as some feminist historians have noted, used their status to invert the usual social patterns of gender control in Puritan society. Witchcraft it may not have been, but certainly in repressively patriarchal cultures such as the Southern Appalachians, where the ritual hung on into the twentieth century, divining (or defining?) one's husband was a dangerous form of play-like deviance.

There were many different versions of the husband-divining ritual, many of which survived into the twentieth century. A number of these were illustrated on postcards, which became popular as seasonal greeting cards around 1910. In one, posted on November 2, 1912, from a rural Illinois town, a young woman is shown tossing a long apple peel over her right shoulder, at the stroke of midnight according to a clock on the wall behind her. A caption reads: "A Twelve O'clock [*sic*] on Halloween / Throw an Apple peel my Sweet Dame / And the Letter which is plainly seen / Is the Initial of your Marriage Name." This ritual, first recorded by the poet John Gay in his *Shepherd's Week*, holds that if a girl successfully peels an apple in one continuous paring and throws it over her shoulder, it will fall to the ground in the same shape as the first letter of her future husband's surname (Opie and Tatem 1989: 3; Santino 1998: 126). Significantly, the postcard shows the girl accompanied by a black cat (an animal that, as we have seen, was associated with witchcraft) and wearing an odd dress decorated with more black cats, the hem ringed with lurid red and blue flames, suggesting hellfire. The apple peel, in addition, looks less like an inanimate object than a living snake. All these details show that this ritual has diabolical implications even as play. Significantly, the message on the postcard reads, "Well did you throw an appel [*sic*] peeling on Halloween night [?] From the other fellow." This suggests that the ritual was still taken seriously when the card was mailed.

Another postcard shows a young woman blindfolded, standing in front of three small dishes with an outstretched finger. Her image is framed in a mirror, which is flanked by a witch and a jack-o'-lantern. The caption reads, "On Halloween by pumpkin's light, this witch will help you choose aright." The image alludes to another divination ritual, in which (as the poet Robert Burns explained in 1787), the dishes are filled with clean water, "foul" water, and nothing. These foretell, in turn, a marriage to a virgin, a nonvirgin, or no marriage at all (Opie and Tatem 1989: 120; Santino 1998: 122–23).

The mirror, which appears only as a decorative frame in this card, in fact turns out to be an important occult device in other Halloween rituals. In one, captioned only "A Joyous Halloween," we see a young woman walking backward down a set of stairs, evidently into the cellar, as the steps are filled with harvested fruit and vegetables. A close look at the mirror shows the face of a young boy; another postcard explicates the ritual with this rhyme: "Let this design on you prevail / To try this trick (it cannot fail.) / Back down the stairs with candle dim / And in the mirror you'll see HIM!" The card shows a jovial young man peeking around the bend of the stairs so as to appear in the girl's mirror, but the verse is somewhat ambiguous, especially as one of the crafts that wizards were supposed to have mastered was to bind a spirit (a devil to the orthodox) to a mirror so that they could use it for sorcery. Thus, although no witch or devil appears in either of these images, the tradition was ambiguous enough that the viewer could see it as potentially a form of witchcraft.

Another series, again featuring a mirror, is the most explicit about defining the depicted activity as a type of witchcraft. In the most benign of these, we see a girl holding a candle to a wall mirror, where she sees both her own image and that of a handsome young man standing behind her. A caption advises, "By the candle's light / He may be seen / At twelve o'clock / On Halloween." The entire picture is framed with rows of apples, a detail that becomes clear in the light of Robert Burns's explanation (again from his notes to the 1787 poem "Halloween"): "Take a candle, and go alone to a looking-glass; eat an apple before it, and some traditions say, you should comb your hair all the time; the face of your conjugal companion, to be, will be seen in the glass, as if peeping over your shoulder" (Opie and Tatem 1989: 252). Two other images make the ritual seem more ominous. In one, captioned "On Halloween look in the glass / Your future husband's face will pass," the girl is again holding a candle to a full-length mirror to see both her reflection and that of a man standing behind her. But in this case, a shadow to the left of her image falls in the form of a stereotypical witch with pointed hat and broom, suggesting that the act of seeing such an image in a mirror is itself a reflection of witchcraft. And yet another, even more ominous postcard shows the woman as if she has just turned around suddenly, the candle extinguished and her hand over her heart in shock. To the right we see the mirror, with the future husband's wraith-like image still in it, and to the left we again see the profile of a lantern-jawed witch with pointed hat and broom. Other images of Halloween fright—an owl swooping down, a black cat hissing with arched back, and a grotesque jack-o'-lantern—complete the scene, which is again framed with rows of apples.

These postcards clearly reflect a living tradition, as the images they show would be difficult, even impossible to interpret unless one were previously familiar with the rituals they depict. The allusive nature of the rhymes likewise convey a knowing wink to the postcard's recipient: "you know this one, don't you?" Unfortunately, like the complex rabbit's foot fetish, these postcards only document the belief's currency and do not give us much background against which to interpret them. And too often folklorists who collected such practices recorded them only in encyclopedia-like compilations of "superstitions" stripped of any kind of background information. Do these items originate in actual behavior in which young engage in a form of conjuring? Or do these reflect traveling legends like "The Sorcerer's Apprentice," which may or may not be traceable to actual events?

A third alternative exists: when American folklorists began collecting adolescents' supernatural legends intensively, they found that the nominal beliefs underlying such stories more often than not had to be taken ironically. That is, a story about calling a lover's spirit, predicting the future, or invoking the devil functioned not as a serious warning but as a form of play. Thus for instance visitors to a "haunted house" can express exaggerated responses to images of monsters and mad killers because they recognize the origins of the images in movie and fiction plots, the people enacting the bogeymen cannot cross certain bound-

Figs. 7–11. Husband-divining rituals on postcards from the early 1900s (on this and following three pages). Courtesy of the author.

Hallowe'en Greetings

On
Hallowe'en,
By pumpkin's light, This witch
Will help you choose aright.

A Joyous
HALLOWE'EN

By the candle's
light
He may be
seen,

At twelve
o'clock
On
Hallowe'en.

ON HALLOWEE'N LOOK IN THE GLASS,
YOUR FUTURE HUSBAND'S FACE WILL PASS.

aries and attack spectators, and the experience is limited to a certain time and place (Magliocco 1985). Sociologist Ikuya Sato likewise notes, "An activity can be playful only when there is an implicit or explicit assumption that a free choice exists between thrilling play and everyday life. Even a thrilling excursion into an extremely dangerous situation presupposes a secure starting point and a safe destination" (205).

The role of adolescents' supernatural legends and rituals are best understood as a form of play rather than as sorcery. For both males and females, such custom involves a playful challenge to adult cultural standards, and as such it is, and is supposed to be, a form of mischief, a ritual crime against community standards. In the case of women, we may expect to find group settings, in which young women engage in "mischievous projects and designes" that in some sense speak to "exulcerated mindes" on some level discontent "(as they thinke)" about male-oriented social expectations. The witch's shadow in many of the postcards is visually balanced against the image of the future husband. In the same way, this form of play-like deviance may hold in balance a form of sorcery (and hence a protest against patriarchal religion) and a form of feminist protest (and hence a protest against patriarchal society).

The Dumb Supper

Many records of the adolescent occult play activity known as the "dumb supper" exist as scaled-down instruction for how to hold one: "Cook a dumb supper and the one you are going to marry will come and eat with you" (McGlasson 1941: 24), or "Cook and do everything backwards. At midnight your lover will come and take his place at the table" (Bruton 1948: 21). A West Virginia report gives a more detailed description: "Three girls would do this together when they had the house to themselves. Walking backward, they set the table just before midnight, not speaking or laughing. A word or a laugh breaks the 'charm' and everything must be done over again. Places and food are set for each girl, and a place opposite each for the expected guest. When all is ready, the girls seat themselves and wait. On the stroke of midnight each maid will see opposite her the man she is to marry" (Keyser 1958: 9). The ritual was not without danger, according to widely circulated legends, for if a girl was fated not to marry, she would see some token of her death. One dumb supper, practiced in Illinois on Halloween night during the 1840s, was said to have concluded this way: "My mother told me the first thing they saw was a soldier come in with a sword and sit in one chair. Then just a man that looked like a farmer sit [*sic*] in another chair. The third thing that came in was a coffin and it floated right under one of the girl's chair. They all screamed. That broke the spell and the rest didn't get to see what would happen at their chair. One girl did marry a farmer, and the one that the soldier sit in her chair married a soldier, and the one that the coffin went under died before the next Halloween night" (Hyatt 1965: no. 9561). Another, collected on tape in 1954 from an "old settler" in the Ozarks reported a similar experience:

> In a dumb supper, you're supposed to set it at the hour of midnight, and two girls has to go backwards and pick up everything they get and put it on the table, till they get nine different things on the table to eat, like pepper and salt and butter and taters, and just anything to make the nine things.
>
> Three girls was at our house one night, a-wanting to do that, so they tried it. [And tradition holds that] they'll come in and whatever they leave in your plate, why that's what they (the new husbands) will be.
>
> One come in and left a switch in the plate, and the other one left a little pen knife, and the other one left three doses of medicine. Well, the one that got the switch, her man (new husband) whipped her to death, nearly all the time, she never had no good time at all. And the one that got the knife, just went and hid it and never would look at it no more. And the (one that got the medicine) was kind of sick. (She kept them until a stranger came to the door) and he said, "I want to stay all night with you," and they said, "Well, if you can put up with our fare, we're poor folks, and got a sick girl in here." "Well," he said, "Probably I might help the sick girl," he says. Well, they let him stay all night, and he left three doses of medicine. And then she took them three doses of medicine and she was well. And that was the man she married. Sure enough. (Van Cleve 2002)

The knife hidden by the second girl is probably an allusion to a very common cautionary legend, found widely enough in both North American and Europe to merit a separate tale-type number (737) and title ("Who Will Her Future Husband Be?") in the standard catalogue of folktales. The Brothers Grimm found it in tradition at the beginning of the nineteenth century:

> In Austria it is said that a lovely maiden once desired to see her future beloved, and she performed the necessary rituals at midnight. A shoemaker appeared to her with dagger in hand. He threw it in her direction and then vanished. She picked up the dagger and put it in her chest for safekeeping. It was not long before that very shoemaker began courting her. Some years after they had been married, on a Sunday after mass, she went to her chest looking for something she wanted to work on the next day. Just as she opened the chest, her husband entered the room and wanted to look in. She held him back, but he shoved her aside, looked into the chest, and saw his long lost dagger. He picked it up and wanted to know how she had acquired it. In her state of dismay and fear she could not think of any other explanation so she openly confessed that it was the dagger he had left in her room the night she had desired him. The man became enraged and shouted a terrifying curse at her: "Whore! So you're the bitch who caused me such wretched terror that night!" And he plunged the dagger into her heart (114–15).

Several versions were collected in the United States in the twentieth century that correspond with this European version in detail. An Illinois text reads:

> I am an old woman but I have heard my mother tell it often about some young girls setting a dumb supper to see who their future husband was to be. There were three girls trying it. They were sitting there and just at twelve o'clock something drop [*sic*] a knife in one of the girl's plate. The other two girls run out of the house, hearing the noise; only, they didn't know it was a knife, and this other girl didn't tell it. This girl put the knife away where no one could find it. Several years after that, this girl married a man and she never told him until one evening he found the knife. They had started to church and had forgot the Bible. He went back to get the Bible on the shelf and in some way the husband found the knife. He wanted to know right away where she got the knife. Then the wife told him about the dumb supper.

"Do you know, when I had this knife I was in hell." And in time this man killed his wife with the same knife that had been dropped in her plate when trying to find out her future. (Hyatt 1965: no. 9557)

If we took such descriptions and legends at face value, we might conclude that the dumb supper was in reality a potent form of witchcraft, drawing men's spirits from their bodies at night and subjecting them to a night in hell. But what really *happened* during such events?

Unfortunately, most reports of the tradition are bare sets of instructions of how to conduct a dumb supper, while stories describing actual visions of spirits are at best secondhand.

Stories told by the source's dead mother told about something she may have done—or was it someone that the informant's dead mother knew? Such "friend-of-a-friend" authority normally suggests the "warranted but unconfirmable" status of urban legends. When we turn to the few sources who describe what happened when they themselves witnessed dumb suppers, we get a rather different image of the ritual. A British collector gave a typical "how-to-do" version, then followed it with this rider: "One old lady told me that she had tried this "charm" when she was a young girl. She and others sat silent for hours. When the clock struck twelve they heard footsteps approaching, whereupon they became so terrified that they all sprang up and rushed to their respective bedrooms" (Billson 1895: 61). A Maryland informant described a similar personal experience:

Now when we were young girls, they used to set Dumb Suppers. . . . We did everything with oil at that time, no electricity, and all the lights were low and we set there by ourselves, nobody but me and this girl, just waiting for people to come in. Just at twelve o'clock, the wind commenced to blow and it blew a gale, and the lights were flickering, and we were both scared expecting something to come in, and Pap had an old horse that he used and she come and poked her head in that door, and I swear, we like to tore that house down getting out of there. We like to broke the door down. (Carey 1971: 207)

And even the teller of the detailed Ozark version quoted above comments: "And they say that just before they (the dead) come, why they'll be dogs a-barking and cats a-squawling, and cows a-mooing, and every-thing like that. And so we heard the cats a-fighting, and here they come, towards the house, just as hard as they could tear, and us a-setting there holding to one another scared to death. And *if we had sat right still, like we was supposed to do,* not whispering nor saying a word, why then they'll come in and ... [*etc.*]" (Van Cleve 2002; emphasis added). In fact, *all* the surviving firsthand accounts of the dumb supper describe the event lead-ing to a tense vigil broken up by some sudden noise or disruptive event—an animal coming in, cats fighting, a bird singing, a gust of wind. Ozark folklorist Vance Randolph says (without giving details) that there were times when "overwrought damsels persuaded themselves that they really saw ghostly figures" (1947: 179). But fellow Ozarker Otto Rayburn was just as certain that the invoked husband-to-be *never* showed up, "but the event caused much merriment for the girls" (1941: 140).

Still, Randolph observes that parents saw the dumb supper as po-tentially dangerous and often forbade their daughters from engaging in them, saying it "smells of witchcraft." The "exchanged knife" story, often reported there too as a mother's cautionary story, suggests an establish-ment warning against dabbling in the occult, even in play. The other stories, in which coffins and the like appear, may have had a different function. A Kentucky "how-to-do" version concludes, "When all is ready for eating, some supernatural sign appears to them. Sometimes it is two men carrying a corpse; or a large white dog may appear. Whatever it may be, it is always very alarming in appearance" (Thomas and Thomas 1920: no. 3879).

This suggests that the ritual was assumed to be open-ended; that is, something was *supposed* to happen at the end. Stories about horrific vi-sions thus may have functioned not so much as warnings as means of generating a properly tense atmosphere for setting the supper. As a West Virginia collector noted, "Various stories of apparitions evoked by this method made it a thrilling experience" (Keyser 1958: 9). The tension created by the stories led participants to interpret any sudden noise or event as a "supernatural" sign. And other youngsters could collaborate with them, through ostensive actions, to "fulfill" the rite. Journalist John A. Day, researching the folkways of rural Kentucky, asked a girl who had described the dumb supper, "Does it ever work?" She responded: "Well, in a way. The girls always let it out there's going to be a dumb supper, so if there's a boy who's been talkin' to a girl some time and is about ready to ask her the question, he may show up. Sometimes even two or three show up. Then sometimes maybe some of the girls' brothers will fix up t' scare them by slippin' a coffin into the room" (1941: 179). Similarly, an Arkansas woman affirmed that boys were informed ahead of time so that they could show up at the right time,[1] and yet another postcard of the mirror-gazing ritual (postmarked in 1912 from Baltimore) features the following sly instructions:

> LISTEN, LITTLE ONE! ON HALLOWEEN TAKE A CANDLE AND LOOK INTO A MIRROR, THEN OVER YOUR SHOULDER YOU'LL SEE YOUR FUTURE HUBBY'S FACE—AND FEEL IT TOO—IF HE KNOWS HIS CUE. IN THE EXCITEMENT THE CANDLE GOES OUT, AND—OF COURSE THIS AFFAIR MUST BE PREARRANGED TO BE SUCCESSFUL FOR THE WITCHES ARE BUSY AND CAN'T TEND TO EVERYBODY. O.U. KID.

Or Damned Supper?

It seems clear that the reality of the dumb supper was often more play-oriented than bare texts would indicate. Still, why did it generate a tradition of being diabolical? What made fixing a meal silently such a potent form of witchcraft? We need to look first at the recorded descriptions, and then at history. In most descriptions, girls are instructed to "do everything backwards," and some accounts elaborate: "Everything they did was to be done backwards. So they got ready and one put a fire in the stove backwards, one cut a little wood backwards. They peeled the potatoes backwards and then set the table backwards" (Roberts 1955: 93). Similarly, "two teen-age girls, desirous of seeing their future husbands . . . prepared a supper backwards in every respect. The tables were set as wrongly as possible; the chairs were turned backward; the meal was to be served, dessert first, and all things were according to the reverse pattern" (Frazier 1959: 88). "You would set the table in reverse order than you normally would; forks would be on the right side and so on. All placements would be handled by two people while the table was being set, even the silverware. You would then serve the food in reverse order as well, beginning with dessert and ending with either soup or appetizers" (Van Cleve 2002). In other accounts, girls are advised to sweep the floor in the reverse direction from usual, stir food the wrong way behind their backs, and set glasses and plates on the table upside down. The food itself was often made in ludicrously small portions, using a thimble for a measuring cup. Or it might itself be virtually inedible: an egg with the yolk replaced by salt; a cake made from meal, not flour; even a kind of pancake made not with water but the girl's urine (Hyatt 1965: no. 9583). As the final touch, the participants might take off their smocks and hang them over the chairs, thus sitting down naked to dinner. Meantime, girls have to take every step backwards and refrain from speaking, laughing, giggling, or even thinking frivolous thoughts. We could take such warnings as an indication that, on some level, participants considered the supper "dumb" both in the sense of "prepared in silence" and "hilariously incompetent" and so had to restrain themselves from laughing at what they were doing.

The practice itself is, moreover, based on a range of many other female adolescent rituals prescribed to catch a glimpse of one's future husband. Generally some kind of "backwards" action characterized these rituals. A British report had two girls invert two pewter pots on a clean hearthstone; then the two "retire to their couch backwards, undressing and getting into bed backwards, and of course in perfect silence." Underneath the pots in the morning would be something by which they could divine the trades of their future husbands (Gurdon 1895: 97). Many less complex rites accomplished similar results by way of some reversed action undertaken while looking into a mirror: walking down stairs backwards; walking backward to a well and looking at the surface of the water in the mirror; sweeping the room backwards then looking in a mirror. One suggestive rite had a woman eating an apple (perhaps a reference to Eve's original sin) while looking in a mirror at midnight on Halloween.

The inversion of everyday activities such as these—particularly the female-specific ritual of cooking and serving a meal—is a kind of domestic equivalent of saying the Lord's Prayer backwards or other commonly recognized "satanic" activities. The term "dumb" literally means that the meal was supposed to be prepared and served silently. Colloquially, it may imply "stupid" or "foolish" behavior. But a third meaning of "dumb" is a euphemism form of "(that) damned supper." And in fact, Jack Santino found that to this day, Northern Irish tradition often assumes a gray boundary between what was a form of adolescent girls' play and what was a potentially dangerous summoning of diabolical forces (1998: 129–37). Following this hint, we find that this teen ritual may have a link with the notorious witches' sabbat.

Recent historical research has, as we've noted, suggested that some of the elements found in witch-trial evidence reflect diabolized versions of real folk practices. Henningsen (1990) found among Sicilian healers a ritual of treating a supernaturally afflicted person by inviting and appeasing the "donne di fuori" or fairies. This was done, according to one healer, by setting out a table for the fairies, with napkins and the usual eating utensils, provided with water, wine, and various pleasant foods. Henningsen finds a number of parallels to this ritual in European folklore, including a 1476 Low Countries description of a similar table-setting *"propter visitationem Perhtae cum cohorta sua"* (for a visit from Perhta [a female nature spirit] and her companions). Another reference that might allude to the pagan ceremony that underlies this tradition appears in a late-medieval saint's life:

> It is said that St Germain, bishop of Auxerre, was once on a journey when he stopped at a village in his diocese. After dinner he saw they were preparing a second dinner for which the table was being re-laid. He asked if other visitors were expected, and was told that the preparations were for the "good women" who walk about by night. [Presumably the *benandanti* or "good walkers-about" mentioned by Ginzburg.] St Germain understood perfectly well what they meant and decided to watch and see what happened.
>
> Some time later he saw a host of devils arrive in the form of men and women and they sat down at the table before his very eyes. St Germain forbade them to leave the room and called all the people of the house to see. He asked them if they recognised any of those who had come to the feast, and they told him they did, and knew them by name. Then the bishop said to them: "Go to their houses and see if they are there." They were all found to be sleeping in their beds, so the bishop adjured the devils to confess that this was how they deceived men into believing that sorcerers and witches exist and have their sabbaths by night. The devils did as they were told and disappeared afterwards in a state of confusion.[2]

The concept of ritually setting a table as part of a religious rite is, of course, ancient. It is reflected in the Jewish Seder, which has a number of "backwards" elements, such as the avoidance of the usual leaven in bread for this particular meal. The Christian Eucharist is also parallel in that it ends with a specific invitation to the divine figure of Jesus to be present in the sharing of the meal. It is also true that a number of folk traditions associated with honoring dead ancestors involved laying out food and other favorite treats on an altar or as part of a ritual. Such traditions are still common in Mexico, as part of "Day of the Dead" customs (Lafferty 1996), and in Japan during the summertime Obon season, in which ancestors are honored by placing food at a domestic altar in their honor. The European dumb supper thus may have been an appropriation of serious folk religious practices.

Elements may well have been *re*appropriated for serious purposes. Neo-Pagan Janice Van Cleve (2002) says that a rural West Virginia custom used the customary "backwards" elements of the dumb supper to make contact with loved ones who had recently died. Extra places would be laid, but instead of being for the future husbands of those participating, they were for the dead souls. "At some point during the meal," she continues, "the recently departed loved one would make contact. One reason to try to reach the loved one who recently died was if the family had had signs or 'feelings' of restlessness, showing the dead might be confused and had not crossed over to the other side. The contact through the Dumb Supper was a way of helping them to cross over and finally find peace." The language of this version suggests the spiritualistic practice of "soul rescue," in which a medium would attempt to contact an "earth-bound" soul and help him or her "cross over" to the other world. If so, then the serious elements of this form of adolescent ritual play were already crossing over to alternative religions such as spiritualism. Certainly in recent years, as Anne Lafferty has documented, the dumb supper has become a fully serious element in the Neo-Pagan repertoire of rituals appropriate for the Samhain or Halloween season, where it is used to silently honor family and friends who have passed on (see Lafferty 2003).

Seen in this light, the dumb supper's *inversion* of usual elements takes on a more serious quality. If an elaborately prepared supper invites benign, healing spirits, then a "backwards" supper might be seen as a way exactly opposite to social rules of calling up supernatural powers. Historian Robert Rowland (1990) makes a similar point about witch-trial accounts of sabbats, which appear, element by element, to violate cultural expectations. An Italian account illustrates this in detail:

It is certain that these banquets are so disgusting that even a starving stomach would be revolted by seeing the display or smelling the odour. . . . And many of the guests say that their hunger and thirst are not satisfied by these foods and beverages. The banquets are followed by dancing in circles, always by the left [i.e., the wrong way]. And whereas our dances have enjoyment as their aim, these dances produce only fatigue, boredom and dreadful torments. When they approach the demons to worship them they turn their backs and retreat backwards like crabs, and to supplicate them they turn their hands backwards. (Quoted in Rowland 1990: 167)

Not that Rowland believes that these sabbats occurred in much this way; rather, he argues that suspects, faced with torture and the interrogators' demand that they come up with a description of these rites, simply inverted the usual social rules of formal meals. Hence, the typical trial account of a sabbat was "an elaborate representation of an anti-world and simultaneously ... an implicit assertion of all the rules which are broken there" (1990: 165–66).

Rowland, however, does concede that such an elaborate demonology might well have started from "[a] single admission made in desperation and derived, perhaps, from local folklore." Such a detail might well have set in motion a process in which prosecutors, through close questioning and torture, elicited an "acceptable" confession. But he leaves open the possibility that some elements of the sabbat might well derive from diabolized accounts of widespread rituals like the magical table-setting ritual, whether conducted forwards or backwards. Alternatively, the enormous attention given the witches' supper might in itself have brought into being a diabolized table-setting ritual among adolescents.

Certainly the details of the contemporary dumb supper can easily be seen as an "antiworld" reaction to repressive adult female role models. The format of the ritual, after all, reflects in a satirical way what most women in a conservative male-oriented society would have had to do to attract a husband: keep their mouths shut and know their housework forwards and backwards. The dumb supper thus was a form of play-like deviance in that it created an "antiworld," a liminal alternative reality where participants could defy male-dominated norms. The ludicrously literal rendition of serving a meal was diabolical precisely because it inverted normal female roles, which is why, in this antiworld, girls could also reverse usual courtship roles and take the initiative in choosing their mates. This element of social protest might also explain why the parental anti-dumb-supper legend always revolves around the future husband's loss of a knife or sword: by taking control of the process of mate-choosing, the girl threatens her mate's manhood, and her appropriating and concealing his knife may symbolize a form of castration. Interestingly, one of the magical powers described in witch-hunters' manuals is witches' ability to steal male victims' penises. Appropriately, when the husband happens on the concealed knife, his first reaction is to penetrate the witch-wife and so regain his "natural" superiority.

The Witch in the Mirror

The old form of the dumb supper, involving the divination of a future husband, was already in decline as British and American folklorists were documenting it, and by 1950 it seems to have survived only as a memory. Gender roles, presumably, had changed to the point that challenging the "marry or see your coffin" choices that women were once given no longer provoked the same thrill. But the impulse for groups of young women to create excitement through deviant supernatural play continued, and elements from earlier rituals still affect contemporary customs. The most complex and widespread of these is the custom of "calling the witch in the mirror." The core of this tradition is the practice of repeating a name (and often a statement of belief or disbelief) in front of a mirror in a dark room to make the form of a mysterious entity appear to you. Beginning in the mid-1960s, this ritual became popular not only in the United States but also in Europe. In Sweden the witch is generally known as "Black Madame"; elsewhere, the name varies widely: Bloody Mary, Mary Whales, Mary Ruth, Mary Weather, Mary Worth. Like other adolescent supernatural play, this rite involves a mood-setting stage, in which participants tell the history of how the witch died. An Indiana report from the mid-1960s gives a full and typical version:

> A long time ago, there lived an incredibly ugly woman named Mary Worth. Some say she was born that way, and others say she was in a bad accident when she was young. Whichever it was, her face was horribly marred. . . . One day, as she looked in a mirror, she could stand her ugliness no more. In a fit of rage and insanity, she put a curse upon the mirror, and shattered it, fatally cutting herself in the process. From that time on, if anyone stares straight into a mirror (providing the room is completely dark),

concentrates and says, "Mary Worth, Mary Worth, come to me; come to me!" she will appear. She will come as a distant shadowy figure at first, that gets more distinct as she comes closer. If you continue to watch and look upon her completely, she will shatter the mirror, trying to mar your face as hers was. (IUFA 71: 697; quoted in Langlois 1980: 219)

But the explanation of who she was and why she haunts mirrors varies greatly from text to text. In some cases she is associated with other widely-known female ghosts. In one complex collected at an Indianapolis Catholic school for African American children, the entity is said to have been a girl run over by a truck on the way to a party; she appears as a hitchhiker trying to get home, but, if picked up, she vanishes from the back seat, leaving only a wet spot.

Added to such "origin stories" are secondhand stories cautioning that others have been killed or injured by carrying out the rite. Some say that the witch will leave some physical sign of her reality, usually by scratching the girl's face. "One girl tried it and was found by her mother in a state of shock, in a pile of shattered mirror glass, with cuts all over her face," one account concluded (Langlois 1980: 219). More elaborate stories say the ritual could end in insanity or death. According to one that circulated in 1972 at Morehead State University in Morehead, Kentucky, a group of local girls became involved in black magic. One of their witchcraft books said that if someone sat in front of a mirror in a totally dark room, she could conjure up evil spirits. A volunteer was tied to a chair in front of a full-length mirror, while the others put towels around all the doors and windows to block out any light, then waited outside the unlocked door.

They didn't lock the door, you know, in case the girl had trouble or anything they were gonna go on in. And so they stood outside for a while and I guess after a half hour or so the girl just started screamin' like crazy inside. And the girls tried to—uh—on the outside, get in and door was locked from the inside. And so they ran down and got the key from the dorm mother there at the school and they came up and opened the door. And the girl's face was just torn to shreds and she was still tied to the chair and the window was still locked and the door that hadn't been locked was locked after breaking in. And one of the girls that went in to see what the problem was went insane and this girl, whose face was just scratched all to pieces, was dead.

The informant positively identified the nursing school and claimed that the local police had records of the incident. When asked if he would try the same ritual, he said he would not, since "there are too many things in the world that we just don't understand" (OSUFA, Rob Roberson, April 1975).

But firsthand versions, in line with the rituals that we have already discussed, describe a tense vigil climaxed by a moment of panic at the first sign of the supernatural. One participant recalled:

> It was tried only once. The feeling standing there in the dark calling the dead was uncanny, even with the other girls. The silence and complete darkness created a sensation of total fright that was unbelievable. We could not have stood there more than a few minutes, though it seemed much longer. Suddenly with one consolidated shriek, everyone headed for the door. It was an unorganized and urgent push on everyone's part to get out as soon as possible. With that, the supernatural was put aside for the night, at least on the surface. Underneath, we were uneasy for the rest of the night. . . . (Langlois 1980: 220)

The same source adds, "I knew of no one who stared until Mary appeared completely, but a couple of girls said they saw her image or shadow, then turned on the lights and ran" (Langlois 1980: 220).

Yet, a number of firsthand descriptions of successful rituals have been recorded. A version from the UC-Berkeley folklore archive adds the detail that, if the ritual is performed, "Bloody Mary's mark would appear later on in the day through bleeding." The informant, who performed the Bloody Mary rite as a fifth-grader, recalled that during the following recess she jammed one of her fingers in play, drawing some blood. "All of the girls who had done the Bloody Mary ritual with me attributed the bleeding to Bloody Mary," she concluded (Dundes 2002: 82). This suggests that the "Bloody Mary" legend-trip discussed at the start of the previous chapter must be linked to this belief complex, since there, too, cursing the witch in the cemetery was punished by some accident that drew blood from the participants. Still, instead of incurring madness, death, or even token physical harm, firsthand versions make the mirror-witch's "victim" a hero of sorts, by allowing her to expand the legend core with her own participation in it. One version makes the actual performance dynamics of the event clearer:

> And then them kids at school they talked about it and stuff and got everybody believing it and so, then we went into the bathroom, and we tried it.
> *Tell exactly what you had to do to call her.*
> Ya, you had to, you could call her ten or a hundred times and call her name and say, "I do believe in Mary Whales" and, a, she was supposed to come.
> *And come in the mirror? That's right?*
> And come in the mirror. And I was back in the corner all by myself. They, they, we said it up to a hundred times and we waited and waited and I closed my eyes and we still waited. And then Leslie said, "Cut on the lights!" and they said, she said, "I saw her, I saw her and you didn't get a chance to see her." And so, I went home and I just got through watching a scary movie and I did it in the mirror myself.
> *And you called her a hundred times?*
> All by myself, I called her a hundred times, and I was saying, "I do believe in you, I do believe in you." And I was by the light switch and she came and her eye started bleeding and then I cut on the light real fast. And then, all that night, I had a dream about her and I dreamed that she was right by my bed. She was about ready to touch me and I, and I, jumped up and looked around. And I thought that the door was open and I thought I saw something in there. And then I pushed Wendy over and got into bed with her! (Langlois 1980: 211–12)[3]

Here, as is often the case with legend-trippers, the person who "trips the farthest and sees the most tangible evidence of the supernatural is 'privileged'" by having the most dramatic story to tell (see Ellis 2001: 189). Paradoxically, calling the witch out of the mirror nominally threatens participants with physical harm, but in fact the terms of the ritual protect them and allow them to come as close as they dare to the supernatural in the darkness before returning to the "lights-on" real world. In order to limit the possibility of a "corruption of play" that results in real anxiety, the ritual needs to provide ways of backing out of such an experience and returning to "reality." As Sato observes, defining play as play, however occult or deviant, assumes a "safe" start and finish. This is per-haps another reason for making the supper "dumb": participants could leave the antiworld they created at any moment by speaking out loud. This is clear in one Illinois account: "I started to do this several times when I was a girl.... But I would always get scared, afraid I would see my coffin and would speak, for that would break the spell" (Hyatt 1965: no. 9559). Similarly, the witch-in-the-mirror ritual allowed participants to close the experience whenever it became too frightening, by turning on the light or leaving the room. It is also less risky: contemporary adolescents *assume* that a horrific vision will appear, and by giving her a history and a name (as we have seen), they give themselves social control over her.

Crised Stra Chru Og

This suggests that the image of the witch is itself an antiworld version of the person looking into the mirror. In examining Swedish versions, Bengt af Klintberg observes that the rite can function as a kind of initiation ordeal, and if one has a dramatic experience, "one can be sure of being, for a while, at the centre of other people's attention. This is a recompense which for many children counteracts the discomfort of exposing oneself to the unknown" (1988: 166). In the account above, we could see this function in the source's resolve to try the ritual alone, after Leslie's "suc-cess" in an earlier group effort. Klintberg suggests that calling the witch helps Swedish youngsters to actively confront and banish supernatural fears, and thus become "vaccinated against the fear of ghosts for ever" (1988: 166).

Interestingly, he notes that the ritual is especially popular among males there; in North America, it is, like the dumb supper, practiced al-most exclusively by young females. The one published North American account of two males attempting the ritual (based on a story heard from girls) records that they did it only after a mutual dare: neither wanted to do it, and they carried it out "only with extreme fear. We both knew nothing would happen but we also both admit we were a bit nervous in doing it" (Langlois 1980: 218).

This gender discrepancy suggests that, for American girls at least, the ritual incorporates concern and willingness to create an antiworld "behind the looking-glass," where the usual male and female gender roles are challenged. Janet Langlois extends this positive function further, suggesting that the mirror "literally reflects the identification of the participants with the revenant. In normal situations, when any of the girls looks in the mirror, she sees herself; in reports of the game playing, she sees Mary Whales, or, at least, expects to. In a sense, then, Mary Whales becomes the girl's own reflection" (1980: 202). She notes that the ritual seems most popular among young girls who are in "a state of disequilibrium [and] of uncertainty," and that the events in the "origin" legend tend to match elements in the participants' own lives. They are often concerned about their physical beauty, or concerned about their ability to get through life without being victimized. In the "Vanishing Hitchhiker" version of the story, Mary Whales is passive, being scratched and killed by forces beyond her control; likewise, as a ghost she is incapable of getting where she wants, and witnesses, too, have no control over her appearances or disappearances.

The vision of Mary Whales in the mirror, though, is, as Langlois says, "a structuralist's dream . . . both revenant and participants move from a passive to an active role" (1980: 200, 202). In fact, the person calling the witch is doubly in control. First, the figure appears only when called in a ritually prescribed way; second, the rite can be terminated at any moment. As with the dumb supper, the play-like elements of this rite allow participants to include ludicrously exaggerated elements from the more mature gender roles such prepubescent girls are then observing and adopting. Alan Dundes (2002) has suggested that, on a psychosexual level, the ritual expresses anxieties about the imminent onset of menstruation, with the blood flowing from the cut in the witch's head displacing the flow of menstrual blood from the young girl's vagina. He argues that the usual location of the rite, a bathroom, is appropriate because it is the place where girls experiencing menarche take care to flush down the toilet any blood that "shows."[4]

On the other hand, the bathroom mirror may be used simply because the rite requires a mirror in a convenient, easily darkened place. The reflecting surface—a mirror, glass, plate, or container of water—is common in related female divination rites. The prevalence of mirrors in rituals intended to reveal the participant's future husband likewise suggests a world like ours, but inverted in important ways to allow women significant power in the marriage game. The two complexes have much in common. A number of dumb supper reports note that the room in which the table was laid was left only dimly lighted. Participants were supposed to gaze into the window, at a dark wall, or even at their own reflection on their plate to see the image of the future mate (Turner 1937: 148; Randolph 1947: 178). The constant feature was that the scene was very dark, and most versions specified a candle or other dim source of light. It is not unlikely, as we will see, that such conditions could help induce an altered state of mind in which visions could appear.

Insight into such a phenomenon was provided by psychiatrists Luis H. Schwarz and Stanton P. Fjeld (1968), who in the 1960s carried out an experiment intended to test the belief that schizophrenics were especially prone to seeing vivid, distorted images in mirrors or other shiny surfaces. To provide controls, 16 diagnosed psychotics were balanced by three other groups of 16 each: sociopaths, neurotics, and "normals." Each of the 64 subjects were taken into a dimly lit room and asked to stare into a mirror for half an hour and describe their perceptions. Oddly, psychotics proved to be the least prone to seeing images in the mirror, although the experimenters noted that the patients chosen were being given medication to control their hallucinations. By contrast, all sixteen of the neurotics reported seeing the reflected face change in some way and most reported violent changes in emotion, feeling predominantly sadness and fear. One woman told of becoming "Panicky, looking in that mirror I have the feeling that I would find something horrible"; another reported seeing "Something frightening, a ghostly face with a vampire's expression." Six openly wept, and two became so agitated that they vomited (280–81).

Twelve of the sixteen "normals" also witnessed changes in the reflected face, in which the image became fluid and distorted. Subjects frequently mentioned a big nose, swollen jaw, and twisted eye, and one "normal" described a vivid image of dancing skeletons. Others described a succession of changing images: "I see several faces.... They change one from another ... are normals ... serious ... short hair ... who are they?" (279–80). All members of the "normal" group likewise experienced mood swings, most often to sadness and fear. While both males and females saw such changes, Schwarz and Fjeld observed that "Women experienced the most severe physical symptoms . . ." (284). They concluded, "The results indicate that vivid fantasies are not the exclusive property of psychotics but are reported at least as frequently and with more apparent vividness and elaboration by other groups. Responses classed as perceptural [sic] distortions were so varied and remarkable that they are comparable to those reported with the use of hallucinogenic drugs" (283). Add this to the intense visions reported from the mirror game and we can easily account for the intensity and popularity of witchcraft experiences. Then as now, this kind of horrific "antiworld" experience is present in most females' (and males') personalities and needs only to be tapped and channeled through ritual.

It seems clear that female adolescents' play-like rituals rely on this physical reaction to the reflected image in a darkened room. The structure of the rite primes participants to experience an antiworld, in which they experience unusual powers or witness things in an altered state of mind. The tense vigil of the dumb supper, the séance, and mirror-gazing are ways to provide this experience. But such experiences could be socially and psychologically dangerous: Randolph notes some parents' fears that the dumb supper "sometimes frightens nervous girls into hysteria" (1947: 178). Possibly this was the case; certainly, the firsthand accounts agree that the vigil usually broke up in a cathartic panic. The "hysterical" response of some participants to the mirror ritual is not a surprise, for if it is based on an empirical "alternative reality" experience, it will genuinely frighten most teens, neurotic or normal. Individuals, Schwarz and Fjeld found, experienced a whole range of vivid fantasies, ranging from horrific to erotic. If there was an experiential dimension to the dumb supper as well, the terms in which it was framed primed participants to an erotic fantasy. But it was particularly dangerous, as a frightening vision could be defined as a death omen.

Calling the witch out of the mirror, by contrast, primes participants to see a vision of fright. The mirror is, normally, a focal point for young females trying to look beautiful and hygienically clean in order to attract a male. Calling the witch out of the mirror, then, inverts the usual ritual of cleanliness (next to Godliness for traditional Americans). Instead of turning *on* lights to see oneself clearly and cleanly, the lights are left *off*, and participants allow themselves to see an "ugly" image rather than one of hygienic beauty. After all, gazing in a mirror at an image that one perceives as beautiful (one's own face) has been an image of narcissistic self-attention from ancient times on. Most children would find such an image in "Snow White," where the stepmother's magic mirror promises to reveal "the fairest one of all." Beliefs supporting traditional role models imply that the penalty for gazing at one's own image is a sort of spiritual deformity. So it is no coincidence that the antiworld figure superimposed on the youths' faces is one of preternatural ugliness, and that she threatens to come through the mirror to disfigure those who gaze too long—that is, to make them more exactly resemble her. If we accept Dundes's reading of the witch as an embodiment of menstruation, then we can see other antiworld inversions: the postmenopausal woman replacing the premenopausal girl; the visible cut face substituting for the bleeding vagina that is hidden out of sight. Above all, the social image of menstruation as a "curse" becomes a widdershins blessing, by allowing participants to conjure it up and experience it in all its alleged ugliness, then use their experience as a token of their courage.

But the ritual must provide ways to channel this antiworld so that participants are not confused or left unable to interpret their encounters. In much the same way, Professor Dumbledore intervenes when Harry Potter becomes fixated on the Mirror of Erised, which is surrounded with the legend *Erised stra ehru oyt ube cafru oyt on wohsi*. This looks like one of the witchy incantations discussed earlier, but actually is no more than mirror-language for "I show not your face but your heart's desire." Fascinated by the images of his dead parents and relatives that appear there, Harry is tempted to spend nights gazing into it, instead of solving the mysteries he has uncovered at Hogwarts. Gently, Dumbledore corrects him: "It shows us nothing more or less than the deepest, most desperate desire of our hearts. . . . However, this mirror will give us neither knowledge or truth. Men have wasted away before it, entranced by what they have seen, or been driven mad, not knowing if what it shows is real or even possible. . . . It does not do to dwell on dreams and forget to live, remember that" (Rowling 1998: 213–24). The fact that the mirror ritual is based on a real means of altering consciousness does not mean that what is seen will necessarily be an image of the future, or even of the present. It does come from deep inside the participant's psyche, and unless carefully prepared or supported, many young people, or even adults, may indeed find themselves in the role of the sorcerer's apprentice, having awakened something that they cannot easily control.

Conclusions

By the early 1970s, such activities were already being viewed as a form of spiritual delinquency—which probably contributed to the rapid spread of the mirror ritual during the same period. Like other contemporary séance activities, the mirror ritual attracts a certain number of teenagers precisely because it is both thrilling and deviant to have the power to call up dangerous supernatural spirits. Charismatic evangelist Nicky Cruz records two instances in which the children of spirit-born Christians came in contact with séance-type activities. In one, the third-grade daughter of a minister found about a dozen girls in her school's rest room "standing in a circle, holding hands and chanting something she didn't understand"; the minister and Cruz concluded it was some form of witchcraft. And Laury Boone, the daughter of born-again actor Pat Boone, once admitted that she had joined school friends "in chanting some witchcraft incantations" and had to be delivered through prayer after her personality changed in a way that her parents found "scary" (Cruz 1973: 110, 122–23). The "devil's hand" had fallen on a contemporary set of "afflicted girls," and probably for much the same reasons.

Such visions, however, were channeled by the rules of the "game," just as when participants succeed in seeing the witch, they "win" by gaining status within their groups. And one remembers Rev. Roberts's description of "weak" females "possessed with unsatiable desire of revenge" who use diabolical means to "bring to pass that rancor which was nourished in their breasts." The origin stories behind the witch agree in making her a victim of some injury that leaves her with an undying grudge. By identifying with her, female teens are simultaneously creating their own "street-corner myth" that implicitly expresses protest over the sex roles offered them by society.[5]

Such seems to have been the case among the tight-knit group of girls, aged nine to eighteen, that regularly met on dreary winter evenings at the home of Salem Village minister Parris. John Hale, a supporter of the witch trials, later wrote:

> I fear some young persons, through a vain curiosity to know their future condition, have tampered with the Devil's tools so far that hereby one door was opened to Satan to play those pranks, Anno 1692. I knew one of the afflicted persons who (as I was credibly informed) did try with an egg and a glass to find her future husband's calling, till there came up a coffin, that is, a specter in likeness of a coffin. And she was afterwards followed with diabolical molestation to her death, and so died a single person—a just warning to others to take heed of handling the Devil's weapons lest they get a wound thereby.
>
> Another, I was called to pray with, being under sore fits and vexations of Satan. And upon examination I found that she had tried the same charm, and after her confession of it and manifes-

tation of repentance for it, and our prayers to God for her, she was speedily released from those bonds of Satan. (Quoted in Hansen 1969: 30)

In the end, female occult activities such as these are rituals of rebellion in the form of play. This is not to say that, as "just" play, they are unimportant: play harnesses individuals' concerns about everyday life and allows them to express those concerns in a freer and safer way than would otherwise be possible. Equally, we should recognize that the nature of play assumes the creation of a *temporary* world that players can create, elaborate, and then leave behind. This temporary world has its risks: corruption of play in this case could lead to anxiety that persists beyond the game itself. But the ritual elements exist to minimize these risks and allow participants to retreat to reality when appropriate. When this process breaks down, as it evidently did in Salem, it may be less the fault of the adolescents than of witch-hunting adults whose overreactions make it more difficult rather than less to leave this "street corner myth" behind. Once the devil is raised, usually the sorcerer's apprentice finds it difficult to spirit him away, a job that falls to the more mature and knowledgeable adults. It was, ironically, the imposition of the adults' conspiracy-focused definition of reality on the Salem girls' corrupted play that trapped them in an adult male-directed deadly fantasy.

Chapter Eight

The @#$%&! Ouija Board

"Last night . . . we were talking to Satan on the Ouija board," a college student in Hazleton began, while chatting with one of my folklore students. The personal experience story that followed was typical of many circulated by American adolescents: it described a conversation with no less than the devil himself. The story, like most, was capped by a mysterious event—in this case, the phone rang but no one was on the line. "Why did you do that?" the student asked the board, "and he goes, 'Because you asked me for a sign and that was my sign'" (PSUHFA, Clinton 1988).

Serious psychics and occultists alike have agreed that amateurs' dabbling with spirit communications could lead to mental instability and even suicide. Most adolescents who have described their experiences for folklorists say this claim is exaggerated, seeing the board as simply an opportunity for entertainment. Still, as I noted in my previous book, many personal experience stories relate dramatic instances in which demons claimed to be communicating through the board, and the messages often became threatening and violent. Further, while the way in which the indicator seems to move "by itself" has been known for a long time to be a physical illusion, the psychological means by which the messages are spelled out are not so well understood. Apparently "automatic" actions like these, especially when carried out in a ritual context that induces an altered state of mind, often produce disturbing and frequently obscene messages. In fact, there is a strong connection between the means by which teens construct Ouija board messages and similar "autonomic" means by which some therapists have elicited violent sexual and mutilation fantasies from their patients in an effort to expose "satanic ritual abuse."

The Ouija board, for this reason, is no party game—and, for many

observers and participants, using it is far more than play, with even occultists frankly admitting the risks involved. This is, again, no new phenomenon: spiritualism, with its own dynamics and agenda, likewise was
no game, but a form of ecstatic religion with important links with world-
wide traditions of shamanism, spirit possession, and exorcism. It, too,
subjected its participants to the risk of contacting an obscene and violent "earthbound spirit." Automatic writing, a common strategy of spiritualists, was particularly known to produce embarrassing messages and
dangerous obsessions.

J.K. Rowling was doubtless aware of this connection when she made
Voldemort, the evil antagonist of the *Harry Potter* books, manifest as an
apparently blank diary. As his victim, the eleven-year-old Ginny Weasley,
discovers, she has only to write a question on one of the pages to have an
answer appear by itself. By initially being sympathetic, Voldemort later
admits to Harry Potter, he encourages her to use the diary more and
more. "If I say it myself, Harry, I've always been able to charm the people
I needed. So Ginny poured out her soul to me, and her soul happened to
be exactly what I wanted.... I grew stronger and stronger on a diet of her
deepest fears, her darkest secrets. I grew powerful, far more powerful
than little Miss Weasley. Powerful enough to start feeding Miss Weasley a
few of *my* secrets, to start pouring a little *my* soul back into *her*" (1999:
310; ellipses in original). In the end, she falls completely under Voldemort's
power, begins killing roosters to allow her Dark Lord more power, and
opens the forbidden Chamber of Secrets. "*Ginny!*" her horrified wizard
father says when he learns what has happened. "Haven't I taught you
anything? What have I always told you? Never trust anything that can
think for itself *if you can't see where it keeps its brain?*" (329).

Rowling, ironically, is absolutely in accord with antioccult crusaders on this point, not surprisingly since, as I noted in *Raising the Devil,*
Christians and occultists often agreed that such strategies were spiritually dangerous, particularly when practiced alone. Still, the Ouija ritual
remains popular in Anglo-American culture. Examining the rituals teenagers improvise around the Ouija board, we can suggest a less extreme,
middle ground, by looking at such activities in the broader tradition of
game-like rituals like the dumb supper and séances. In my previous book,
I argued:

> There are important differences between occultists' approach to
> this device and that of the adventure-seeking teenager: in par-

ticular, the sincere occultist may perceive it as a way to create an *alternative* world to that of official science and religion. Rather than accepting religious verities second-hand, the occultist constructs his or her own supernatural worldview. The adolescent, however, will use it to create an *antiworld* to challenge and reject. Both approaches, however, allow participants to participate *directly* in myth. In much the same way, the device allows teens a two-way dialogue with the devil. In official religion the concept of Satan can be used to threaten adolescents; with the Ouija board they can talk back to him. (2000: 66)

While not doubting that such rituals allow "other voices" to speak to the participant, the main point we will follow in this discussion is that participants are rarely as passive and pliable as Ginny Weasley. If "Satan" speaks obscenely to teens, they know enough of the argot to give the devil back his own, in spades. And, in this dirty double-talk, we can find yet other ways in which the Ouija ritual is a way of subverting adult social norms.

Origins of the Ouija Board

Use of some mechanical means to contact spirits has been common in western cultures since Biblical times, when the mysterious "urim and thummim" were used as an oracle to consult Yahweh before important decisions. Whatever these devices were, they gave "yes" and "no" answers to a series of questions, by which the presiding priest constructed Yahweh's will (see I Samuel 14:37–42 and passim). Still, the ancient Israelites harshly proscribed private communication with spirits, an attitude that was eventually adopted by the early Christians. Nevertheless, mechanical means of receiving answers were practiced underground as a form of charming. The sieve-and-scissors method, in which a precariously supported colander falls down at the correct answer, has already been discussed as a common form of "little sorcery" during the time of the witch craze. Other methods of using mechanical devices include the use of a needle, key, or other object suspended by a thread. Using some prearranged code, the users ask questions and determine the answers by watching how the object swings. In elaborate cases, the pendulum may spell out words by being suspended above an alphabet; more often a yes/no code is used. A still-common form of this method of spirit communication is used to predict the sex of an unborn child: typically, a back-and-forth motion means the child will be male, and a circular motion means female.

Another especially common form of divination involved tying a key on a string into a Bible and then suspending it. Participants then asked a series of questions, and the motion of the book gave answers. A rather serious nineteenth-century British ritual identified a thief through this method: after reading two passages from the Bible (one being the story of the Witch of Endor), the charmer instructed the victim and another person to support the ring of the key between the tips of their forefingers. A list of suspects was then repeated, and the key turned and fell off the fingers when they came to the thief (Henderson 1866: 195–96). More play-like variations were practiced both in Europe and America, in which adolescent girls divined the name or initials of the future husband. A Sheffield collector explained, "A key is put into the centre of the Bible with the ring outside. A garter, made of tape, is then tied round the Bible to keep the key in position, and the key is suspended on the fingers of two persons. A question, which must be answered by 'Yes' or 'No,' is then put to the Bible. If the key and Bible turn, the answer is 'Yes,' if they do not the answer is 'No.'" This collector adds that twirling the Bible on the garter and reciting the alphabet was another way of constructing messages, the letter named just before the Bible wound up at one end and stopped being the letter indicated (Addy 1973: 74).

Such folk practices lie behind the techniques used with the Ouija board. Its immediate history, however, begins with the rise of spiritualism that spread from upstate New York in the late 1840s and influenced popular culture in both the United States and Europe during the 1850s. At first, this interest focused on "spirit rapping," mysterious sounds that could be used to construct messages through yes/no questions or by reciting the alphabet. While these were believed to have a supernatural origin, in the case of the Fox Sisters (among the earliest and most influential of the "spirit-rappers") the sounds were eventually proved to have come from their toe joints, which they had learned to crack on cue (Isaacs 1983). The method of constructing a message through this yes/no process later became attached to a puzzling physical phenomenon first observed in Europe: when two or more people sat at a table and held their hands and legs in a certain way, the table would begin to tilt or even turn around. By 1854, the practice of "table-turning" was widespread in Continental society, and soon after it was discovered that top hats and upturned glasses placed on top of tables would do the same (Goss 1991: 10–11; Klintberg 1988: 163).

The two traditions merged in a long-lived folk tradition of "table-tapping." In this ritual, once the table begins to tip up, the participants ask questions of the "spirit" raising it, which it answers by rapping (usually) once for "yes" and twice for "no." By the 1890s, the phenomenon had largely died out as a serious spiritualistic device, but it remained a living tradition in folk culture. In 1918, W.J. Crawford, a lecturer in mechanical engineering at Queen's University, Belfast, published a detailed account of experiments with levitating tables, in which he eventually became convinced that the rapid twisting movements of the tables could not be explained by voluntary or involuntary movement by the participants and so must be the acts of spirits (1918: 61). Evangelist Kurt E. Koch heard of a club in Germany where the table-turning ritual was practiced "amid solemn ceremonies," from a maid who had used it for years to get advice about important decisions. Introduced to the practice by her mistress, she found when she attempted it by herself that the table would not move until she told it, "If you won't move in God's name, then move in the devil's name!" Thereafter, the table cooperated, nodding toward her for "yes" and moving from side to side for "no" (1972: 45–46).

In the United States, Richard Dorson found detailed memories of table-tapping as a supernatural ritual in coastal Maine (1959: 128–29; 1964: 57–60), and sporadic reports of it come from contemporary rural America.[1] We have only fragmentary evidence of how these rituals were carried out. Dorson's records show that, as with the scissors-and-sieve ritual, it could be used to identify petty thieves, but another memory he recorded shows that participants would also use the ritual to contact *evil* spirits for entertainment. An informant recalled occasions from around the turn of the century, in which his uncle called up the spirit of Mother Hicks, a woman remembered in the area as a notorious witch.

> *But she was supposed to be a bad spirit, wasn't she?*
> Oh, gee, you couldn't believe nothing she told you.
> *Well, why would he ask for her?*
> I don't know. You wouldn't believe—I wouldn't believe
> nothing. . . . [One time] Harmy Alley come in the door, and there

was a pair of scissors on the table, and [my uncle] says, "Fire them scissors at Harmy." And them scissors and that table tipped quick, and them scissors struck right over his head in the door. I was there, and I seed that when they done that, by gorry. It scairt me. I didn't want to be around when he was following that up. And a lot of people got scared . . .

Dorson, understandably, assumed that this activity was a form of witchcraft and asked, "Well, what would he do? Would he be able to do bad things after he talked to the spirit? Your uncle?" But his source simply responded, "Why, he'd just ask her questions, that's all" (Dorson 1964: 57–58).

A more recent report from Lancashire, England, confirmed that villagers used table-tapping to contact the spirit of Elizabeth Sowtherns, or "Old Demdike," the focus of a sensational series of seventeenth-century witch trials. The informant recalled, "when we did 'table-rapping' . . . the tumbler[2] always spelled out 'Demdike' and the table itself careered round the room in no uncertain fashion" (Seth 1969: 164). The Ohio State Folklore Archive contains reports from the 1970s and early 1980s with similar details of contacting entities who would make the table react violently. The Lima séance occasionally reached "evil spirits" who would literally slam the table onto the floor; a heavy dining-room table had to be reglued the next day because of the punishment it took (OSUFA, Burden 1976). A Marion teen recalled calling for "Jack the Ripper," to ask if he now regretted his crimes: "the table would go crazy bouncing up and down very hard. Sometimes the table would take after the person who asked the question" (OSUFA, Wakeley 1983).

The device now known as the Ouija board, however, came out of several ways developed in the nineteenth century to facilitate receiving spirit messages. Some spiritualists practiced "automatic writing," in which communications would be traced by the medium's hand while she sat in a trance or meditative state. This practice was facilitated as early as 1867 by what was called a "planchette." This was a small table on wheels or felt pads that held a pencil against a sheet of paper underneath. It gave users a firmer place for their hands and allowed them to produce messages by moving the planchette over the paper (Goss 1991: 11; Cavendish 1974: 172; Klintberg 1988: 163). Not all individuals were adept at automatic writing, however, even with a planchette, so simpler methods were invented in which the letters of the alphabet were printed on a "spirit board."

The planchette then spelled out a message by pointing to the letters in sequence (Fodor 1966: 270).

By the end of the nineteenth century, several "spirit boards" were being sold by Sears Roebuck and other firms, but the most successful was "Ouija, the Mystifying 'Oracle' Talking Board," patented on 19 July 1892 by William Fuld, a Baltimore customs inspector. This familiar device combines the planchette (in this case, a triangle-shaped stand large enough for two persons to rest their fingers on it) with a rectangular board featuring the letters of the alphabet, numbers, and the words "yes," "no," and "good bye" added. Fuld, perhaps facetiously, claimed that once he had built the board's prototype, he contacted a spirit and asked it what he should call the device: it spelled out "O-U-I-J-A" (Gruss 1975: 25–26). A simpler explanation is that Fuld probably was thinking of the then-popular writer "Ouida" (Louise de la Ramée, 1839–1908), who published a series of melodramatic novels set in exotic settings. The pen name "Ouida" was constructed from the French and Russian words for "yes," and "Ouija" likewise combines the words for "yes" in French and German. The name may thus recall familiar folk forms of divination, like "sieve and scissors," that give only "yes/no" answers.

At first, the boards were made by William and his brother Isaac in a home workshop, but by 1899 demand was strong enough that the brothers opened a small factory in Baltimore (Gruss 1975: 25–26). Fuld's board was further popularized by the success with it of American "channelers" like the St. Louis housewife Pearl Curran, who has been studied in detail. Beginning in 1913, she and a friend began to receive complex messages from "Patience Worth," who claimed to have been a seventeenth-century farmwife killed in an Indian raid. Curran soon found the Ouija board too slow, and cultivated the ability to dictate Patience Worth's messages by voice, though she often placed her hand on the planchette idly while doing so. No concrete evidence of the spirit's previous earthly existence ever emerged, but this persona allowed Curran to produce a huge corpus of literary works—poems, plays, short stories, even five novels—in an astonishingly short period of time. The works produced had a brief vogue, being thought surprisingly good by literary critics of the time, though once the novelty of their origin had passed, they faded quickly from notice. Still, the facility with which Curran produced them was beyond the capacity of most trained writers. Indeed, when challenged to produce two poems on different topics, dictating them simultaneously by alternate lines, "Patience Worth" had no difficulty doing so. In addition, this spirit used an unusual archaic English dialect, consistently, from the first messages to the end (Litvag 1972; Scott and Norman 1986: 292–304).

The entry of the United States into World War I also encouraged many people to try to communicate with loved ones at the front, and sales of the board increased to the point that Fuld quit the customs service, built a larger factory, and went full time into the board-game business. By 1920, the Ouija board was reported to have "succeeded the Bible and the prayer-book in fraternity houses and students' rooms" at the University of Michigan, and one professor there solemnly warned that "the lure of the Ouija is becoming a serious national menace." Another critic called it "the Bolshevik of the psychic realm," adding that "her *Soviet* of Ghosts threatens to ... lay in ashes the little Swiss republics of our certainties" (Ouija Board 1920: 64, 67). At this point, establishment religions began to publicize its diabolical side. J. Godfrey Raupert, commissioned by Pope Pius X to warn American Catholics against spiritualism (Wickland 1968: 19), attacked the device in the *American Ecclesiastical Journal,* noting that "So rapidly has this practice spread in this country that there are few families to-day who have not come in touch with these experiments in one way or another" (1918: 463).

Sales of the device peaked again in 1929, at the start of the Great Depression, and then again in 1944 at the height of World War II, when again it was used to gain information about distant sons and husbands on the various fronts (Hall 1944; Ouija Board 1945; Gruss 1975: 34–35). As the 1960s brought a widespread revival of interest in the paranormal, Ouija boards again came into demand, and on 23 February 1966, Parker Brothers, a leading American manufacturer of board games, bought out William Fuld's trademark. Parker Brothers' president at once announced plans to double production of the Ouija board (*New York Times* [24 February 1966]: 50). The device received a further boost that year from Jane Roberts's *How to Develop Your ESP Power,* which included a description of how she had contacted "Seth," a helpful spirit, through experimentation with a Ouija board. Roberts soon learned to "channel" Seth directly, and a series of popular "Seth Books" followed. Sales of the board, however, were most popular among teenagers, who, according to employees at one toy store, mainly used it to ask about "their dates and the school exams" (Gruss 1975: 59). The game remains one of Parker Brothers' most popular items, reportedly second only to Monopoly in sales, and the firm has recently brought out a model with glow-in-the-dark letters to facilitate its use in darkened rooms.

Ouija Board Groups: Cults or *Communitas?*

Among the long-lasting effects attributed to the Ouija board by some crusaders is that the messages received may in some fashion organize teens into dangerous cults that will proceed to commit suicide or antisocial acts. This fear may be an extension of partly justified concerns about the board's effect on individuals. As we have seen, many occultists have made long-term efforts to communicate with the spirits they contact, and the result has been a number of lengthy books. Chief among these are Jane Roberts's communications with "Seth," which she began on the Ouija board and ended by becoming a trance medium, dictating her messages out loud. Chelsea Quinn Yarbro's communications from "Michael" (1986) were received by four cooperating mediums, partly on the Ouija board, partly through automatic writing. Each of these contacts led to the formation of persistent groups organized around learning, pursuing, and putting into effect the teachings received, which generally reflect a Theosophical tradition based on reincarnation and working out of "karmic debts" from one life in the next. While not diabolical in appearance, many fundamentalist Christians would rate these mythologies as unorthodox and spiritually dangerous. Since the intensive, sophisticated use of the board by occultists differs only in degree from the casual, improvisatory techniques used by adolescents, crusaders worry that uncritical acceptance of "spirits'" messages may entice such youths into more serious forms of satanic activities.

College-age students do in fact sometimes form Ouija board groups that, like the professional occultists, carry out intense, daily communications with the entities contacted. E.L. Quarantelli and Dennis Wenger (1973) provide a detailed description and analysis of a group of eight young women who lived in adjacent dormitory rooms at an American university. The group formed after two of the girls had separately brought Ouija boards to the campus and involved their roommates and other acquaintances in its use. Though the two boards were used for some time in nearby rooms, no stable group formed around their use until three girls using one board asked the spirit for a "sign." "At precisely this moment, a study light went on 'by itself,' and a cigarette flew out of the hands of one of the girls. The three girls were frightened and ran screaming into another room, where two other girls were working the other board. They were soon joined by three other dormitory residents who also had worked the board in the past" (385). Unable to come up with a rational explanation for the event, the group turned back to the Ouija board and at once contacted a spirit who claimed to be a Welsh nobleman from the thirteenth century. For the next two-and-a-half months the eight young women met almost every night at midnight to contact the spirit and record its answers to questions. The group was anxious to keep their "own private Ouija" to themselves and became increasingly secretive; in general their activities were well known among other dormitory residents, who termed the group "weird," "screwy," or even "silly" (386–87).

It seems unfair to call such groups "cults," however much their beliefs contrast with fundamentalist Christianity. The term "cult," at least as used by crusaders, implies a secretive, tightly-organized group that recruits individuals and keeps them in control though some kind of psychological coercion. It also implies that the group is prone to commit antisocial acts of some kind, ranging from drug use and vandalism to child abuse and murder. The highly public groups organized around medium-type revelations by such people as Roberts and Yarbro do not fit this characterization. Nevertheless, Quarantelli and Wenger argue that the term "cult" is an apt one to describe the group of college students they studied, at least in nonjudgmental sociological terms.

This kind of cult, they argue, has four characteristics. First, it is a *diffuse group,* whose members organized a set of rules governing when they would meet and how they would work the Ouija board; nevertheless, they continued to attend school and interact normally with relatives and others outside the group. "Cult behavior is typically not all-embracing," the researchers comment, and when it threatens to become so, they say it represents "an extreme case of a cult rather than the more modal type we are discussing." Second, the group exhibited *innovative behavior* in the context of its emergence; that is, it was seen as relatively new and different from the everyday, casual activities of the other students in the dormitory. Further, both the group and its observers recognized the Ouija board activities as "more than a passing act and something that in all likelihood would continue to recur."

Third, the dormitory culture at large reacted to the Ouija group as "deviant" and its participants as "abnormal," so the group became *differentiated* from their peers outside the group and *conformed* more closely to the group's self-generated expectations. Quarantelli and Wenger comment, "Cult members became increasingly secretive so as to protect their activities and themselves from 'nonbelievers.' This had the dual effect of increasing the separation between participants and nonparticipants and of bringing the participants even closer together in sharing something exclusive. . . . To remain a member of such an exclusive group, however, each participant, clearly had to conform to the expectations and rules that had developed, that had, in a genuine sense, become semi-institutionalized" (391). Finally, they argue, the group rationalized its activities with an *ideology* that claimed "the superiority of the cult activity over that of the larger society." To this extent, they continue, "the ideology represents an open challenge to the traditional views and beliefs of the larger society" (388–92).

The researchers, however, do not provide much detail on the exact nature of the communications they recorded. At the start, they note, the questions had to do with "such topics as dating, parent and friend relationships, marriage, academic success, and so forth," but the final session is briefly characterized as dealing with "the impending death of certain participants, 'Ouija attacks' upon two other members of the group, and expressed fear of 'falling into the fourth dimension'" (385–86). Without further details, it is impossible to say for sure, but this session seems to have become a "confrontation" like those we have seen, with a spirit who has ceased being a benign spirit guide and has become threatening. It was, however, the end of the academic year, and the group's activity was destined to ceased soon after in any case. Two members left the university, another moved to another dormitory, and the girl acknowledged as the group's leader lost interest; hence the "cult" dissolved at this point (387).

We can define a number of differences between this understanding of "cult" and the more popular concept. The researchers note that although the group generated rules of conduct to which all eight members conformed, there was no coercion involved: rather, the researchers characterized the structure of such a group as "a radical, participatory democracy" (392). Ironically, the main force causing the group to withdraw even into moderate secrecy was the general hostility that their activities met with among their peers. Besides, the group's "secrecy" meant only that witnessing or performing the ritual was limited to certain insiders; just as in the case of the Meddlers' possession and use of *The Sixth and Seventh Books of Moses* in rural Franconia, discussed in Chapter 2, virtually everyone in the dormitory knew who was involved and what was going on. Finally, while involvement in the group was at times intense and time-consuming, it did not survive the normal reshuffling of students at the end of the semester. No "Chamber of Secrets" was opened, nor were any roosters strangled.

Quarantelli and Wenger use the term "cult" cautiously and in a sociologically limited sense, but it has been used so frequently as a negative term that it may still be misleading to apply it to groups such as these. To begin with, the formation of the group had little to do with "recruiting" or any predetermined agenda. In fact, far more young people use the Ouija board casually than form any similar coherent group. And the "ideology" that the sessions developed seems not to have had any permanent impact on the members beyond the end of the school year. Folklorist Kenneth A. Thigpen (1971) made similar observations after surveying the supernatural beliefs and legends of a rural Indiana high school. Some 14 percent of students, he found, were familiar with various forms of the legend-trip, but only six young males had formed a coherent group devoted to the ritual. These had focused on investigating "The Watcher," a malign spirit said to wander back roads after having been invoked by secret covens of witches. Legend-tripping, which frequently includes drinking and recreational drug use to heighten the mood, has strong links with the Ouija ritual. Despite their use of the supernatural to generate "fun," Thigpen concluded, overall their participation had no "profound or stable influence on [their] belief system" (1971: 207). Similarly, one student collector of this folklore explained, "Many people who use the Ouija feel as one informant put it, 'You really don't get any answers that mean anything. We just get drunk and have a good time'" (Gans 1970: 7; cited in Pimple 1985).

The same dynamic is clear in this Hazleton-area manuscript account: "On another [instance] a group of my friends were just messing around with the board in the woods. As normal half of the group didn't believe. My friend Dave and myself were calling on Mr. Crowley[;] we wanted the head of the Church of Satan[3] to answer us. Everybody else were drinking, [and] we were drinking [too] but we were so focused on the board. The board was moving to our questions spelling out satanic words. Dave ask[ed] Mr. Crowley's spirit to give him a sign because he wasn't totally sure of the board's power. Moments pasted [*sic*] and the triangle stopped dead and I looked at Dave and his face was dark green. I was in a state of shock" (PSUHFA: Haney 1988).

It would make more sense to see such transient relationships not in terms of cults and institutions, but as *folk groups,* or collections of individuals that generate their own specialized beliefs and practices through common interests and face-to-face contact. Folk groups may become semi-institutionalized, particularly if they are stable and enduring. But in most cases they are short-lived and serve as stabilizing social structures in contexts like universities where students simultaneously have to cope with a depersonalizing environment and also are under pressure to achieve. The dormitory setting is by definition temporary, and so normally is one's relationship with roommates and neighbors; hence it is common for intense but transient groups to form around common interests and activities.

The goal here is what anthropologist Victor Turner (1977) termed *communitas*, a strong egalitarian comradeship developed among people going through a process of being initiated into a higher status. College students have left their home environments and their usual circle of friends, but cannot return home for good or enter an adult profession until they have finished their degrees, or at least until the end of the academic term. They are thus in what Turner termed a *liminal*, or "in-between" phase of their lives, being no longer part of their previous social life but not yet having the rank of independent adults. Turner found that this phase existed in a variety of world cultures, where it was marked by the formation of profoundly felt but short-lived friendships. The college environment tends to foster such small groups, and some of these, such as fraternities and sororities, have institutionalized the process through a formal practice of hazing and initiation.

But such groups also form spontaneously around folk rituals such as the Ouija. Interestingly, the initiation process described by Turner shows organizers subjecting members of the new group to a ritual "lowering of the high" to reshape them into their new roles: this process requires humility, submission to rules, and stripping away social elements belonging to the old rank. But in my work on the formation of *communitas* among young males attending institutional summer camps (2001: 165ff.), I found that sometimes the process creates a topsy-turvy situation in which the group becomes socially elevated and the nominal "masters" become subordinate. During "ostensive ordeals," in which counselors tell them that a monster, maniac, or some evil supernatural force threatens them, the young campers often are given rank and privileges superior to counselors, who role-play characters that do things their inferiors recognize as stupid.

For instance, one camp carried out a tense "Snipe Hunt," in which the "snipe" were not birds but dangerous, vampire-like creatures. Leaders made it clear that everyone who had touched a magic stick was protected from attack; but two vocal "disbelievers" (counselors who had chosen the roles ahead of time) refused, and went off the trail ahead. The rest stayed with the group and were "protected." Hence it came as no surprise that when they came around a trail bend, they found the two counselors, now realistically made up as "victims," and the rest of the adventure became a kind of quest to get them bandaged up and evacuated back to safety. The young males reacted with mock fright that barely covered admiration for the skill with which the ordeal had been put together, and they readily cooperated in the effort to "save" the counselors. They could enter, experience, and leave the dangerous world as spectators rather than as potential targets of attack. Thus, I argued that these events were actually a form of folk drama.

Such activities may frighten younger children, but around the age of twelve, youths master the skill of becoming *engrossed,* or play-acting emotional involvement in such situations. Without openly stating that the danger is not real (for this would spoil the fun for everyone), the participants adopt mutually supportive roles and pull together in an intense way that would not have been possible without the "monster." However, such activities generated *communitas* only when the dangerous activity was set up in terms of familiar narrative structures, so that the youths could predict what was likely to come next. It also needed to be focused onto a set place or object. The participants could then engage in role-playing without fear of being put in physical danger.

When such ritual structures were not provided, however, or when campers were too young to recognize such activities as dramatic in nature, the result was often literal panic. In such cases, *communitas* did not develop, and campers were left bitter or resentful of being terrorized by a "hoax." For this reason, it seems likely that the Ouija ritual, for most adolescents, is casual but still carefully structured, with a regular opening and the option of some kind of termination, in which the board is destroyed, discarded, or simply not used again. Such traditions are not just signs of "semi-institutionalization," but are folk techniques that limit the context in which spirits contact humans, both in terms of location (the board) and of a structured ritual.

Seen this way, the confrontation stage of the ritual makes sense as a "lowering of the high." The "spirit" adopts the role of a hyper-authority figure, but in a way that makes its blasphemous and often sexist opinions easy to reject. And, if the spirit is a mirror-image transcription of adult authority, then nothing seems more appropriate at the climax of the rite than mockery and belittlement of its powers. Even if we look at the rite literally, as the summoning of a real spirit, we arrive at something like the comic interlude in Marlowe's *Doctor Faustus* (scene 9), when Mephistopheles, ex-angel and potentate of Hell, is reduced to materializing to a group of rustics who have snitched the magic book and summoned him all the way from Constantinople "only for pleasure." The very idea that a demon—even Satan himself—could be reduced to the status of a moving planchette, performing tricks and answering trivial questions for a group of college students, is in itself a fundamentally comic concept, however many risks the tradition says accompany it. The group that succeeds in contacting and harnessing the devil has to that extent managed to reverse the mythological order by subjecting supernatural forces to natural conditions.

Like ostensive ordeals, engrossment in Ouija rituals may become intense at times, and the content of material received and discussed may be psychologically unsettling. Quarantelli and Wenger note that one of the participants had heard that a fortune teller had told her mother that her daughter would die at the age of twenty, and she believed that some of the board's communications had confirmed this prediction (she was then nineteen). Some concern seems justified.

But often, those who participate in such groups do so not because they seriously accept the messages as coming from a supernatural world, but because acting as if they were in the presence of some kind of supernatural threat enables them to cooperate on a more intense level than would be otherwise possible. And the script of this play-acting, as we will see, may in fact come not from Satan but from the religious establishment against which the participants are nominally rebelling.

Suck the Greasy Cock of the Dark Lord

Is it true, in any case, that Ouija board participants *generate* an ideology that claims "the superiority of the cult activity over that of the larger society"? We might be able to make a case for this claim in the theosophist circles in which contact with spirit guides is pursued and used to generate complex alternative religions that compete with mainstream Christianity. In the case of adolescent users, however, the Ouija ritual is more often a way of expressing an *anti-ideology* than generating an alternative ideology. That is, the messages received from spirits conflict with the beliefs and attitudes of the participants, and the termination of the rite often implies a rejection of these "evil" ideas and an affirmation of the mainstream ideology from which the teens have temporarily escaped. This is not to say that the Ouija board involves no conflict with social norms: particularly in the case of female participants, the Ouija board could provide an opportunity to express feelings of anger about gender roles that might otherwise be difficult to express. For some, the ritual may continue the reaction against male-dominant restrictions on "proper" female behavior.

The world of spiritualism, historian Alex Owen notes, was intimately tied to issues of women's empowerment. On the surface, such mediumship apparently endorsed conservative social norms: the religious and ethical norms of sentimental motherhood are endorsed, and social ills such as drinking and brawling are condemned. Even the mode of spiritualism seems to have proceeded along norms of male dominance: séances and healings might ordinarily be conducted under the nominal leadership of a male, while the female who typically served as the medium adopted a posture of complete "passivity" in the face of the spirit world. "A medium gave herself, sacrificed her 'self' to another," Owen says. "The possessed woman was inert, inactive, never responsible" (1990: 233).

Anthropologist I.M. Lewis, describing Third World spirit possession cults, likewise observed this nominally passive role played by female participants. But, she notes, such a surrender of responsibility in fact empowered women in a paradoxical way. Being "controlled" by another personality allowed females to speak with a liberty not normally allowed in their own culture. In terms of the mythologies accepted by these cultures, women who become possessed cannot help themselves when they utter obscenities or insult powerful males in their communities, because such statements are seen as coming from the spirits who are controlling them. "They are thus totally blameless," Lewis observes; "responsibility lies not with them but with the spirits" (1989: 27). In a similar way, Owen shows, women participating in spiritualism could engage in religious and social discourse and indeed penetrate into forbidden social areas, frankly discussing adultery and uttering "unprintable" obscenities. Such communications, interspersed as they were with messages of the utmost orthodoxy, were usually interpreted as contacts with evil spirits. Nevertheless, Owen comments, the séance was predicated on "the ritualized violation of cultural norms," so "unwomanly" behavior was to be expected. Overall, spiritualism "effected a truly radical challenge to cultural orthodoxy and the stunning subversion of the nineteenth-century feminine ideal" (1990: 202–03, 209–15).

Obscenity, being itself a formalized way of violating social norms of conversation, is often itself a "sign" of a satanic spirit, which explains why many antioccult crusaders were quite willing to believe the part of the *Onion*'s satire that claimed that J.K. Rowling had told a *London Times* reporter that her books were intended to "guide children to an understanding that the weak, idiotic Son Of God is a living hoax who will be humiliated when the rain of fire comes, and will suck the greasy cock of the Dark Lord while we, his faithful servants, laugh and cavort in victory" (*Harry Potter* Books Spark Rise in Satanism 2000). This quote, intended to be the most outrageous part of this burlesque of the crusade against the *Harry Potter* books, was in fact accepted on faith as wholly authentic by many horrified Christians. In various forms, it formed the centerpiece of most of the tracts and chain letters inspired by this hoax, many of which called special attention to it by inserting the following:

> warning: the following quote contains highly graphic descriptions of a pornographic nature and should not be viewed by minors!

Such a warning, of course, made sure that virtually every reader of every age would read the quote carefully and, when it was bowdlerized, guess which obscenity was being left out.[4] Even though Rowling is a professing member of the Church of Scotland who has consistently told inquiring reporters, "I believe in God, not magic" (Film Forum 2002), the impact of the bogus obscenity matches that of the real ones uttered by female spiritualists exercising their "evil, male" personas.

As we saw in *Raising the Devil* (Ellis 2000), occultists and Christian antioccult crusaders agree that one of the possible outcomes of incautious dabbling with the board may be oppression by a spirit who engages in a form of sexual harassment, subjecting the victim to repeated obscenities and, in the most dramatic cases, a rape-like incubus experience. The experience of this spiritual obsession is doubtless real, but it also derives its structure and probably part of its emotional impact by being a close parallel to the kinds of sexual domination and harassment to which some women have been subjected in real life. Whatever the response of the victim, the experience is charged with gender politics, and her reaction to it likewise is a political act. In this sense, Ouija board involvement may in fact generate a kind of "cult" ideology, in the nonjudgmental sense suggested by Quarantelli and Wenger, in that it challenges conventional views about gender roles. The intense involvement by many women in the confrontation stage of the ritual suggests an anti-ideology of gender roles, in which women, not men, assert their identities by appropriating and triumphing over nominally "male" expressions of obscenity and ridicule.

We already see this "battle of the sexes" in spiritualistic practice of the 1870s, when mediums began to diagnose mental or behavioral problems by going into trance and speaking in the persona of a deceased soul that was "obsessing" the victim. Chandos Leigh Hunt, an especially popular mediumistic healer, treated chronic alcoholics by suggesting that the spirit of a "drunken sailor" had taken over the personality. Through mesmeric passes, she could induce this obsessing spirit into a child medium. Such treatment often involved a violent personality change on the part of the child, who would use obscene language mixed with coarse laughter. Nevertheless, Chandos could converse with the obsessing spirit, best him in debate, and, typically, consign him to the care of his angel mother in heaven (Owen 1990: 132–33, 213).

A similar methodology was used in the United States by clinical psychologist Carl Wickland, who began in the 1890s to treat a variety of mental cases with the help of his wife, a gifted medium. He used an actual electric shock to jolt the obsessing personality loose from the victim and into Mrs. Wickland's body, where he could enter into lengthy dialogues with the earthbound spirit and encourage it to leave the patient's personality alone and seek the light. These dialogs, published in his *Thirty Years among the Dead* (1974), do not show the obscenity characteristic of Chandos's (the most violent spirits' tirades tend to be paraphrased, perhaps for this reason). But they do show a characteristic violence against women, similar to Ouija spirits' attitudes, as in this communication from "John Sullivan," a violent male spirit afflicting a female patient and channeled through Mrs. Wickland: "I wouldn't hang on to a woman for love or money, for I hate women. I would like to crush every woman; they are all deceitful creatures. God never made such a thing as a woman. . . . I swore revenge on all women, and I will have that revenge. I could have had a good home once if it hadn't been for a woman. Revenge is sweet and I will have it." As with Chandos's treatment, aid comes from an angelic mother figure. At the end of this exchange, "John Sullivan" describes seeing the spirit of his mother approaching him, saying "I have been hunting for you for years." Cowed by her presence but unwilling to repent of his sexist attitudes, he is led away to a spirit-world "dungeon" (1974: 99–102). Dr. Wickland became chief psychiatrist at the National Psychopathic Institute in Chicago and later practiced privately in Los Angeles. His dialogs with obsessing spirits have remained in print in spiritualist circles, and he influenced a number of later psychologists who used regressive hypnosis to explain mysterious psychological problems in terms of trauma that occurred in "past lives" (see Rogo 1987).[5]

In more recent times, psychic investigators have recorded a number of obscene verbal duels between Ouija board users and the spirits they contact. Arnold Copper, in his popular book *Psychic Summer,* describes several sessions in which his group contacted a number of evil spirits. The language became quite obscene, and in one instance a violent confrontation developed between the damned soul "Beth" and Melissa, one of the mortal participants.

> The glass spun around the letters in a fury of speed, spelling out vicious, vile insults against Melissa.
>   whore cunt fucking bitch
>   "You think you can scare me with your filth?" Melissa shouted, enraged. "You are filthy and weak. You can never hurt me."
>   fucking whore which cock will you fuck tonight big cock not here howard fuck howard fucking cunt.
>   . . . we were all dumbfounded at the obscenities. . . . But [Melissa] would have none of it. She had read the message with the rest of us. "Filthy bitch!" she shouted. At that moment the heavy glass ashtray with the lighted candle lifted itself off the table and hurled itself at Melissa. There was a cry and the crash of glass against the opposite wall. (Copper and Leon 1976: 101)

In a somewhat less dramatic form, medium Susy Smith describes a conflict with a potentially dominating spirit voice. Like a number of victims featured in anti-Ouija stories, Smith began receiving messages through a Ouija board, then graduated to automatic writing and finally to directly hearing voices. She, too, was plagued by an especially abusive spirit who whispered profanities and threatened to kill her. She, like Melissa, was not disposed to be a passive victim, especially when she found that the spirit did not like to be ridiculed.

> "All right, Sam, you son of a bitch," I said. "I've been around, too, you know. Just because I don't use dirty words is no sign I don't know at least some of them." Then I said a few choice epithets to show him. After that, whenever he spoke profanity in my mind, I matched him aloud with some of my own. And I addressed him as Sam every time.
>
> Then it wasn't a fight anymore. My intruder degenerated from an infamous fiend of magnitude coming from outer space to do me great harm into a petulant invisible derelict who didn't like being referred to snidely as Sam and didn't want to be laughed at. He particularly could not understand my mirth. (Smith 1974: 23)

Such verbal confrontations are also found in folklore archives' accounts of Ouija rituals. The Ohio State Folklore Archives contain a transcript of a Ouija board session sponsored by "Lana,"[6] a self-proclaimed ex-satanist, who with some pride showed around a "black magik" spell she had written with her own blood. In the session recorded, she did not touch the planchette (which was controlled by two girls), but when they contacted an evil spirit, she joined the conversation, determined not to be intimidated by the "demon."

> Hey! Is this cocksucker? Hello? Is this all masterful what's his face of the house? You won't tell me your name. If it is, you're really weak.
> *Board:* YES.
> Oh. How ya doing? So, got anything exciting to say? Oh great. What's he saying?
> *Board:* K.I.L.L.
> You can finish spelling the name.
> *Board:* L.A.
> Well let me guess. [*Laughter*].
> *Board:* N.A.
> Because I didn't suck your dick, right? [*Laughter*].
> *Board:* YES.

See. Why? I don't understand if I didn't, but you said I didn't suck your dick yet and I'm going to suck your dick when I see you in hell. Okay. Is that why you want to kill me, so I can suck your dick? So then I'll be in hell to suck your dick, is that it?

Board: YES.

Veq le vouz [*sic*][7]

What's that?

I said veq le vouz, "fuck you." [*Laughter*]. Well, you're really exciting to talk to. You guys have anything to ask him?

Who is this?

Um, he won't tell us his name. Why don't you tell us something to call you, anyway. It's like—or I'll just keep calling you asshole.

Board: M.A.S.T.E.R.

Master, my ass. [*Laughter*].

Master? Why master?

Yeah, why master? Well, no. Because he said he's the master of all of us. Because he thinks he is.

Later she commented:

Well, he [the spirit] thinks he's like Satan devil number one. Big time. Bad, evil person. And he wants to kill me as you found out.

What, 'cause you're trying to. . . .

'Cause I didn't suck his dick right. That's his only reason why. I didn't suck his dick. . . . He likes to believe I'm only nineteen, but see I am the master of the house, or we are the masters of the house and we control him.

Yeah.

This is our house, so we can, you know, play with him whenever we want. All he can do is talk on the board and drop an occasional penny jar. If he were the quote unquote master the way he thinks, he'd be able to do a lot more. (OSUFA, Birch 1990)

Such exchanges seem best understood as a supernatural form of "the dozens," or contest of insults. This verbal dueling, ironically, has been characterized as a distinctively masculine pastime, which can become quite serious in some cultures: one partner's ability to come up with a more vulgar obscenity than the other implies his greater sexual knowledge and verbally "rapes" the loser. But among African Americans it often includes a string of obscene comments about the opponent's girlfriend, mother, and grandmother. Roger Abrahams has noted that such insults deflect verbal aggression away from the males participating and can continue without deteriorating into violence because both parties share low opinions about women in general. Hence the insulting contest, even though it nominally is a form of sexual battle among males, actually expresses a collective sexist attitude by "putting down" as many females as possible (1970: 54–55). Thus, the aggressive response of female Ouija board users to threats from the other world reverses the usual political roles in this world. By capping their opponents' vulgarity, such users indicate unwillingness to submit to harassment and in fact turn the tables by harassing and belittling the powers of "demons."

    This sexual dimension may explain why groups of women continue to form folk groups around the Ouija ritual despite the commonly expressed (and genuine) risk of "opening the door" to psychic rape. When the messages embody an extreme sexist point of view, in which vulgarity is a means of becoming and remaining "master" of women, the participants' response may become intense. And when the "demon's" weapon is

Fig. 12. Photo of 1920s Ouija board. Courtesy of the author.

simply appropriated and used against him, the result reverses cultural expectations and makes them ridiculous. The *communitas* here results from creating a seemingly invulnerable male opponent, then cutting him down to size through ritual insults. There are psychological dangers here, in that women with deeply seated fears of domination may not be ready to cope with the intensity of this confrontation; but many women find this kind of morality play a satisfying way of confronting male prejudice.

In conclusion, we can see a number of reasons why the Ouija board has gained and maintained popularity among adolescents. In depersonalizing contexts, it is a way of generating a brief but satisfying form of *communitas* among young adolescents in the face of a danger that they feel they can ritually control. By generating and reacting to aggressive messages, the ritual allows them to tell off, often in obscene ways, representatives of the adult world who try to be their "master."

Ultimately, as a semi-insulated form of achieving an alternate state of consciousness, it is a way of getting in direct touch with a mythic realm outside of adult-moderated institutions. If you want to get a call, why not have a phone? If it rings, it's a sign that there *is* someone there.

Chapter Nine

The Welsh Revival

Evangelical Christianity Meets the Occult

We have demonstrated that witchcraft, magical ritual, and contact with the supernatural constitute stable and generally functional folk traditions in cultures in both Europe and North America, up to the present day. Such traditions have often been at odds with social norms, allowing young people an opportunity for deviant play and providing a matrix for alternative religions such as the Neo-Pagan movement and satanic organizations. Elements drawn from folklore have been used by religious and secular institutions to justify claims that witchcraft and magic are promoted by evil, underground organizations and orchestrated by malicious people. In this sense, folk magic is not just ignorance and superstition but a rival institution that endangers both those who practice it and the legitimacy of true religions in leading culture away from brutality. We see a modern statement of this theme in evangelist Berit Kjos's warning that believers must remember the lessons of history.

> The witchcraft and wizardry in Harry Potter books may be fantasy, but they familiarize children with a very real and increasingly popular religion—one that few really understand. Far removed from the terrors of tribal witchcraft and shamanism, Americans are oblivious to the bondages that normally follow occult favors. But historical and archeological records have traced the earth-centered myths, practices, and consequences through the millennia. . . . the human cruelties involved in pagan worship included torture, mutilation and human sacrifice. Many of these practices continued in parts of the world until the 20th century, when the spread of genuine Christianity (totally different from

cultural Christianity) with its emphasis on love and the value of life, made most of these cruelties intolerable. But now the world turns, once again, from God's truth to the world's gods and rituals. (Kjos 1999)

From this point of view, any contact with the occult, even in the context of a fictional children's book, results in a slippage backward in human progress, with blood sacrifices and slavery at the bottom of this slippery slope. The alternative, developed elsewhere in Kjos's website, is a return to biblically based Christianity, a movement that she sees emerging no earlier than the beginning of the twentieth century.

The beginnings of the last century were indeed marked by events that led to major developments in evangelical religion. In *Raising the Devil*, I mentioned the birth of the Pentecostal movement in 1901, which led to a revival of the use of divine "gifts of the spirit" in worship. The most widespread and visible of these was the "gift of tongues," or use of glossolalia in worship. But closely aligned with it was a gift of discerning and exorcising demons. In the "deliverance ministry," which arose from Pentecostalism, this gift became the primary focus of believers, who interpreted a wide range of medical and moral ills as due to the influence of supernatural entities who followed or even inhabited the personalities of Christians. Like the Ouija board "cults" that we looked at in the previous chapter, small groups formed to invoke, question, confront, and finally dismiss these demons in ceremonies that often included obscene and disgusting language or even behavior (see Ellis 2000: 73ff.). But unlike the Ouija "cults," the deliverance ministry formed coherent ideologies, subversive of mainstream Christianity (which it saw as lukewarm or even demon-inspired), which were circulated through media-enhanced conduits and maintained strongly over time and space. The deliverance ministry was a genuine act of mythmaking, and it therefore is instructive to trace it to events in the early part of the twentieth century, when its key ideas were formulated.

An important and dramatic event in this origin was the religious revival that occurred in Wales late in 1904 and early in 1905. This intense but short-lived religious movement exploited many formerly private rituals that were often practiced in folk or even occult settings. At the same time, it gave prestige and influence to women, previously excluded from positions of power within Christian institutions. While nominally Christian, the movement often criticized mainstream denominations, which in turn meant that establishment critics saw it as hysterical or even dia-bolical in nature. More importantly, it was clear from the outset that this movement was heavily influenced by folk religious traditions that ran parallel to spiritualism. Not surprisingly, then, it developed its own con-cepts of the devil and how to detect and combat demonic influence. The methods and theories so developed persisted in fringe networks long after the revival itself, and continue to motivate much of the present antioccult propaganda.

Spiritualism and Revival

The deliverance movement sprang from the groups that emerged from a religious mania that broke out late in 1904 in South Wales. It is therefore important to spend some time reviewing the history of the so-called Welsh Revival and the religious practices that fed into it.

"Deliverance," in fundamentalist Protestant Christian teaching (e.g., Matthews 1970), is a theological concept parallel to the Catholic sacra-ment of confession or reconciliation. When Christians search their hearts for occasions in which they sinned and hence rebelled against God, name them, and ask forgiveness, they progressively free themselves from the influence of the devil. In the mythology that arose from the Welsh Re-vival, deliverance was increasingly supernaturalized. The benefits of de-liverance were seen as dramatic, visible signs of the Holy Spirit, and, conversely, the sins thought to impair individuals' ability to have reli-gious experiences were associated with demons. These were not simply base desires of the sinner but active, intelligent beings foreign to the per-sonality who blocked religious development and often caused men-tal and physical illness.

The positive side of this mythology had been widespread in En-gland and North America at least since the rise of Methodism in the early 1700s, which under the Wesleys had stressed the importance of individual religious experience. This took the form of a dramatic con-version, often in the context of intense camp meetings or revivals that had the effect of breaking down individuals' normal ways of thinking through lengthy sermons, singing, or even forms of dancing (see Sargent 1961). While the devil formed an important part of the theology sparked by such revival-oriented movements, demons or possession did not—perhaps because symptoms that might earlier have been interpreted as diabolical illness were now seen in terms of a more optimistic movement toward recognizing sin and being reborn. Traditions of demon possession were kept alive, though, within the alternative religious movement represented by nineteenth-century spiritualism. From the 1840s on, small groups both in North America and Europe had communicated with spirits in a variety of ways, including the forms of automatic writing, table-tipping, and Ouija-style automatism described above.

While some mediums attracted considerable attention, Owen (1990) notes, there were as many who quietly practiced automatic writing, trances, or healing within a family or village setting. And while certain scientific and feminist groups strongly supported spiritualism, its appeal was not limited to urban privileged classes. In fact, from the outset its strongest adherents were working-class communities in areas such as West Yorkshire and the Midlands. There it often mingled with or competed directly with Methodism, as well as even more marginal movements, such as the followers of Joanna Southcote, one of the many "female Messiahs" of nineteenth-century Anglo-American culture. Margaret Fuller, in her feminist classic *Woman in the Nineteenth Century,* alluded to Southcote and Mother Ann Lee, founder of the Shaker movement, as signs of a change in the status of females in Western culture. "If larger intellectual resources begin to be deemed needful to woman," she said, "still more is a spiritual dignity in her, or even the mere assumption of it, looked upon with respect. Joanna Southcote and Mother Anne Lee are sure of a band of disciples; Ecstatica, Dolorosa, of enraptured believers who will visit them in their lowly huts, and wait for days to revere them in their trances." She noted that mystics often alluded to concepts such as "the mothers" as a token of an "oracular promise as to Women": "Whenever a mystical whisper was heard [she concluded] sprang up the thought, that, if it be true, as the legend says, that humanity withers through a fault committed by and a curse laid upon woman, through her pure child, or influence, shall the new Adam, the redemption, arise. Innocence is to be replaced by virtue, dependence by a willing submission, in the heart of the Virgin Mother of the new race" (Fuller 1994 [1845]: 284–85). Certainly, Fuller spoke for many smaller, less visible, but tightly-knit groups of women who discussed, originated, and followed new avenues in religious expression. Hence it is striking that the Welsh Revival sprang up precisely among such small, loosely coordinated, female-dominated groups.

For some time preceding, the Welsh religious scene had been characterized by "prayer circles," small groups of religious-minded persons who met to join in prayer at a certain hour every day. Frequently led by a layman or deacon rather than a priest, they functioned parallel to denominational religion rather than within it. At the turn of the century, a wave of millennium-seeking led some participants to ask for a revival of divine grace. In some cases, their practices were similar to séances, as in the practice termed "waiting on the Spirit." In this, the prayer circle "prayed and waited in a prayerful spirit," expecting that at "some time the Holy Spirit would come to them" (Goodrich et al. 1905: 10). This form of "waiting" seems to have been similar in dynamics to rural folk rites such as dumb suppers and legend-trips. In both, participants "summoned a spirit" (in the prayer circle's case, a Holy Spirit), then waited anxiously for some supernatural sign that their rite was successful.

In themselves local in influence, such circles collectively constituted a widespread form of folk religion, parallel to the equally active circles of spiritualists and needing only a network to coordinate their efforts into a broad-based movement (Stead 1905: 65–66). Late in 1903, such circles began individually to pray for a more dramatic sign of the spirit, which led to several small-scale revivals. The movement was galvanized by the emergence in October 1904 of Evan Roberts (1878–1951), a coal miner from near Swansea. Roberts's religious quest began when his prayer group practiced "waiting on the spirit," which led to a solitary spiritual quest. At length he was rewarded by an ecstatic vision of God, in which "for the space of four hours I was privileged to speak face to face with Him as a man speaks face to face with a friend" (Goodrich et al. 1905: 55).

For several months he experienced regular mystic encounters with God, and subsequently entered a seminary to prepare for the ministry. However, he found the courses spiritually deadening, and also found that his mystic experiences left him. After only one month, a second series of visions instructed him to return home, so he left the college to organize a revival there. The revival initially spread through South Wales in a grassroots fashion from these early meetings, without overt advertising or coordination by existing denominations. However, as it became clear that it was no isolated or passing craze, a number of influential persons became interested, for their own reasons, in witnessing and describing it. Among these were reporters from the *Western Mail*, whose dramatic accounts of the revival meetings led by Roberts were influential in drawing attention to the movement from other parts of Great Britain (see Lewington 2001 and Evan Roberts 1996).

A crucial figure in promoting the Welsh Revival was the journalist William Thomas Stead (1849–1912). Stead is best known for his editorial work for the *Pall Mall Gazette,* a daily paper that held considerable political influence during the late 1880s. In addition to his role in influencing foreign affairs (he was largely responsible for Charles Gordon's fatal mission to Khartoum in 1885), he campaigned for stronger laws against the abduction and sexual abuse of children. In one of the key incidents of his life, however, he was jailed in 1885 after it came out that he had "bought" a thirteen-year-old virgin and had her chloroformed and delivered to him at a brothel, ostensibly to gather information for an expose he was planning for his paper (see Schults 1972).

Stead left the *Gazette* in 1890 to found a periodical of his own, the *Review of Reviews,* and soon after admitted that for at least a decade he had been increasingly involved in spiritualism. A series of popular books on the survival of the soul, communication with the otherworld, and ghosts followed, during the course of which he told how he had been able to establish a continuous source of psychic advice. More dramatically, in 1892, Stead found that he could communicate instantaneously with associates without the use of any telegraphic instrument: "I simply ask the question, and my hand automatically writes out the answer." Interestingly, he found that it made no difference whether his contacts were alive or dead, and that while his living friends generally were unaware that Stead was taking messages from them, as a rule, their contents were "astonishingly correct" (1911: 16, 20–21; Shepard 1970: vii–viii).

His automatic writing experiments eventually developed into a series of communications from Julia Ames, a deceased editorial colleague, who gave him friendly business advice and warnings in this form for the rest of his life. Stead also found that he could communicate easily through automatic writing with a second, living associate, whom he identified only as "E. M." In the most bizarre twist to this story, E.M. committed suicide after Stead received a series of warning messages from her. But her death in fact led to no break in the communications E.M. sent to Stead; she "apparently [found] it just as easy to use my hand as she did when still in the body" (1911: 37). For the remainder of his life, Stead relied on such spirit advice and eagerly promoted automatic writing as evidence for a benevolent life after death. Oddly, both his spirit guides kept silent when Stead booked a cabin on the April 1912 maiden voyage of the Titanic, the sinking of which ended his terrestrial career as a spiritualist.

Stead, who claimed to have had a peaceful but undramatic religious experience during an earlier revival at the age of twelve, was among the first journalists to arrive in Wales. Interviewed soon after for *The Methodist Times,* he described his first impressions in terms closer to his occult interests than to orthodox Christianity: "Well, you have read ghost stories, and can imagine what you would feel if you were alone at midnight in the haunted chamber of some old castle, and you heard slow and stealthy steps stealing along the corridor where the visitant from the other world was said to walk. If you go to South Wales and watch the revival you will feel pretty much like that. There is something there from the Other World" (1905: 30).

Part of Roberts' appeal, like that of the leading spiritualists, was tied to his ability to produce explicit signs of otherworldly power. The revival expressed itself from the start as being in some palpable sense governed by supernatural forces. One participant said, "there's something funny about it. They say you feel it as soon as you're inside the building where [Roberts is] going to speak" (Goodrich et al. 1905: 7). During the meetings, Roberts usually made a formal appeal to his audience to summon the Holy Spirit. Stead summed up this appeal as follows:

> Do you desire an outpouring of the Holy Spirit?
> Very well. Four conditions must be observed. They are essential.
> (1) Is there any sin in your past life that you have not confessed
>   to God? On your knees at once. Your past must be at peace.
> (2) Is there anything in your life that is doubtful? Anything you
>   cannot decide whether it is good or evil? Away with it. There
>   must not be!
> (3) Obey the Spirit.
> (4) Confess Christ publicly before men. (1905: 59; cf. Evans 1969: 84)

Roberts's explicit message focused on the first two—confessing and renouncing dubious practices—while the direction of the meeting itself embodied the third. Several witnesses attested to the seemingly random, yet somehow orderly nature of the revival meetings. One commented, "I am speaking with diffidence, for I have never seen anything like it in my life; while a man praying is disturbed by the breaking out of song, there is no sense of disorder, and the prayer merges into song, and back into testimony, and back again into song for hour after hour, without guidance. These are the three occupations—singing, prayer, testimony"

(Goodrich et al. 1905: 39). Another remarked, "The very first thing that strikes one is the absolute 'liberty of prophesying' which characterises the meetings. There is no leader, and yet there is an unseen control. . . . No one is asked to speak, sing, or pray; all are invited to follow the guidance of the Spirit. The missioner [Roberts] is frequently interrupted in the course of his address. Sometimes his words are drowned in a chorus of song, sometimes by the liquid notes of one of the soloists accompanying him. But there is no sense of discord, no break in the harmony" (Goodrich et al. 1905: 79).

Enormously popular among young people, Roberts made much of his lack of formal training. Of his revival meetings, he explained, "Why should I teach when the Spirit is teaching? . . . And why should I control the meetings? The meetings control themselves, or, rather, the Spirit that is in them controls them" (Johnson 1906: 349–51; cf. Evans 1969: 127–28). When Roberts was asked about his methods, he responded that he never prepared a sermon. "I leave all that to Him." This, he said, was a sign that he was not personally the source of the revival's power. "I am not moving men's hearts and changing men's lives; not I, but 'God worketh in me.' I have found what is, in my belief, the highest kind of Christianity" (Goodrich et al. 1905: 5).

Roberts's theology, sketchy as it is, reflects the rhetoric of spiritualism, particularly in the way his passivity in the face of the Spirit in fact leads to a "liberty of utterance," which is attributed to divine inspiration rather than to his own thoughts. The "unguided" nature of his meetings thus extended the folk religious practice of "waiting on the spirit" in a way that allowed large groups to participate directly in the creation of a liminal realm between the natural and the supernatural, exactly parallel to the séance.

Being a practical spiritualist, W.T. Stead felt immediately at home in the Welsh Revival. Much of his account of Roberts' ministry reads like standard religious literature; in fact, his reports (stripped of the most obviously occult references) were widely reprinted by evangelical presses. In his own collection of essays, though, his essentially occult point of view comes to the fore several times. In presenting Roberts's account of his mystic trances, Stead adds footnotes drawn from William James's newly published *Varieties of Religious Experience* (1902). These make it clear that Stead saw the motivating spirit of the revival not as distinctively Christian, but as part of a supernatural impulse common to all world religions. In much the same way, a standard spiritualist tenet held that Jesus was not in fact a unique "son of God" but simply a representative of healing and teaching powers available to any charismatic religious leader (see Owen 1990: 174–75). Stead suggests that Roberts's source of divine power is not the Jesus Christ of standard religion, and clinches this point by interrupting Roberts's testimony for a significant exchange:

> "May I ask," I said, "if he of whom you speak appeared to you as Jesus Christ?"
> "No," said Mr. Roberts, "not so; it was the personal God, not as Jesus."
> "As God the Father Almighty?" I said.
> "Yes," said Mr. Roberts, "and the Holy Spirit."
> "Pardon me," I said, "but I interrupted you. Pray go on."
> (1905: 50–52)

Indeed, while Roberts regularly included the injunction for believers to "confess Christ" publicly, he made rather little of this article of faith. Confession, renunciation of sins, and implicit trust in the commands of the Spirit were far more crucial. This aspect of his theology made it more attractive to those oriented toward an eclectic, spiritualist-oriented faith that accepted supernaturalism and a benign god-force but distrusted the exclusivity of traditional Christianity.

Furthermore, Stead made the most of several of Roberts's practices that suggested that he was functioning essentially as a medium. He notes, for instance, that Roberts clearly had developed a facility of making decisions through "thought-prayer": asking for guidance, pausing a moment, and then receiving an answer from some divine source (1905: 58). In recording and commenting on this habit, Stead could hardly have missed the link with his own practice, in which he mentally asked for guidance, then found his hand automatically writing an answer from one of his associates, dead or alive. Finally, Stead concludes, "The truth about Evan Roberts is that he is very psychic, with clairvoyance well developed and a strong visualizing gift. One peculiarity about him is that he has not yet found any watch that will keep time when it is carried in his pocket" (1905: 63). In fact, to this day the spiritual "charge" emanated by psychics is sometimes said to stop the watches they wear, particularly the digital kind that rely on quartz crystals.[1] Whatever the truth of this claim, Stead includes it almost as a code phrase to identify Roberts as an "authentic" clairvoyant to his fellow spiritualists.

Overall, the Welsh Revival, whatever its consequences for mainstream religion, had its immediate roots in folk religious movements that paralleled and shared ideas with spiritualism. Roberts was seen less as a religious leader actively directing the meetings than as a kind of medium whose presence enabled crowds to submit passively to a supernatural control that, if all went well, would lead to signs of the Spirit parallel to the climax of a séance or occult rite. The obvious links to female-oriented rituals also made it likely that the movement would appeal strongly to women and incorporate references to female empowerment, which indeed proved to be the case.

Feminism and Fire from Heaven

While Roberts and most of the nominal leaders of revival meetings were male, many commented on the dominant role of women in the revival. Even Evan Roberts often took a role subordinate to the "Singing Sisters," a group that performed revival hymns during meetings. And Stead noted that a sentimental gospel song featuring this verse "was sung over and over again":

> Tell mother I'll be there
> In answer to her prayer,
> This message, blessed Saviour, to her bear.
> Tell mother I'll be there,
> Heaven's joys with her to share,
> Oh, tell my darling mother I'll be there.

He commented, "It is perhaps an indication of the swing of the slow pendulum back to the days of the matriarchate that in Wales today the father takes a back seat. It is the mother who is always to the front" (Stead 1905: 37–38).

Accounts of Roberts's meetings are filled with sentimental scenes in which parents and children are reconciled. In one, "a quaint, pitiful little figure in black" was said to kneel and, in words just loud enough to hear, ask for the conversion of her erring son. Instantly, a young man rushed up the aisle, knelt beside her, and embraced her "in tears and happiness" (Goodrich et al. 1905: 27). In nearly equal numbers, however, converted children prayed for their fathers, whose testimony reflected the common sentimental image of males as prone to vices such as drinking and swearing. A number of commentators note that, in fact, consumption of alcohol declined dramatically during the revival, and a common anecdote held that horses refused to work in the coal mines because they missed the curses and profanity with which miners used to give them orders (Goodrich et al. 1905: 46; McClure 1995: 2).

Roberts's work in the populous south of Wales was matched, though in a less visible way, by Mary Jones in the more rural North Wales. Not much is known for certain about Jones, who seems to have been a farmer's wife of about thirty-five when she burst into prominence in December 1904. According to the few biographical items that appeared during her brief fame, she had had no particular religious training, though her husband regularly attended services and weekday prayer meetings at a tiny chapel in Egryn, a farming community near Harlech. Mary Jones had indeed been hostile to Christianity for some time after the deaths of her young son and her only sister. "I do not believe," she told a reporter, "that anyone ever had harder thoughts of Him than I did then" (McClure 1995: 4).

A vast amount of sentimental poetry and parlor song memorialized the passive, suffering mother as an icon of faith. But Mary Jones was not the only woman deeply ambivalent about God the Father. One of the winning entries in a 1904 American contest, in which readers sent in their favorite sentimental poems, was one by Josephine Dodge Daskam, simply entitled "Motherhood." Its narrator, a bereaved mother, is hardly passive, but resembles a female Job tempted to curse God for allowing her infant son to die:

> If thou allow it that my child forgets
> And runs not out to meet me when I come—
>
> What are my curses to Thee? Thou has heard
> The curse of Abel's mother, and since then
> We have not ceased to threaten at Thy throne,
> To threat and pray Thee that Thou hold them still
>
> In memory of us. See Thou tend him well,
> Thou God of all the mothers.
> (*Heart Throbs* 1905: 447)

Jones, by her own account, was reconverted not through a revival or even through Bible reading, but instead by picking up another Victorian sentimental classic, Sidney Sheldon's *In His Steps*. This advised readers to solve moral problems such as drink and the proper use of money by asking themselves "What would Jesus do?" Comforted, she returned to chapel meetings, though in a quiet role in which she did little more than lead hymns.

For Jones, though, acting as Jesus would mean more than self-denial, and she began to pray to be the vehicle of a local revival. Early in December 1904, her prayers were answered when she had a vision of Jesus Christ "in bodily form clothed in bright raiment." Paradoxically, Jesus told her that the mission she sought had been given to another woman in her community, and she was told to go and tell her so. When Jones sought out her neighbor and explained the vision, the woman, alarmed, refused the charge, whereupon Jones felt secure in claiming it for herself. A contemporary report said, "That evening Mrs Jones attended the little chapel at Egryn, related her vision, told of the proffered commission being refused, and added: 'She has missed the one opportunity of a lifetime, and my service is accepted.' From that night forth she threw herself into revival work with a zeal and energy that nothing could damp—and with a success beside which, in proportion of converts to the relative population dealt with, even that which accompanies Evan Roberts' movement in Glamorgan, pales into insignificance." By December 15, 1904, the sensation she had created was already making the local newspaper, which said, "It is a remarkable thing that at Egryn a lady ... has taken the lead, and those who were eye-witnesses admit that no-one could have been better entrusted with it" (McClure 1995: 4–5).

Mary Jones was by all accounts rather shy outside of her ministry, which was far more limited in scope and publicity than Roberts's. She granted few interviews with journalists and never traveled far from her rural community. After three months of local prominence, she returned permanently to her obscure farming life. No detailed accounts of her messages exist, as relatively few reporters heard her preach and, like Roberts, she in fact said relatively little during the meetings, giving them over to songs and public testimony by converts. The few mentions that exist, however, indicate that accounts of the devil played an active role in these testimonies, and that she and her followers enthusiastically shared accounts of supernatural visions and encounters.

One such, related to a reporter on the spot at which it happened, involved a strange man whom she met on the way home. When she sang part of a revival hymn, the man suddenly changed into "an enormous black dog, which ran from bank to bank across the road in front of her as though preventing her advance. 'And then,' she told me, 'I knew it was the Devil himself, angered at my assault upon his kingdom.'" Another such story told of one of Mary Jones's supporters, whose bedroom was visited repeatedly at midnight "by a man dressed in black, whose appearance corresponds with that of the person seen by Mrs. Jones." The man in black, whose appearance suggests the "Old Hag" encounters already discussed, was said to have given the woman a message that, unfortunately, "she is forbidden to relate" (McClure 1995: 16).

Most attention, however, was given to the mysterious lights that were associated with her revival meetings. From the start, she told the meetings, she had seen "stars and lights" appear around the chapel, rising from the surrounding marshes and hills. These infallibly indicated the success or failure of the prayer meetings, sometimes forecasting the exact number of conversions to expect. One reporter explained:

> The star seemed to rest above particular houses, whose rooves are thrown out in bold relief amidst the surrounding darkness. When occurs in the Egryn district a convert or converts invariably turns up at the next meeting from that particular house; when it occurs at a distance the house is the one selected for the Revivalist's temporary lodging. Similarly it glows placidly on the roof of the chapel where her service is held, and when it does so the spiritual character of the meeting is very marked. On two occasions only, so far as I know, has the star or light stopped short of the chapel fixed for the service—and on each occasion the service proved a frost. (McClure 1995: 5)

These mysterious lights were visible not just to Mrs. Jones, but also to her followers and, inexplicably, to a number of skeptical journalists who visited Egryn specifically to investigate this phenomenon. These airborne lights, sometimes dim and reddish, other times blindingly white, captured the attention of the communities among which Mary Jones circulated. A number of scientific explanations were proposed, but none verified, nor were the lights ever proved to be hoaxed. They suggested a literal manifestation of the Holy Spirit's "tongues of fire" and did much to establish her reputation as a prophet.

This aspect of her ministry, more than any other, made Mary Jones famous outside of her Welsh district. For about a week, national reports appeared describing her connection with these mystery lights. The early teams investigating spiritualism and other paranormal phenomena were intrigued: accounts appeared in the *Journal for the Society for Psychic Research* and *The Occult Review*. Along with these mystery lights, a whole range of anomalous events were reported in the press during this time, ranging from mystery animals that were killing and mutilating livestock to poltergeists and mysterious deaths blamed on spontaneous human combustion. Charles Fort, a tireless researcher of odd news reports, noted that he never came across any other period of time in which so many uncanny events had been reported in the press (1941: 651ff.). Since this time, these sightings have regularly been mentioned in a variety of paranormal publications as an early analogue to modern UFO sightings (Clark 1998: 2, 925; McClure 1995). It is clear that, whatever Jones's theology or methods were, her claim to fame was her apparent ability to provoke objective supernatural phenomena. This, like Roberts's "psychic" tendencies, was the source of much of her power within the circles in which she moved and of all the attention she gained outside.

War by Satan upon the Womenhood of the World

A second key female figure in the revival was Mrs. Jessie Penn-Lewis (1861–1927), a native of South Wales. Unlike Mary Jones, she took a supporting role in the revival itself, but her background role was hardly one of submission: she ultimately proved to be the most important organizer and long-lasting publicizer of the movement. An early and active supporter of the London YWCA movement, she formed a small prayer group there in 1892, devoted to studying the role of the Holy Spirit in leading revivals. Confused by the various theological works they read, as she later said, she became convinced that "there was a work of God to be done *in themselves*" before God would allow a revival to begin. Accordingly:

> I said, I will go straight to God and ask Him to *prove* to me where there is *for me* an enduement for service that will liberate me in utterance, as it did Peter at Pentecost. I will put it to the proof for myself! Away went the books, and away went the various views and theories. In desperation I said, I WILL GO TO GOD. . . .
> I cried, "I want the deliverance that Peter got at Pentecost. I

do not care what the Christians call it. If "The Baptism of the Spirit" is not the right term, give me the right words to use. I do not care about the words, but *I want the thing.* (Quoted in Garrard 1947: 21–22; emphasis hers)

After a period of doubt and frustration, Penn-Lewis had a series of ecstatic visions that confirmed her special mission and removed her nervousness about speaking in public. In a phrase that echoed spiritualist rhetoric, she found herself "able to speak with liberty of utterance."

A wide-ranging ministry followed in several parts of the world, including Russia and India, and she was frequently invited to participate in evangelical conferences. As a woman, though, she frequently found her role limited to presentations before auxiliary prayer groups for women. This discrimination concerned her deeply, and, toward the end of her career, she admitted that she had frequently asked God to show her a man to whom she could entrust her ministry. "Many tears did I shed over this, and with anguish of heart I would go into the open doors that were plainly set before me, until at last, when I saw and could say with the Lord, 'I beheld, and there was no man,' I had to settle it that for some unexplained reason, God had committed this message to me, and at whatever cost, I must go forward." As for Paul's notorious Biblical injunctions against female participation in church services, she commented, "I was certain in my mind, as I walked with God and found His will and guidance, and as His message came to me, that if we only knew the exact original meaning of these passages, they were bound to be *in harmony with the working of the Holy Spirit* in the Nineteenth Century" (quoted in Garrard 1947: 267; emphasis hers). To this end, she incorporated her unorthodox views about the female role in revivals in a religious pamphlet entitled *The Magna Charta of Women.* In the end, she became convinced that mainstream Christianity's discrimination against women was no less than satanically inspired, a cornerstone of his plot against humanity.

In an unusual but closely argued reinterpretation of the Adam and Eve incident, Penn-Lewis argued that the devil had exploited not Eve's weakness, but her "highest and purest desires" to know God. Her only fault was that she was innocently deceived, and Penn-Lewis interpreted God's response as pardoning Eve and laying the heaviest blame on the serpent, or Satan. The prophecy that Eve would produce a "seed" destined to bruise the serpent's head, is, for her, in fact a blessing, since she interprets this issue as the Messiah, Jesus Christ. While the immediate result of Eve's sin is ruin, she adds that, "in effect, the beguiled victim is blest, for through her will come the 'Seed' which will triumph over the devil and his seed" (1973: 4–5).

This paradoxical blessing of Eve and her descendants explains why Penn-Lewis found institutional Christianity hostile to her mission. She concludes, in an eloquent passage unique to evangelical Christian writing of the day:

> Henceforth it is . . . war by Satan upon the womenhood of the world, in malignant revenge for the verdict of the garden. War by the trampling down of women in all lands where the deceiver reigns. War upon women in Christian lands, by the continuance of his Eden method of misinterpreting the Word of God; insinuating into men's minds throughout all succeeding ages, that God pronounced a "curse" upon the woman, when in truth she was pardoned and blessed; and instigating men of the fallen race to carry out the supposed curse, which was in truth a CURSE UPON THE DECEIVER, and not the deceived one (Gen. iii. 14).
> "I will put enmity between *thee* and the woman," said God, as well as between "*thy* seed and her seed," and this vindictive enmity of the hierarchy of evil to women, and to believers, has not lessened in its intensity from that day. (1973: 5; emphasis hers)

In short, Penn-Lewis labeled those who imposed gender limitations on her role as evangelist as "the seed of Satan" and the patriarchy itself as "the hierarchy of evil"—bold words indeed, but characteristic of the antipathy both fringe religion and spiritualism showed toward mainstream Christianity.

Indeed, the enmity of which she spoke has not entirely disappeared, even in the time since the Welsh Revival. Recent church historians concede that women took an unusually large role in the movement. Dr. Eifion Evans complimented the Welsh sisters for their valuable missionary and nursing work, but he rebuked the movement for breaching scriptural limits on the ministry of women. "Women's nature is such as to follow rather than to lead," Evans insisted, continuing, "Her spiritual equality with man as a recipient of God's grace is unquestioned, but for the purpose of public worship the woman is not constitutionally equipped by God for a teaching rôle. Her part is one of submission rather than authority. At the time of the revival this Scriptural norm was not always observed. Its omission left the movement open to emotional excesses and to a related failure in providing adequate doctrinal foundations" (1969: 175–76). Nevertheless, Penn-Lewis proved to be the key figure in introducing the methods and the lessons of the revival to prayer groups, which in turn developed its demonological side.

Meanwhile, Evan Roberts's meteoric career was cut short when he began to suffer from attacks of anxiety, which he blamed on evil influences present in the meeting halls. As early as 29 January 1905, he halted a meeting to say that he had received a sign that two prominent persons present were so antagonistic toward each other that he could not continue unless they reconciled or left the hall. At this point, a report said, "He fell forward on the pulpit desk in a violent paroxysm of agony, completely giving way, and sobbing and groaning." After a deacon warned that Roberts was "going to pieces," a number of people left, and he was eventually able to continue leading the meeting. Shortly after, he was forced to skip a meeting because of "an attack of nervous prostration," and by March was reported to be suffering from a "nervous breakdown" (McClure 1995: 2–3). Later in the year, as he attempted to spread the revival to Liverpool, he repeatedly complained that evil forces were present at public meetings, hindering his ministry and even, on one occasion, trying to "hypnotise" him (Evans 1969: 140). By the end of the year, he had virtually ended his public appearances.

It was at this point that Jessie Penn-Lewis offered her house as a haven for Roberts to recuperate. There, her biographer relates, Roberts "began to open his mind to his hostess on many experiences of supernatural forces witnessed during the Revival" (Garrard 1947: 231). Mrs. Penn-Lewis's theology insisted on the primacy of Jesus' crucifixion to Christian faith, to such an extent that even fellow evangelists termed her ministry "rather-one-tracked" (Evans 1969: 30). She must have seen Roberts's vision of the deity, which pointedly excluded Jesus, as dangerous, possibly even satanic in nature. Certainly, her biographer relates, she told Roberts of "the dangers attendant upon souls who, having experienced such a breaking-through into the supernatural realm, do not know *identification with Christ in His death* as the place of safety from the wiles and assaults of the devil" (Garrard 1941: 231; emphasis hers).

As a result, Penn-Lewis became henceforth a kind of protector of the burnt-out evangelist, who appeared only in her company for the next several years. Indeed, she managed his affairs to such an extent that his former supporters felt he had been co-opted. A historian of the affair comments, "This reluctance to allow Roberts unhindered converse with the outside world may have been due to legitimate motives, such as concern over his physical health, but it could not fail to create an impression of secrecy, suspicion, and mistrust. . . . it seems as if the revivalist had been commandeered for Jessie Penn-Lewis's private deployment. At any rate, she was the only one who had free access to him" (Evans 1969: 174). Except for a few appearances in 1928–30, where he performed faith healing and exorcisms, he lived the life of a "solitary contemplative" for the next forty-five years, praying for some eight hours a day (McClure 1995: 3).

One result of this closeted collaboration was the publication in 1912 of *War on the Saints,* the doctrinal cornerstone of Protestant demonology. As her biographer Mary N. Garrard put it:

> This God-given knowledge and experience, together with the insight into the devices of the enemy gained by Mr. Roberts in his experiences during the Revival, are conserved to the Church of God in "War on the Saints." Issued only after seven years of testing, proving, and praying through the truths given therein, this book has been the means, by the grace and power of God, of the deliverance of hundreds of His children from the wiles and deceptions of the great adversary of God and man, which, when recognized, can be resisted and defeated in the victorious Name of our Lord Jesus Christ. (1941: 232)

The title page describes it as "by Mrs. Penn-Lewis in collaboration with Evan Roberts," but the work exhibits the incisive rhetoric of Penn-Lewis's other work, punctuated by her characteristic emphases through italics, quotation marks, and capitalization. Since Roberts's few published statements are limited to a few pages, giving his standard revival message, it is difficult to believe that he actually wrote much, if any, of the book, and Penn-Lewis's followers attribute the basic arguments to her without qualification.

Clearly, the book is based on Penn-Lewis's critique of the revivalist's practices, particularly his emphasis on mental passivity and "obeying the spirit." But it would be unfair to suggest, as did Penn-Lewis's critics, that she simply exploited Roberts's mental breakdown for her own purposes. She also pointedly criticized Mary Jones's female-focused ministry of stars and lights, reminding readers that one of Satan's weapons in the end times "will be supernatural signs from heaven, when a counter-feit 'lamb' will do 'great signs,' and *even 'make fire come down out of heaven'* to deceive the dwellers on the earth" (1993 [1912]: 23; emphasis hers). At first, such a book seems an astonishing recantation of the main elements of the Welsh Revival and the feminist advances it embodied. But a closer look at the work, which has never gone out of print, shows a subversive aim similar to that of the séance, which often nominally endorsed social norms only to challenge them radically.

1) *Challenging the Norm.* In fact, Jessie Penn-Lewis's book was a logical outgrowth of the Welsh Revival. To the superficial observer, the affair was a brief and illogical craze, a fad of a few months for the local population and a nine days' wonder for the British print media. In the short run, though, the results were real enough: membership in main-stream churches in Wales did increase and petty crime and alcohol abuse did for a time decrease. At the same time, the supernaturalism of the meetings soon attracted harsh criticism from establishment media and religious authorities. Stead's occult-oriented magazines and Penn-Lewis's revivalist networks circulated accounts sympathetic to the movement, but most mass-circulation publications treated it as a bizarre anomaly and its participants as close to lunatics.

Penn-Lewis did not deny the fanatic and mentally unstable ele-ments among many of its participants, especially Roberts. But by defin-ing these as the result of demon possession, she shows that embarrassing excesses in fact validate the divine origin of the revival. Indeed, she ar-gues, revival movements have historically been short-lived precisely be-cause Satan and his demons introduced such flaws into them. Satan recognized that, if they were allowed to continue, spirit-filled movements such as these would destroy his control over the world. "To put it in bluntest language," she asserts, "the Revival hour is the occasion for evil spirits to obtain 'possession' of spiritual believers, AND REVIVAL CEASES BE-CAUSE OF SUCH POSSESSION" (283). Penn-Lewis argued, in fact, that expo-sure to demonic influence was the *normal* state of practicing Christians: And, even as she argued for a much wider range of demonic influence than had previously been accepted, Penn-Lewis stressed that the mecha-nism by which one could become obsessed or possessed was nothing es-pecially supernatural. It consisted simply of ignorance and honest error.

"Giving ground to Satan," an important term for Penn-Lewis, meant refusing to consider the possibility of error in any part of religious life. Once certain experiences or tenets were considered infallible, the devil would introduce errors or misleading conclusions. Even if these untruths initially constituted only a small part of the believer's thoughts on the subject, if they were never to be doubted, they would, in her view, eventually corrupt the integrity of the whole. In particular, she attacks the self-righteousness of certain authorities who cite Scripture for their position: such persons are unaware of the depths of evil spirits' craft and wickedness, she counters, "and are under the impression that they will not quote Scripture, whereas they will quote the whole Book if they can but deceive one soul" (20).

In one of her strongest attacks on the critics of the Welsh Revival, Penn-Lewis suggests that they, not the enthusiastic converts, are in fact the ones who are possessed by demons and thus functionally insane. In an explicit inversion of her opponents' position, she in fact equates her Christian critics' arguments with satanism: "when thinking he is 'fighting for truth,' it is possible for a believer to fight for, defend, and protect evil spirits, and their works, believing he is thereby 'defending' God, and His works; for if he thinks a thing Divine, he will protect and stand for it. It is possible for a man through ignorance to stand against God and to attack the very truth of God, and also defend the devil, and oppose God, unless he has knowledge" (2–3). The effect of this argument is to turn the tables on mainstream theology. Doctrinal orthodoxy, even when apparently supported by Scripture, was as likely to lead to demonic possession (perhaps even more so) than the direct religious experiences that the orthodox denounced as "fanaticism."

2) *Ubiquity of demons.* Penn-Lewis described demonic possession as motivated by supernatural powers of vast cunning and depravity. In a detailed "diabolical medicine" section, she attributed a vast range of mental and physical disorders to the actions of demons, ranging from premature graying of the hair to auditory and visual hallucinations. In general, she considered any compulsive impulse demonic, and the breadth of symptoms she attributed to possession was vast: "Feverish activity which accomplishes nothing is manifested occasionally, or else perpetual occupation which gives no moment of rest; difficulty with work in the day time; 'dreams' at night, with no sense of rest or leisure at any time; suffering, confusion, difficulty of action, embarrassment, perplexity, all emanating directly, maliciously, and deliberately from evil spirits, unrecognized by the man" (158–59). She gives particular attention to the eyes, which she feels more affected by evil spirits than any other part of the body. Evil spirits may make them roam around during conversation,

"ofttimes in a most unseemly or discourteous manner." Conversely, a "set or fixed gaze" into another's face may induce "a mediumistic attitude," particularly in a public setting. She warns both speaker and audience to avoid staring at each other, lest a kind of hypnotic state result in which evil spirits could operate, presumably an allusion to Roberts's fear of being hypnotized during meetings (167).

Penn-Lewis's chief point, that Satan attacks certain people by sending demons to afflict them, was hardly a new idea for the time. Spiritualists had been healing mental illnesses by identifying the "earthbound souls" that were obsessing the living, and psychic books describing similar practices in terms of demon possession had appeared shortly before the Welsh Revival. American missionary John Nevius, for instance, had in 1895 published *Demon Possession and Allied Themes*, an account of exorcisms he and other missionaries to China had witnessed. Previously, such cases were felt to be rare, the result of witchcraft or occult sins such as participation in spiritualism and related rituals. Yet, even as Penn-Lewis chided mediums for cultivating a passive mind conducive to demons, she just as forcefully rounded on the "Christian men [who] think they are free from spiritism because they have never been to a séance, not knowing that evil spirits attack, and deceive every human being" (40). She had no particular use for public exorcisms, though, perhaps finding them too redolent of Catholicism and spiritualism. While she cites the exorcisms described in Nevius's book, she at once says such rituals are perhaps unnecessary, and in any case only temporarily effective, unless the root cause of possession is removed.

In a significant passage, she says, "for believers who have become possessed by evil spirits as a RESULT OF DECEPTION, the main principle of deliverance is the being UNDECEIVED" (111). Deliverance was best achieved through this undramatic method rather than through any extraordinary crusade, she argued. The more so, in fact, because Satan could seem to fight against himself, in order to gain further control over certain believers. Indeed, she concludes, "a deceived believer may be more deeply deceived, by seeing nothing but Satan's counterfeits everywhere" (148). Hence she devotes only a few pages in an appendix to discussing details of conventional possessions and exorcisms.

3) *Empowerment of Women.* For Penn-Lewis, the only remedy to satanic influence was a mind actively ready to challenge orthodoxy. During the Welsh Revival, the practice of "Waiting on the Spirit," involved continuing prayer meetings indefinitely until some manifest event oc-

curred that gave a sign of the Holy Spirit's presence. The success of the public meetings during the Welsh Revival seems to have been based on the numbers of such conversions that took place that night. Indeed, both Roberts and Jones said they received divine messages foretelling the numbers of such conversions to expect that night, and so the meetings were continued, often for hours, until the requisite number of collapses occurred. By 1912, Jessie Penn-Lewis described such "waiting meetings" as common among charismatics. In some cases, she noted, prayer groups used this idea to justify regular meetings, over a period of months and even years, intended to create an atmosphere in which spirit-led experience occurred. Such waits were more apt to end "in an influx of deceiving spirits which has rudely awakened some of the waiting souls," she ironically concludes (61–63). As we have seen, this practice has clear links to similar ritual elements in occult folk rituals like dumb suppers, which often ended in fright rather than enlightenment.

Penn-Lewis, in fact, was quick to notice the similarity of many Pentecostal practices to those of spiritualism, and so defined *every* activity in which believers' minds were encouraged to be passive in the face of external spirits, even "holy" spirits, as by definition diabolical. In many cases, she argues, Christians took Roberts's injunction to "obey the Spirit" so literally that they became a kind of unreasoning "medium," demanding spirit leadership in even the most trivial matters. In addition, the spiritualist Stead had already implicitly compared Roberts's "thought-prayer" to his own automatic writing; Penn-Lewis extended the analogy and compared those who relied on advice from the Holy Spirit in an unthinking way to curious youngsters operating a Ouija board. "In some cases [demons] even establish communication with [the believer] from within his own bodily frame. If he desires to know whether he shall go here or there, he turns inward for guidance to the inner voice—supposed to be the 'voice of God'—the answer 'Yes' being by a movement of his head, caused by the spirit in possession, or 'No' by no action at all; evil spirits making use of the body of the man in the same way as they reply to those who consult them through a 'planchette' in other cases" (142–43). Penn-Lewis's link between spirit-guidance and the Ouija is perceptive and looks ahead to the later fallacy found among some therapists of Multiple Personality Disorder, of using semiautomatic finger motions to "recover" memories of ritual abuse.

But Penn-Lewis boldly extended this argument to critique even the orthodox Christian arguments that were used to critique the Welsh Revival. Even her own church, she argues, was penetrated and interpenetrated with "a vast realm of *doctrinal* deception by deceiving spirits . . . by which evil spirits, in more or less degree, influence the lives even of Christian men, and bring them under their power" (16; emphasis hers). Satan fostered this deception, she alleged, by encouraging religious passivity, assuring believers that obstinate reliance on doctrinal tradition would somehow protect believers from error.

In fact, active reexamination of every belief was necessary: "God does not do anything instead of a man, but by the man's co-operation with Him; neither does He undertake to make up for a man's ignorance, when He has provided knowledge for him which will prevent him being deceived" (49). Elsewhere, she stresses that "The powers of darkness would make man a machine, a tool, an automaton. Therefore God never says to any faculty of man, 'Be thou idle' . . . Believers who surrender their wills, and all they have and are to God, yet who WALK BY THE USE OF THEIR NATURAL MINDS, are not the ones who are open to the 'passivity' which gives ground to evil spirits" (70–71).

So, actively defying the patriarchal power structure of mainstream Christianity was conforming with God's wish to cooperate with human beings' thirst for knowledge, while submission to the received traditions of mainstream Christianity was a diabolical trick to make unthinking robots out of believers. This, ironically, was based on an inversion of one of spiritualism's key tenets, the subversive use of passivity. "Although it was thought to guarantee weakness and submissiveness in the female sex," Alex Owen observes, "passivity was the key concept in a spiritualist understanding of the mechanics of spirit possession. Believers acknowledged it to be an innate element of the female make-up, but . . . validated it as a powerful and facilitating quality" (1990: 209). Penn-Lewis, as might be expected, powerfully denounced spiritualism and the mental passivity that it advocated. But by so doing, she demonstrated that the only valid stance for the religious-minded woman was to cultivate intellectual strength and aggressively question the status quo.

Spiritualism, as we have seen, frequently allowed females under the control of other personalities to use obscene language and adopt behavior unthinkable within normal social conventions. In a parallel fashion, Penn-Lewis's description of demon encounters is developed in openly erotic terms:

> The counterfeit presence of God is given by deceiving spirits working upon the physical frame, or within the bodily frame,

upon the senses. . . . It is deepened by these sense-manifestations being repeated, so gently, that the man goes on yielding to them, thinking this is truly "communion with God" . . . as the believer responds to, or gives himself up to these "conscious" manifestations, he does not know that his WILL-POWER IS BEING SLOWLY UNDERMINED. At last through these subtle, delicious experiences, the faith is established that God Himself is CONSCIOUSLY IN POSSESSION OF THE BODY, quickening it with felt thrills of life, or filling it with warmth and heat. . . . From this point the lying spirits can work as they will, and there is no limit as to what they may do to a believer deceived to this extent. (130–31)

The pronoun references ("the man," "he") are masculine, following conventions of the day, but Penn-Lewis's description suggests not only Evan Roberts's repeated ecstatic communions with God but her own much-desired ecstatic baptism in the spirit. The orthodox position implied that such spirit baptisms themselves were signs of mental instability; Penn-Lewis counters that they are in fact not only genuine but indications of *"the believer's highest experience of union with the Lord,* and . . . the 'high places' of the spiritual maturity of the Church" (13; emphasis hers). The baptism of the Holy Spirit, she affirms, is an ineffable and genuinely motivating event for Christians like herself. It is a mistake, however, to assume that such an experience immediately and permanently banishes all demons that might afflict believers. Indeed, the genuinely supernatural nature of such experience identifies the believer as especially dangerous in Satan's eyes and therefore an immediate target for demonic attack.

More importantly, she seems to have found in such analysis an opportunity to express her own ambivalence about her mission in a male-dominated realm. Several times she notes that the satanic counterfeit can sometimes appear in the form of the deity to which the believer is most attached. Since Penn-Lewis was committed to the dominant role of Jesus in her faith, it is significant that she warns her readers about demonically inspired "visions of Jesus" as "Bridegroom" to those who "crave love" (e.g., 106). Even in the ecstasy of the divine encounter, discernment was necessary. Otherwise, spirit baptism becomes nothing less than a form of psychic rape similar to those frequently reported by female practitioners of automatic writing and the Ouija board. Thus, on the surface, she appears to be renouncing the ecstatic baptism in the spirit as demon-inspired, but the intensity of such supernatural encounters in fact validates the charismatic original that Satan counterfeits. The possibility of demonic rape, in other words, demonstrates the reality and importance of intercourse with the Holy Spirit. The main difference, in yet another paradox, is that demonic "baptism" asks women to submit passively to patriarchal possession. Genuinely divine spirit baptism empowers the true female Christian, like the Ouija board users and the psychic discussed in the previous chapter, to talk back to the spirit, in the full "USE OF THE NATURAL MIND," and by so doing effectively challenge the patriarchal status quo.

Conclusions

In different ways, Stead's and Penn-Lewis's works inspired by the Welsh Revival proved influential in the modern deliverance ministry. Stead's emphasis on the supernatural elements of the revival attracted audiences interested in the occult. This ensured that the movement, although nominally Christian, in fact appropriated the grassroots, small-group dynamics of spiritualist circles, as well as their emphasis on dramatic, visible "signs of the spirit." His account of the affair was widely circulated in pamphlet form and in fact translated into German as *Die Erweckung in Wales.* There it influenced the youth ministry movements in which Kurt E. Koch, one of the most prolific of antisatanism crusaders, was later to rise to prominence (see Scharpff 1966).

Penn-Lewis, for her part, founded a journal called *The Overcomer,* devoted to completing the work begun in *War on the Saints* of exposing the psychic excesses begun during the revival. Even as World War I disrupted religious networks, she noted that the book was able to inspire informal networks devoted to deliverance throughout France and Switzerland, where one correspondent was "able to form prayer groups to pray against the forces of darkness" (Garrard 1947: 259). These prayer groups formed yet another influence on the movement that Koch was able to mobilize later in the century.

Though Penn-Lewis mentioned glossolalia and other practices resembling spirit possession as "satanic counterfeits," *War on the Saints* proved invaluable to crusaders inside the emerging Pentecostal movement. Her arguments for the ubiquity of demonic possession and analysis of its diagnostic signs created models for later generations of "spiritual warfare" manuals. Yet the value of the book's demonological sections was muted by what even her followers considered as theological errors. Hence even the "official" edition of her book was by the 1960s available only in a heavily abridged edition. At least one of her modern advocates objected to this editing, saying that it "emasculated" her argument by eliminating "the main thrust of her vital book" (1973: vii).

Such controversy confirms the central place the Welsh Revival commands in early twentieth-century demonology. Its main appeal stemmed from the appropriation and use of spiritualist and folk beliefs, as we can see from W.T. Stead's fascination with the affair and the attention Mary Jones's "stars and lights" received from occultists and paranormal investigators. The enormous but short-lived success of Evan Roberts drew partly from his successful use of séance-type tactics to produce religious experiences. But his willingness to empower women was seen in his use of sentimental themes in meetings and his incorporation of women in important roles in his ministry. His long "convalescence" under the care of the feminist evangelist Jessie Penn-Lewis was perhaps providential: otherwise, the intensity of his ministry and his lack of writing skills meant his public life probably would have been as brief as Mary Jones's.

Thus *War on the Saints* capped and encapsulated the lessons of the Welsh Revival in a way that infused them into a multitude of prayer-group conduits in Europe and in North America. Defining traditional Christianity as contaminated by demonic doctrines, it gave charismatics, and especially charismatic women, instructions on how to wage war on Satan by subverting establishment religion and treating a wide variety of mental illnesses through Christian counseling. The Welsh Revival stressed direct contact with spirits and supernatural occurrences, and created a mechanism for encouraging religious experience. While Jessie Penn-Lewis critiqued this mechanism, it was successful enough to motivate the long-lasting networks of prayer groups that became the cornerstones of the modern deliverance ministry.

Chapter Ten

Learning from Lucifer

What do we learn from this survey of grassroots occultism?

First, we see that magical practices are far more common and pervasive than might initially be suspected, and many of them, like the rabbit's foot practice or chain letters, are in fact so common that even folklorists ignore their roots in conjure or cabalism. Indeed, many of the practices in the antioccult movement are themselves entangled with "Satan's counterfeit," the magical and spiritualist practices in which they are historically rooted.

Second, such practices commonly are vehicles for protest against existing adult or institutional social structures. As such, they are especially attractive to adolescents who are going through the process of internalizing these structures. Teens are not drawn to satanism by opportunistic "recruiters" or even by the media, but find in occult or "satanic" practices a useful frame for deviant play, in which they can temporarily redefine their activities as an "antiworld" in which adult norms can be defied and mocked in the form of supernatural "witches" and other bogeymen. By calling such activities "play," I do not mean to trivialize their importance, as they may often engross participants to the extent that serious crimes such as grave-robbing may result. Further, the supernaturalism of the Welsh Revival gave impetus to new religious movements within Christianity, which to this day use the miraculous nature of the gifts they practice as ground for rejecting the doctrinal orthodoxy of mainstream denominations.

Third, we see that witchcraft often reflects a desire to return to an "original" state of religion, as seen both in the growth of secret or occult societies allegedly preserving ancient wisdom, and also in the growing interest of evangelical Christianity in "gifts of the spirit" exercised in the early days of the Church. Paradoxically, the growth of such movements functions synergistically: religious movements providing models for

223

"antiworld" folk rituals of rebellion such as legend-trips, dumb suppers, and mirror rituals, which in turn incites the mainstream to demonize these traditions, while alternative religious movements appropriate the strategies of folklore to broaden their appeal to seekers dissatisfied with orthodox religion. The result is an increased emphasis on supernatural phenomena, and, consequently, a greater interest in incorporating them into religious mythologies. Thus, while we affirm that witches and satanists have existed over a long period of time, we need not presume any underground conduit for their activities when those activities and strategies have been repeatedly revived and publicized in detail by those who decry them, even as they appropriate such strategies for their own purposes.

Lucifer, the bearer of light, was, as Albert Pike suggested, not at all a principle of evil opposing religion but rather an essential part of the "Universal Equilibrium": ultimately, every experience is the work of God's wisdom and love, and so "there is no rebellious demon of Evil, or Principle of Darkness co-existent and in eternal controversy with God." The two principles are not antagonists, no more than the Earth's centrifugal force is an "enemy" of the Sun's gravitational pull. Both are, in Pike's illuminated view, part of the plan of the Eternal Architect of the Universe, and the result is not strife but harmony and mathematical accuracy (1947: 859–60). We could therefore propose that religion and the occult form a "Luciferian dialectic" in that the theological impulse creates an equal and opposite mythological force, and vice versa; the two counterbalance and ultimately harmonize. The occult, by showing that individuals can participate in myth, challenges the conservative social standards and dictates of religion. In a Luciferian way, the occult thus forces religion to come to terms with the totality of human experience, at times checking or repressing it, at others times finding ways to incorporate it into its own practices. And religion, in turn, provides a stable ground and safe destination for those wishing to experiment with alternative points of view, even alternative states of consciousness.

We see the Luciferian dialectic clearly in the way in which evangelical movements seem to develop synergistically with the outbreak of supernatural phenomena. The Welsh Revival, as we have seen, brought news of many supernatural experiences, as did subsequent revivals. During a subsequent Canadian revival, the same phenomenon was noted by antioccult crusader Kurt E. Koch. A Mennonite minister from British Columbia brought an interesting story to Koch's attention, and he found it so impressive that he repeated it in several of his antioccult books. It had happened, the minister said, to the eleven-year-old son of a friend of his (note the FOAF frame). During a break at school, the boy observed a group of children playing with a Ouija board. The users were demanding to know who gave the board its power, and the planchette told them first "Hitler," then "Lucifer," and finally (since the children were obviously not satisfied by these replies) "Satan." "At this moment," the minister said, the eleven year old, "whose parents had been affected by the revival," stepped up and cursed the board in Jesus' name. "What do you think happened?" he later told his parents. "The game suddenly stopped. The board would not work anymore." "But that was not the only thing," the child added. "After it had happened, another boy told me, 'If there is so much power in the name of Jesus, I will start coming to Sunday School in the Church. I want to hear more about this Jesus.'"[1] "All these events prove that the Light is driving out the darkness," Koch concluded (1973b: 49–50; cf. 1973c: 157–58 and 1978: 153), adding that similar experiences always come to light during evangelical revivals:

> In times of great visitation by God the inward structure of man is open both for good and evil influences. Times of revival reveal the nearness of the Holy Spirit, and at the same time the presence of demonic powers. That is why at such times of divine blessing many supernatural events occur. . . . The unseen world is always interlocked with the world we see, even if in our spiritual blindness we cannot see it or do not want to know about it. At times of revival, when God creates strong points of contact between the natural and supernatural worlds, many individual examples illuminate the close connection between the unseen and the seen. (1973b: 82–83)

A folklorist would view such stories differently: the Ouija board story looks like a foreshortened account of a typical "confrontation" narrative, which teens and preteens would pass around as a "good trip." Satan was successfully summoned, played with, and then rebuked and banished. We note also that the Canadian revival also gave Koch his story of a spiritual attack by a "black figure," already discussed in chapter 2 as an "old hag" paralysis attack. Both are relatively common experiences, but rarely reported outside the folk culture of individual communities. As with the supernatural experiences reported during the Welsh Revival, it is unlikely that either experience would have been narrated outside of the revival context, much less committed to print.

Revivalist movements likely do not *produce* cycles of supernatural or demonic phenomena, but they do provide ready opportunities in group meetings for people to describe their experiences and fit them into a shared mythology. Hence, large numbers of previously unshared odd phenomena enter into oral discourse and, often, print media, as they are distributed by media-enhanced conduits or by critics of the revival. They *appear* to have been caused by the revival; indeed, those who record them often assert that they were so caused. But, in fact, the revival may only have caused them to be recounted and recorded in larger numbers than would otherwise have been possible.

In essence, events like the Welsh Revival broadened the cultural language available to evangelical Christianity, so that it could incorporate beliefs and practices that otherwise would fall into the gray areas of legend, fetish, and subversion myth. Such revivals, because they held that supernatural power was directly at work, implicitly subverted existing religious institutions, allowing factions that had previously been blocked from leadership to control religious events. If the witch-hunts were a "war against women," then events such as the Welsh Revival allowed intelligent, incisive women such as Penn-Lewis a chance to even the conflict by taking the high ground. Her work in constructing a theology based on Roberts's spiritual experiences allowed her to critique the power of male-dominant Christian institutions as a "war by Satan upon the womenhood of the world."

She was thus able to encompass within a nominally orthodox theology supernatural phenomena that had previously belonged to witchcraft and occult play. Her descriptions of quasi-sexual experiences with supernatural beings recall both the old claim that witches copulated with the devil, and Vance Randolph's enigmatic comment that Ozark witches gave their bodies to "the devil's representative," which "women who claim to have experienced both" call "a much more moving spiritual crisis than that which the Christians call conversion." In an earlier time, she might well have been accused of being a witch, having unlawful knowledge of the occult, showing insubordination to her spiritual mentors, and in general displaying one of those "exulcerated mindes" that, as Rev. Roberts said in 1616, seek a diabolical "meanes by which they may bring to passe that rancor which was nourished in their breasts." However, in the early decades of the twentieth century, with orthodox religion on the defensive, Penn-Lewis was able to expand Christianity to include elements of witchcraft, and by so doing advance the role of women within contemporary revival movements.

This advance came at a price, however. When her demonology emerged among charismatic sects later in the century, it had become, as I have shown, a "diabolical medicine" practiced (like witch-mastering) overwhelmingly by male therapists on passive female patients. Again, those who were exorcised or otherwise treated for ritual abuse were not typically feminists, Wiccans, or dabblers in the occult, and the content of SRA stories did reflect a modern critique of child abuse and wife-battering. Still, the late-twentieth-century use of demonology differed from Penn-Lewis's theological worldview in an important respect. She believed that demons afflict believers through their own intellectual errors, and she strongly argued that the female Christian mind must be well educated, flexible, and ready to question everything. The tradition of witchcraft holds that demonization is caused by the malice or unconfessed sin of others. Historically, witch-finders and antioccult crusaders have put unusual stress on witches' ability to afflict small children with malefic spells. In short, Penn-Lewis's demonology soon was compromised. Even the trustees of the Overcomer Literature Trust, an antioccult organization she founded, saw fit to reissue her book in an abridged version, since "First and foremost they felt that they could not endorse the teaching that a born-again, Spirit-filled Christian can at the same time be demon possessed" (1993: 9). If Pentecostal Christians could be assumed free from demonic influence, then the evils blamed on Satan could be projected onto cultural Others who did Satan's bidding on Earth.

Still, Penn-Lewis's argument for the ubiquity of demonic influences became a mythological principle that proved useful to many Christian thinkers, chief among them the authors C.S. Lewis and J.R.R. Tolkien. In *Raising the Devil*, we noted that both had access to the magical ideas generated by the turn-of-the-century occult group the Order of the Golden Dawn, through their mutual friend Charles Williams, a one-time apprentice to A.E. Waite. Lewis made use of Penn-Lewis's concept of demonization in his *Screwtape Letters*, an influential satire that purported to be advice from one demon to another on how to secretly influence the behavior of a young Christian. While Tolkien did not use this concept directly, the obsessing influence of the One Ring in his *Lord of the Rings* trilogy has much in common with Penn-Lewis's demonology. In her turn, J.K. Rowling repeatedly uses demonic obsession as a motif in the *Harry*

Potter books, most visibly in the ways in which the satanic antagonist Voldemort takes over first Professor Quirrell, then Ginny Weasley, in order to try to reincarnate himself and seize control of the magical community.

And so we return to the flap created when *The Onion* announced, facetiously, that ten million children had been converted to satanism by the *Harry Potter* books. One Christian observer commented, "If you are guided by the Holy Spirit—and not blinded by superstitious fear—how can you fail to discern that *The Onion*'s article is a spoof?" (Satire Mistaken for Truth 2000). Jessie Penn-Lewis would have been unrelenting in her critique of this flap, calling those who circulated it self-deceived and passive confederates of the devil, for all their protestations of godliness. "Truth of every kind makes free," she begins the first chapter of *War on the Saints,* "while lies bind up in bonds. Ignorance also binds up, because it gives ground to Satan. Man's ignorance is a primary and essential condition for deception by evil spirits."

Any discussion of how Rowling's fictional magic relates to real-life traditions of the occult, and hence to Christianity, is thus terminated, because, from the inflexible fundamentalist point of view, only one answer is available: "The very creation of Harry openly blasphemes God, and promotes the practice of sorcery, seeking revenge upon anyone who upsets them by carrying out rituals, performing spells, and exercising demonic powers" (Wright 2003). Between God and the demonic world, no dialogue seems possible. J.K. Rowling showed similar dissatisfaction with the way in which her critics really seem unwilling to discuss matters of faith. In an interview with the *Vancouver Sun,* she reiterated her belief in God, but added that her profession of faith "seems to offend the religious right far worse than if I said I thought there was no God. Every time I've been asked if I believe in God, I've said yes, because I do, but no one ever really has gone any more deeply into it than that . . ." (Grace 2002).

But it is never as simple as that, even inside the world of the *Harry Potter* books, which repeatedly show that what appears to be sure knowledge of right and wrong in fact is ambiguous. By going outside the strict rules of magic, Harry learns, in a Luciferian way, that received wisdom, however well founded, must always be balanced and harmonized with ongoing experience. "Harry frightens only those who want the answers to be the same every time the question is asked," children's literature critic Amanda Cockrell concludes. Still, such a realm demands an active mind, one prepared to see that being willing to learn more about traditions that challenge one's religion does not necessarily mean that one's faith is weak. Using Pike's analogy, we could concede that relying on supernatural experience alone leaves one without a focus, like a planet detached from its orbit around the sun and left spinning randomly into space. But, by the same token, passive reliance on standard religious tenets alone dooms one to terminal passivity, like the same planet plunging directly into a black hole from which it cannot escape.

The Luciferian dialectic suggests that it is no accident that the occult and religion perpetually attract each other, but without either ever absorbing or destroying the other. As a common bumper sticker notes, religion tries to become a magic device for turning unanswerable questions into unquestionable answers. Magic, we could say, makes the process reciprocal, questioning what religion tries to make unquestionable and proposing a wider range of answers to the unanswerable.

Notes

Acknowledgments

1. Some of the material in this book appeared in tentative form in the following articles and is reprinted with permission: "Speak to the Devil: Ouija Board Rituals among American Adolescents," *Contemporary Legend* 4 (1994): 61–90; and "Why Is a Lucky Rabbit's Foot Lucky? Body Parts as Fetishes," *Journal of Folklore Research* 39 (2002): 51–84. Indiana University Press, publisher.

Chapter 1. Wizards vs. Muggles: A Long-Standing Debate

1. An odd detail, as noted by *BreakTheChain.org*'s reporter Astor: why is Cerberus, a figure from Greek mythology, being identified as a "demon" in an alleged satanic rite? This detail is perhaps explained by the debut of the Japanese anime series *Cardcaptors* on American television in July 2000. This series centers on a third-grade girl who discovers that she has magical powers when she opens a magic book she finds in her father's library. She is tutored by the book's "gatekeeper beast," a flying teddy-bear-like creature named Cerberus (or Kero-chan for short). The series, based on Shinto religious beliefs that do not include the good/evil struggle central to Christianity, never attained mass popularity in the United States, unlike its competitor *Pokemon*. It did create a brief flap in January 2002, when Taco Bell proposed to give out replicas of the magic cards used in the episodes in kids' meals, to promote the series. This promotion was quickly squelched when the Christian organization American Family Association complained that it implicitly encouraged children to dabble with *tarot* cards. A spokesperson called the cards an attempt to exploit "the 'Harry Potter' craze of black magic" and warned parents that "[The tarot card promotion] is part of an occult [*sic*] because these cards teach kids that they can predict [their own] future . . . simply by turning over a playing card . . . This is very dangerous, especially when you look at the occult [and] the controversy that Harry Potter brings with magical spells and sorcery." See Pugh 2002.

2. The United Religions Charter, a project of William E. Swing, Episcopal Bishop of California, was signed on 26 June 2000, a date designed to coincide with the fiftieth anniversary of the signing of the United Nations Charter. The "United Religions" project, intended to create an interfaith forum to comment on social problems and work toward faith, was, like the United Nations, widely seen by fundamentalists as a "One-World" project intended to facilitate the coming of Antichrist.

Chapter 2. What Were Witches Really Like?

1. For more on this idea, see Ellis 2000: 4–5.

2. See the essays collected in Ellis 2001, particularly those in the section headed "The Life of Legends" (3–92).

3. In his introduction to *Objects of Special Devotion: Fetishism in Popular Culture* (1982), Ray B. Browne compares fetishes to *icons,* objects that mainstream institutions agree are charged with sacred power and which often express the same power, strength, and social rationale. But because fetishes lack respectability, Browne argues, they find their place in a shadowy world, out of the public's eye. Even though they may express a culture's core values in an especially direct way, he concludes, "They are to icons as devil worship is to religious practice" (1982: 1).

4. For folklorists' collections of this story type, see Baughman 1966: Motifs D2083.2.1, G271.4.1(i); Kittridge 1929: 103, 167, 485–486; Hand 1961–64: no. 7547; Goldberg 1974: 93–94.

5. See Baughman 1966: Motif D2083.3.1(h); Kittridge 1929: 163 ff., Goldberg 1974: 94.

6. See Baughman 1966: Motifs D655.2, G275.12; Kittridge 1929: 179; Hand 1961–64: no. 5592; Goldberg 1974: 89–93.

7. A Hazleton-area variation holds that if you could ever snatch the entity's hat (an impossibility, given the nature of the paralysis) you could make it "shit gold" and make you wealthy.

8. Charismatics H.A. Maxwell Whyte (1973b: 49) and Don Basham (1972: 49–50) likewise described similar attacks during their ministries.

9. Brooks cites Koch's *Between Christ and Satan* (1962) as a reference in her bibliography, so it is possible that she or her friend were recalling the case cited above.

10. For other modern examples of charming by the moon, see Hand 1961–64: no. 1550; Hyatt 1965: no. 5127; Townsend and Bird 1970; Townsend 1971.

11. Cf. the statement, commonly repeated by Wiccans, that "A witch who cannot hex cannot heal" (Budapest 1989: 43).

Chapter 3. Black Books and Chain Letters

1. What was it doing there? The legend doesn't explain. But a related Danish tradition about a grimoire titled *The Book of Cyprianus* says that, once obtained, the book cannot be destroyed, sold, or given away, unless one leaves it "in a secret place in the church, together with four shillings clerk's fee" (Thorpe 1851, 2:186–87). Another Scandinavian belief held that priests secretly possessed a "black book" of their own that they could use to bring supernatural punishments on those who disobeyed God's law (Stokker 1992).

2. As I showed in *Raising the Devil*, antioccult crusaders in the Pentecostal movement made a similar point about spiritualism and other forms of divination, which they saw as "Satanic counterfeits" of true gifts of the spirit. See Ellis 2000: 32 ff.

3. Augustine (*De Doctrina Christiana* 2:20) refers to a number of common types of folk belief as examples, including hiccup cures, precautions to be taken if something comes between two people walking, and omens of bad luck, such as stumbling when walking out the door on a journey.

4. In the Theodosian Code (438 CE), for example, a distinction is made between explicitly magickal practices, which deserved to be punished severely as sacrilegious, and "remedies . . . innocently employed in rural districts" which deserved no severe punishment, "since by such devices no person's safety or reputation is injured" (quoted in Pietz 1987: 32).

5. Because its practitioners frequently insisted that its teachings be transmitted only to a small elite, many of the major texts of the Qabbalah remain untranslated from Hebrew and are often unedited even in their original languages. The most authoritative survey of qabbalistic thought is in the *Encyclopedia Judaica* (Scholem 1971); briefer accounts are provided by Moshe Idel in *The Encyclopedia of Religion* (1987: 117–24) and by J.L. Blau in *The Encyclopedia of Philosophy* (1967, 2:1–3). To avoid confusion, I refer to the concepts of these authentic Jewish mystical movements as the Qabbalah and their proponents as qabbalists. The spurious or distorted occult versions circulated among Christian and communities thus are referred to as the Cabala and their proponents as cabalists.

6. Fogel explains, "The Bishop, to whom reference is made, was one of the Bishops of the Methodist Church, if I mistake not, who however refused to countenance or sanction the sending out of such a letter" (1908: 307).

7. A shorter version archived by Van Arsdale (1998) reads: "An Ancient Prayer/ Oh Lord I implore thee to bless all mankind. Keep us from all evil and take us to dwell with thee eternally. This prayer was sent to me. It is being sent all over the world. It was said in Jesus [*sic*] time that all who would write it and pass it on would be delivered from all calamities. Those who would not write it on would meet with some misfortune. Those who write it before nine days, stating the day received, to nine of their friends will on the ninth day receive some great joy. So do not break the chain."

8. Beginning in 1982, the dominant versions say he lost his *wife* (Van Arsdale 1998), and one parody version adds that breaking the chain made him so unlucky that he eventually got her back.

9. A similar insight is offered by a number of popular horror writers and movie makers. The famous British supernatural author Montague R. James based one of his best-known short stories, "The Casting of the Runes," on a similar idea: an occultist who dooms his enemies to death within a certain number of days by passing a slip of paper to them containing a mysterious inscription. The story concludes when the last of his attempted victims manages to return the slip to him without his noticing. Similarly, the Japanese horror movie *Ringu* ("The Ring," or, more accurately, "The Chain") (2000) is based on the premise of a mysterious video whose viewers mysteriously die a week after watching it. At the end of the movie, the protagonist realizes that the curse can be avoided by making a copy of the videotape and giving it to someone else (with the warning that he or she must likewise make a copy and pass it on within a week, and so on).

Chapter 4. Satanic Bibles

1. Charles V is remembered in occult history as one of the patrons of arch-mage Johannes Faust. However, this particular attribution must be fictitious, as Charles V was only one year old in 1520.

2. For the practice of removing warts with the help of a corpse, see Hyatt 1965: nos. 6598, 6607, 6609.

3. A similar incantation is given in the German American spell book *Albertus Magnus* under the heading, "For Cunning Thieves, may they be ever so sly. Pronounce this grace every morning three times, over all thy possessions, with devotion" (n.d.: 31). This version does not include the invocation of the devil, and it asks that the thief "stand still, like a stick, and see like a brick."

4. A similar ritual is given in *Albertus Magnus* under the heading *A particular Way to recover Stolen Goods* (n.d.: 37). It includes the rhyming caution, "The wheel, thou must not rapidly turn, or the soles of his feet may blister and burn, he will in pain and anguish cry, and ere you catch him, thus may die."

Chapter 5. Why Is a Lucky Rabbit's Foot Lucky?

1. In his *Discoverie of Witchcraft* (1584), Reginald Scot notes that using a horseshoe as a protection against witchcraft was "observed in manie countrie houses." Scot also observes that "children and some old fooles" were diligent in looking for "foure leaved grasse" (Opie and Tatem 1989: 88, 202). The custom of breaking a wishbone to gain a wish was recorded first in 1688 by antiquarian John Aubrey, who remarks that the custom then was "common" (Opie and Tatem 1989: 448).

2. Reginald Scot recorded in 1584 that people carried a hare's or rabbit's foot to ward off cramp or arthritis. But doing so as a charm or amulet was not recorded in British tradition until 1827, and even then it was mentioned rather specifically as a guard against witchcraft (Opie and Tatem 1989: 193–94). The modern custom apparently was introduced from the United States early in the twentieth century, as a correspondent to *Folk-Lore* observed in 1908 that rabbits' feet made in America were being commonly sold in England (Simpson and Roud 2000: 289). By 1932, a British observer noted that "it is astonishing to find it a common custom, not only among the ignorant but the cultured classes" (Opie and Tatem 1989: 194).

3. The following beliefs, from various folk belief collections, are summarized in a helpful way in the notes to Hand 1962–64: nos. 5796–802.

4. This was an inexpensive perfume readily available in drug stores at the time. See Hyatt 1970–74: 586–87.

5. Hyatt's unorthodox way of recording his informants' dialect, along with his use of underlining and other typographical peculiarities, have been preserved verbatim in quotes, although most folklorists now would avoid the use of "eye dialect" spellings like "whut" or "wus."

6. They note that many people misunderstood "gravestone rubbers" as "robbers" (1982: 139).

7. A ghoul is a person or creature that carries off human cadavers or body parts from graves.

8. See also 1970–74: 3304–8, nos.7549ff..

9. See Puckett 1926: 256–59; Hand 1962–64: nos. 5591–92, 5771, 5788; Hyatt 1970–74: 74–96 and passim.

10. Baughman 1966: motif G275.12 ff.

11. Carter 1925: 354–55; Chase 1943: 76–82; Long 1955: "Jack and the Sop Doll"; Painter 1994: 251–52; Smith 1998: 60–61, 124–26.

12. Other references to African American versions of this story include Cross 1909: 251–52; Parson 1917: 196; and Puckett 1926: 149.

13. Mail order firms such as Sears and Roebuck aggressively advertised their willingness to work up such items on commission, provided one sent in a quantity of a loved one's hair, plus a fee of $1.50 to $15.00, depending on the complexity of the item desired. Contemporary legends of the era held, as one might expect, that such firms regularly misplaced the authentic hair and sent back jewelry made from a stranger's hair—or, worse, from horsehair. An instruction manual published at the time stressed the advantage of learning to make such display items oneself at home, thus gaining "the inexpressible advantage and satisfaction of *knowing* that the material of their own handiwork is the actual hair of the 'loved and gone'" (Miller 1982: 103; emphasis added).

14. Also a common ingredient in African American folk magic: see Puckett 1926: 233 ff.; Hand 1962–64, nos. 5565 ff.

15. Surveys of these warnings include Victor 1993: 66–67; Hicks 1991: 283–85; Raschke 1990: 73–74; Johnson 1989: 290; and *The D.I.O.S. Informant* 2: (July-August 1991):3.

16. See also nos. 8019–22; nos. 8030 ff. discuss reducing such bones to powder, thus creating a substance that, like graveyard dust, could be used to cause illness.

17. I Samuel 18:25–27.

Chapter 6. Visits to Forbidden Graveyards

1. "'Ghost' Scares Teenagers," *Tonbridge* [Kent] *Free Press* (29 November 1963): 3.

2. Photographs and information on these crop circles were widely distributed through the British crop circle conduit and posted on a number of Internet sites, among them the *Cambridge (UK): Crop Circle web site* <http://www.cam.net.uk/home/Nimmann/events/cropcircles.htm>.

3. We recall from chapter 4 that Saint Cyprian lent his name to the most commonly circulated *grimoire* in Scandinavian countries.

4. This is in itself a very old belief: a common legend holds that Swithun, Bishop of Winchester (d. 862), modestly asked to be buried in the churchyard outside the cathedral where he presided. In local eyes, he attained the status of a saint (though this designation was never confirmed by Rome), and so, on 15 July 971, his grave was opened against his wishes and his bones moved to an impressive shrine inside the building. Tradition holds that the bishop's offended

spirit caused a violent storm to break out, either then or on an anniversary of this date. Certainly, St. Swithun's Day became a date commonly associated with rain in British folklore. See Opie and Tatem 1989: 337–38 and Simpson and Roud 2000: 312.

5. The British tradition inspired a scene in the award-winning film *Chariots of Fire*, though for cinematic reasons the contest was held at noon rather than at midnight.

6. Dorson incorrectly calls the building "Havoline Hall"; for information correcting and explicating Dorson's 1959 reference, I am indebted to Michael Shapiro of the Network Information eXchange (NIX), San Diego, California.

7. "'Ghost' Scares Teenagers," *op. cit.*

8. A number of witches did come from this area, but none were burned or buried with stakes through their hearts. Such details probably leaked over from post-*Dracula* vampire-hunting traditions.

9. The widely available Avon paperback prints ". . . one that is *not* in vogue to parody." In response to a query, LaVey confirmed "*now* in vogue" as the correct reading. It is a telling comment on the book's alleged influence on American culture that no one had previously pointed out this typo.

Chapter 7. Table-Setting and Mirror-Gazing

1. Parler Arkansas Collection, No. 7144. UCLA Folklore Collections, Los Angeles, California.

2. Julio Caro Baroja, *The World of the Witches*, trans. O.N.V. Glendinning (Chicago: University of Chicago Press), 64. Baroja cites a 1746 Paris tract as his immediate source but also notes that it was widely attested to (in *The Golden Legend*, among other common collections of saints' legends).

3. Interestingly, when the same girl was later interviewed in a group, she gave a different account of this vision, saying that the face of "Mary Whales" was "how a semi-trailer smashes you!" but admitting that she got no results the first time she tried the ritual alone. Laughing nervously, she said the second time "I kept looking and I think maybe my imagination went wild 'cause [Laughing.] she was looking at me right back and she wasn't doing nothing. She was sitting up there looking at me and I looked at her. [Laughing.] So then I got scared and clicked on the lights!" (Langlois 1980: 216).

4. This, however, does not explain why the ritual is predominantly practiced by males in Europe. A close comparison of the two traditions remains to be done.

5. The movie *Candyman* (1993) makes this point explicitly by focusing on a female graduate student who is victimized by her pompous and unfaithful husband. After she dies, her husband inadvertently calls out her name four times in the bathroom, and so allows her to appear as a "witch in the mirror" who wreaks a bloody revenge. When I saw this movie, the audience delightedly urged the husband to "say it one more time," and cheered the revenant when she appeared.

Chapter 8. The @#$%&! Ouija Board

1. My sister was introduced to table-tapping in the 1960s by Navy wives in rural Maryland, and two recent archive reports show that it remained a popular party entertainment in rural Ohio into the 1980s. One informant from Findlay recalls learning the technique in the military, and the collection describes a séance that he and friends conducted in Lima on Halloween 1974 (OSUFA, Burden 1976). Another teen likewise described table-tapping as a popular adolescent party game in rural towns near Marion (OSUFA, Wakeley 1982).

2. The ritual evidently included a form of improvised Ouija board. In Europe, a tumbler or shot glass is often used in place of a planchette.

3. The informant confuses the British occultist Aleister Crowley (often characterized by crusaders as a satanist) with Anton LaVey, founder and head of the Church of Satan.

4. The chain letter reprinted nearly the entire passage, only replacing "cock" with "****." Other accounts likewise gave enough of the passage to let readers guess at the obscenity mentioned. Pastor Porter (2000), for instance, quoted nearly the entire passage, replacing "the greasy cock" with "@#$%," while Pastor Meyer (2000b), warning the reader that he cannot "print every word because it is disgustingly filthy," bowdlerized more fully to "will ____ the _____ ____ of the Dark Lord." Interestingly, this way of censoring the passage makes the passage potentially obscene in other ways. Coming across this version before I traced the original, I assumed the blanks stood for "kiss the sweet ass of the Dark Lord," following a practice mentioned frequently in witch trial records of witches' sabbats.

5. As we saw in *Raising the Devil* (2000), this spiritualist-influenced approach to psychological therapy was the basis for much of "satanic ritual abuse" therapy, which likewise explained adult problems in terms of unremembered childhood traumas.

6. Here and in the transcript, the real first name of the Ouija board user has been altered at her request.

7. Presumably improvised by the informant. "Fuck you" in French is "vas te faire enculé."

Chatper 9. The Welsh Revival

1. For contemporary observations of this phenomenon, see Watson 1991: 156–57 and the e-mailed personal experience stories archived at Weird Science Page (2002). Self-identified psychics and UFO contactees have often mentioned to me that a battery-operated wristwatch would always malfunction when they wore it next to their skin.

Chapter 10. Learning from Lucifer

1. It is worth noting that the comments of "Ashley Daniels" in *The Onion*'s satire on the anti–*Harry Potter* crusade are an obvious parody of this kind of homiletic story: "I used to believe in what they taught us at Sunday School . . .

But the *Harry Potter* books showed me that magic is real, something I can learn and use right now, and that the Bible is nothing but boring lies" (*Harry Potter Books Spark Rise in Satanism* 2000).

Sources Cited

Abrahams, Roger. 1970. *Deep Down in the Jungle: Negro Narrative Folklore from the Streets of Philadelphia.* Chicago: Aldine.

Addy, Sidney Oldall. 1973 [1895]. *Folk Tales and Superstitions.* Totowa, N.J.: Rowman and Littlefield.

Albertus Magnus; or, Egyptian Secrets. N.d. N.p. [Probably ca. 1916, Chicago: The de Laurence Company].

Ankarloo, Bengt, and Gustav Henningsen, eds. 1990. *Early Modern European Witchcraft: Centres and Peripheries.* Oxford: Clarendon Press.

Astor. 2000. Harry Potter: Good Reading, or the Work of Satan? *Break TheChain.org.* October 6, 2000. Available: http://www.breakthechain. org/ exclusives/harrypotter.html

Baker, Ronald L. 1988. Ritualized Violence and Local Journalism in the Development of a Lynching Legend. *Fabula* 29:317–25.

Baroja, Julio Caro. 1965 [1961]. *The World of the Witches.* Trans. O. N. V. Glendinning. Chicago: University of Chicago Press.

Barstow, Anne Llewellyn. 1994. *Witchcraze: A New History of the European Witch Hunts.* San Francisco: Pandora.

Basham, Don W. 1972. *Deliver Us from Evil.* Washington Depot, Conn.: Chosen Books.

Basham, Don W., and Dick Leggatt. 1974. *The Most Dangerous Game: A Biblical Exposé of Occultism.* Greensburg, Penn.: Manna Christian Outreach.

Bastien, Joseph William. 1982. Good Luck Fetishes: Andean Amulets. In Browne, ed. 1982: 352–61.

Baughman, Ernest W. 1966. *Type and Motif-Index of the Folktales of England and North America.* The Hague: Mouton.

Bennett, Gillian. 2003. "Saint" William of Norwich: A Medieval English Ritual Murder Accusation, Its Creation and Aftermath. Paper presented at the Rockefeller Foundation Conference on the Social Consequences of Rumor and Legend, Bellagio, Italy, April 2003.

Billson, Charles J. 1895. *Folk-Lore of Leicestershire and Rutland.* London: Folk-Lore Society.

Blake, William. 1970. *The Poetry and Prose of William Blake.* David V. Erdman, ed. Revised Edition. Garden City, N.Y.: Doubleday.

Blau, J. L. 1967. Cabala. In *The Encyclopedia of Philosophy,* 2:1–3. N.Y.: Macmillan.

Bord, Janet and Colin. 1972. *Mysterious Britain: Ancient Secrets of the United Kingdom and Ireland.* London: Grafton Books.

———. 1978. *The Secret Country: More Mysterious Britain.* London: Grenada.

———. 1986. *Sacred Waters: Holy Wells and Water Lore in Britain and Ireland.* London: Grafton Books.

Boyer, Paul, and Stephen Nissenbaum. 1974. *Salem Possessed: The Social Origins of Witchcraft.* Cambridge: Harvard University Press.

Briggs, Katharine. 1971. *A Dictionary of British Folk-Tales.* Bloomington: Indiana University Press.

Bronner, Simon. 1988. *American Children's Folklore: Annotated Edition.* Little Rock, Ark.: August House.

———. 1990. *Piled Higher and Deeper: The Folklore of Campus Life.* Little Rock, Ark.: August House.

Brooks, Pat. 1972. *Out! In the Name of Jesus.* Carol Stream, Ill.: Creation House.

———. 1978. *Healing of the Mind.* Fletcher, N.C.: New Puritan Library.

Browne, Ray B., ed. 1982. *Objects of Special Devotion: Fetishism in Popular Culture.* Bowling Green, Ohio: Bowling Green University Popular Press.

Brunvand, Jan Harold. 1981. *The Vanishing Hitchhiker: American Urban Legends and Their Meanings.* New York: Norton.

Bruton, Hoyle S. 1948. Miscellaneous Beliefs and Home Remedies. *North Carolina Folklore* 1:20–26.

Budapest, Zsuzsuanna. 1989. *The Holy Book of Women's Mysteries.* Berkeley, Calif.: Wingbow Press.

Budge, E. A. Wallace. 1978 [1930]. *Amulets and Superstitions.* New York: Dover Publications.

Buffy Draws Children to Witchcraft. 2000. *BBC News.* August 4, 2000. Available: http://news.bbc.co.uk/1/hi/entertainment/864984.stm

Buhler, Rich. 2000. Email Chain Letter Brands Harry Potter Series an "Encyclopedia of Satanism." *Urban Myths.* 14 September 2000. Available: http://ship-of-fools.com/Myths/HarryPotter.html

Burl, Aubrey. 1976. *The Stone Circles of the British Isles.* New Haven: Yale University Press.

———. 1985. *Megalithic Brittany: A Guide to Over 350 Ancient Sites and Monuments.* London: Thames and Hudson.

Carey, George. 1971. *A Faraway Time and Place: Lore of the Eastern Shore.* Washington D.C.: R. B. Luce.

Carter, Isabel Gordon. 1925. Mountain White Folklore: Tales from the Southern Blue Ridge. *Journal of American Folklore* 38:340–74.

Cavendish, Richard, ed. 1974. *Encyclopedia of the Unexplained: Magic, Occultism and Parapsychology.* New York: McGraw-Hill.

Chai, Danny. 2000. Short Thoughts: October–December 2000 [on-line journal]. November 14, 2000. Available: http://www.dannychai.com/short/short3.html

Chase, Richard. 1943. *The Jack Tales.* Boston: Houghton Mifflin.

Child, Francis James. 1965 [1882–98]. *The English and Scottish Popular Ballads.* New York : Dover Publications.

Clark, Jerome. 1998. *The UFO Encyclopedia,* 2nd ed. Detroit: Omnigraphics, Inc.

Clements, William M., and William E. Lightfoot. 1972. The Legend of Stepp Cemetery. *Indiana Folklore* 5:92–141.

Cockrell, Amanda. 2002. Harry Potter and the Witch Hunters: A Social Context for the Attacks on *Harry Potter*. Paper presented at the Children's Literature Association Conference, Kingston, Penn., June 2002.

Cohn, Norman. 1975. *Europe's Inner Demons: An Enquiry Inspired by the Great Witch-Hunt*. N.Y.: New American Library.

Connell, Evan S. 1984. *Son of the Morning Star: Custer and the Little Bighorn*. San Francisco: North Point Press.

Cooper, St. John. 1944. The Witch Walks at Scrapfaggot Green! *Sunday Pictorial* (8 October): 11.

Copper, Arnold, and Coralee Leon. 1976. *Psychic Summer*. New York: Dial Press.

Covina, Gina. 1979. *The Ouija Book*. New York: Simon and Schuster.

Crawford, W. J. 1918. *Hints and Observations for Those Investigating the Phenomenon of Spiritualism*. New York: E. P. Dutton.

Crosby, Rev. John R. 1927. Modern Witches of Pennsylvania. *Journal of American Folklore* 40:304–9.

Cross, Tom Peete. 1909. Folk-Lore from the Southern States. *Journal of American Folklore* 22: 251–55.

Cruz, Nicky. 1973. *Satan on the Loose*. Old Tappan, N.J.: Fleming H. Revell.

Davies, Owen. 1998. Charmers and Charming in England and Wales from the Eighteenth to the Twentieth Century. *Folklore* 109:41–53. Available: http://www.findarticles.com/cf_0/m2386/v109/21250630/print.jhtml

Day, John F. 1941. *Bloody Ground*. New York: Doubleday, Doran and Co.

Dégh, Linda. 1971. The "Belief Legend" in Modern Society: Form, Function and Relationship to Other Genres. In *American Folk Legend: A Symposium*, Wayland Hand, ed., 55–68. Berkeley: University of California Press.

———, ed. 1980. *Indiana Folklore: A Reader*. Bloomington: Indiana University Press.

Dieffenbach, Victor C. 1976. Powwowing among the Pennsylvania Germans. *Pennsylvania Folklife* 25 (2): 29–46.

Dorson, Richard M. 1959. *American Folklore.* Chicago: University of Chicago Press.

———. 1964. *Buying the Wind: Regional Folklore in the United States.* Chicago: University of Chicago Press.

———. 1973. *America in Legend: Folklore from the Colonial Period to the Present.* New York: Pantheon.

Downs, Douglas. 2001. Movie Review of *Harry Potter: Witchcraft Repackaged. Christian Spotlight on the Movies.* Available: http://www.christiananswers. net/spotlight/movies/2001/harrypotterwitchcraft repackaged.html

Drennan, Miriam E. 2000. Musn't [*sic*] tarry when it comes to Harry. *Children's Bookpage.* Available: http://www.bookpage.com/0007bp/childrens/ harry_potter.html

Dundes, Alan. 1991. The Ritual Murder or Blood Libel Legend: A Study of Anti-Semitic Victimization through Projective Inversion. In Alan Dundes, *The Blood Libel Legend: A Casebook in Anti-Semitic Folklore,* 336–76. Madison: University of Wisconsin Press.

———. 2002. *Bloody Mary in the Mirror: Essays in Psychoanalytic Folkloristics.* Jackson: University Press of Mississippi.

Dundes, Alan, and Carl R. Pagter. 1992 [1975]. *Work Hard and You Shall Be Rewarded: Urban Folklore from the Paperwork Empire.* Detroit: Wayne State University Press.

Ellen, Roy. 1988. Fetishism. *Man.* N.S. 23:213–35.

Ellis, Bill. 1978. The "Blind Girl" and the Rhetoric of Sentimental Heroism. *Journal of American Folklore* 91: 657–74.

———. 1996. Legend-Trips and Satanism: Adolescents' Ostensive Traditions as "Cult" Activity. In *Contemporary Legend: A Reader,* ed. Gillian Bennett and Paul Smith, 167–86. New York: Garland.

———. 2000. *Raising the Devil: Satanism, New Religions, and the Media.* Lexington: University Press of Kentucky.

———. 2001. *Aliens, Ghosts, and Cults: Legends We Live.* Jackson: University Press of Mississippi.

Ensign, Grayson H., and Edward Howe. 1984. *Bothered? Bewildered? Bewitched? Your Guide to Practical Supernatural Healing.* Cincinnati: Recovery Publications.

Erikson, Erik. 1970. Reflections on the Dissent of American Youth. *International Journal of Psycho- Analysis* 51: 11–22.

Ernest, Victor H. 1970. *I Talked with Spirits.* Wheaton, Ill.: Tyndale House.

Evan Roberts and the Welsh Revival of 1904. 1996. *The Christian Bookshop.* Available: http://www.christian-bookshop.co.uk/free/biogs/roberts1.htm

Evans, Eifion. 1969. *The Welsh Revival of 1904.* London: Evangelical Press.

Film Forum: Intelligent Believers on the Big Screen? 2002. *Christianity Today.* January 28, 2002. Available: http://www.christianitytoday.com/ct/2002/103/41.0.html

Fogel, Edwin M. 1908. The Himmelsbrief. *German American Annals* 10:286–311.

Fort, Charles. 1941. *The Books of Charles Fort.* New York: Henry Holt. Includes *The Book of the Damned* (1919), *New Lands* (1923), *Lo!* (1931) and *Wild Talents* (1932).

Frazier, Ian. 1989. A Reporter at Large: Great Plains II. *The New Yorker* (27 February): 35–65.

Frazier, Paul. 1959. The Dumb Supper. *Midwest Folklore* 9(no. 2): 87–88,

Fuller, Margaret. 1994 [1845]. Woman in the Nineteenth Century. In *The Portable Margaret Fuller, ed. May Kelly.* N.Y.: Penguin Books.

Gardner, Emelyn Elizabeth. 1937. *Folklore from The Schoharie Hills, New York.* Ann Arbor: University of Michigan Press.

Garrard, Mary N. 1947. *Mrs. Penn-Lewis: A Memoir.* Westbourne, Bournemouth, Hants: The Overcomer Book Room.

George, Diana Hume, and Malcolm A. Nelson. 1982. Man's Infinite Concern: Graveyards as Fetishes. In Browne, ed. 1982: 136–50.

Gesta Romanorum. 1891. Trans. Charles Swan, rev. Wynnard Hooper. London: George Bell & Sons.

Gide, André. 1951 *The Journals*. Trans. Justin O'Brian. New York: Knopf.

Ginzburg, Carlo. 1990. Deciphering the Sabbath. In Ankarloo and Henningsen, eds. 1990: 121–37.

———. 1992. *The Night Battles: Witchcraft and Agrarian Cults in the Sixteenth and Seventeenth Centuries*. Baltimore: Johns Hopkins University Press.

Goldberg, Christine. 1974. Traditional American Witch Legends: A Catalog. *Indiana Folklore* 7:77–108.

González-Wippler, Migene, ed. 1982. *The New Revised Sixth and Seventh Books of Moses and the Magical Uses of the Psalms*. Bronx, N.Y.: Original Publications.

Goodrich, Arthur, et al. 1905. *The Story of the Welsh Revival*. New York: Fleming H. Revell Co.

Goss, Michael. 1991. Old Hat New Hat. *Magonia* 40:9–11.

Grace, Kevin Michael. 2002. Tolkien's Ring Triumphs over the Uncomprehending to Shed a Christian Light on Our Times. *The Report: Canada's Newsmagazine*. January 7, 2002. Available: http://report.ca/archive/report/20020107/p34i020107f.html

Graves, Tom. 1986. *Needles of Stone Revisited*. Glastonbury: Gothic Image Publications.

Greeley, Andrew M. 1975. *The Sociology of the Paranormal: A Reconnaissance*. Beverly Hills, Calif.: Sage Publications.

Grimm, Jakob and Wilhelm. 1981 [1816]. *The German Legends of the Brothers Grimm*. Trans. Donald Ward. Philadelphia: ISHI.

Grinsell, Leslie V. 1976. *Folklore of Prehistoric Sites in Britain*. North Pomfret, Vt.: David & Charles.

Grumbine, Dr. E. 1905. Folklore and Superstitious Beliefs of Lebanon County. *Lebanon County Historical Society Historical Papers and Addresses* 3:252–294.

Gruss, Edmond C. 1975. *The Ouija Board: Doorway to the Occult*. Chicago: Moody Press.

Gurdon, Lady Eveline Camilla. 1895. *County Folk-Lore, Volume 1, Part 2: Suffolk.* London: David Nutt.

Hall, Gary. 1973. The Big Tunnel: Legends and Legend-Telling. *Indiana Folklore* 6:139–73.

Hall, Manly Palmer. 1944. The Devil's Flatiron. *Horizon* 4 (Fall–Winter): 71–77.

Hand, Wayland D., ed. 1961–64. *The Frank C. Brown Collection of North Carolina Folklore, Volumes 6–7: Popular Beliefs and Superstitions from North Carolina.* Durham: Duke University Press.

Hansen, Chadwick. 1969. *Witchcraft at Salem.* New York: George Braziller.

Harris, Trudier. 1984. *Exorcising Blackness : Historical and Literary Lynching and Burning Rituals.* Bloomington: Indiana University Press.

Harry Potter Books. 2001. *Providence Baptist Ministries.* July 2001. Available: http://www.pbministries.org/Parachurch/sorcery/harry_potter_books.htm

Harry Potter Books Spark Rise in Satanism Among Children. 2000. *The Onion* 36, no. 25 (June 15, 2000). Available: http://home.swipnet.se/~w-49954/English/Potter/onion.html

Hawthorne, Nathaniel. 1985. Northern Volunteers: From a Journal. *The Hawthorne Society Newsletter* 11, no. 1 (Spring): 1–2.

Heart Throbs in Prose and Verse Dear to the American People. 1905. Boston: Chapple Publishing Company.

Heindel, Ned D. 1976a. Unorthodox Practitioners of Medicine in Old Northampton County. In Northampton County Bicentennial Commission, *Two Hundred Years of Life in Northampton County, PA,* vol. 9, 17–33.

———. 1976b. *The Hexenkopf: Mystery, Myth & Legend.* Easton, Penn.: Ned D. Heindel.

Henderson, William. 1866. *Notes on the Folk Lore of the Northern Counties of England and the Borders.* London: Longmans, Green and Co.

Henningsen, Gustav. 1990. "The Ladies from Outside": An Archaic Pattern of the Witches' Sabbath. In Ankarloo and Henningsen, eds. 1990: 191–215.

Hettinger, Virginia A. 1982. The Ghost at Stepp's Cemetery and Related Events. Indiana University Folklore Archives, Bloomington, Indiana.

Hicks, Robert D. 1991. *In Pursuit of Satan: The Police and the Occult.* Buffalo: Prometheus.

Hohman, John George. 1904. *The Long Hidden Friend,* ed. Carleton F. Brown. *Journal of American Folklore* 17:89–152.

———. 1992. *Pow-Wows: Or, The Long Lost Friend.* State College, Penn.: Yardbird Books.

Hopkins, B., D. M. Jacobs, and R. Westrum. 1992. *Unusual Personal Experiences: An Analysis of Data from Three National Surveys Conducted by the Roper Organization.* Bigelow Holding Corporation, Nevada.

Hsia, R. Po-chia. 1988. *The Myth of Ritual Murder : Jews and Magic in Reformation Germany.* New Haven: Yale University Press.

Hufford, David J. 1982. *The Terror That Comes in the Night: An Experience-Centered Study of Supernatural Assault Traditions.* Philadelphia: University of Pennsylvania Press.

Hughes, Pennethorne. 1965. *Witchcraft.* Baltimore: Penguin.

Hyatt, Harry Middleton. 1965. *Folk-Lore from Adams County Illinois.* Rev. ed. Hannibal, Mo.: Alma Egan Hyatt Foundation.

———. 1970–74. *Hoodoo—Conjuration—Witchcraft—Rootwork: Beliefs Accepted by Many Negroes and White Persons These Being Orally Recorded Among Blacks and Whites.* Hannibal, Mo.: Memoirs of the Alma Egan Hyatt Foundation.

Idel, Moshe. 1986. Qabbalah. In *The Encyclopedia of Religion,* 12:117–24. N. Y.: Macmillan.

———. 1988. *Kabbalah: New Perspectives.* New Haven: Yale University Press.

Isaacs, Ernest. 1983. The Fox Sisters and American Spiritualism. In *The Occult in America: New Historical Perspectives,* ed. Howard Kerr and Charles L. Crow, 79–110. Urbana: University of Illinois Press.

James, Ken. 2001. Is "Harry Potter" Harmless? *ChristianAnswers.net.* Available: http://www.christiananswers.net/q-eden/harrypotter.html

Johnson, F. Roy. 1974. *Supernaturals among Carolina Folk and Their Neighbors.* Murfreesboro, N.C.: Johnson Publishing Co.

Johnson, Henry. 1906. *Stories of Great Revivals.* London: Religious Tract Society.

Johnson, James P. 1983. Ouija. *American Heritage* 34 (February–March): 24–27.

Johnson, Jerry. 1989. *The Edge of Evil: The Rise of Satanism in North America.* Dallas: Word Publishing.

Jones, Malcolm. 2000. The Return of Harry Potter! *Newsweek* (July 10): 56–60.

Keyser, Blanche W. 1958. Divining the Future. *Keystone Folklore Quarterly* 3:5–9.

Kittridge, George Lyman. 1929. *Witchcraft in Old and New England.* Cambridge, Mass.: Harvard University Press.

Kjos, Berit. 1999. Bewitched by Harry Potter. *Crossroad: Kjos Ministries.* September 1999. Available: http://www.crossroad.to/text/articles/Harry9–99.html

———. 2002. Twelve Reasons Not to See Harry Potter Movies. *Crossroad: Kjos Ministries.* September 12, 2002. Available: http://www.crossroad.to/articles2/HP-Movie.htm

Klintberg, Bengt af. 1988. "Black Madame, Come Out!": On Schoolchildren and Spirits. *ARV: Scandinavian Yearbook of Folklore* 44:155–67.

Koch, Kurt E. 1962. *Between Christ and Satan.* Grand Rapids, Mich.: Kregel.

———. 1970. *The Devil's Alphabet.* Berghausen: Evangelization Publishers.

———. 1972. *Christian Counseling and Occultism: The Counselling of the Psychically Disturbed and Those Oppressed through Involvement in Occultism.* Grand Rapids, Mich.: Kregel.

———. 1973a. *Demonology, Past and Present.* Grand Rapids, Mich.: Kregel.

———. 1973b. *Revival Fires in Canada.* Grand Rapids, Mich.: Kregel.

———. 1978. *Satan's Devices.* Grand Rapids, Mich.: Kregel. Rpt. 1980 as *Occult ABC.*

Koch, Kurt E., and Alfred Lechler. 1970. *Occult Bondage and Deliverance: Advice for Counseling the Sick, the Troubled and the Occultly Oppressed.* Grand Rapids, Mich.: Kregel.

Lafferty, Anne. 1996. Feeding the Dead. *EarthSpirit Newsletter.* Late Autumn 1996. Available: *The EarthSpirit Newsletter Archives,* http://www. earthspirit.org/ newsletter/feedead.html

————. 2003. The Roots of the Contemporary Pagan Dumb Supper. Unpublished essay.

Langlois, Janet. 1980. "Mary Whales, I Believe in You": Myth and Ritual Subdued. *Indiana Folklore* 11: 5–34.

Langmuir, Gavin I. 1972. The Knight's Tale of Young Hugh of Lincoln. *Speculum* 47:459–82.

LaVey, Anton Szandor. 1969. *The Satanic Bible.* New York: Avon.

Lewington, Jay. 2001. The Welsh Revival of 1904. *Heath Christian Bookshop Free Downloads Page.* Available: http://www.christian-bookshop.co.uk/free/ r04.htm.

Lewis, I. M. 1989. *Ecstatic Religion: A Study of Shamanism and Spirit Possession.* 2nd ed. New York: Routledge.

Lewis, James R. 2002. The Satanic Bible: Quasi-Scripture/Counter-Scripture. Paper presented at the 2002 CESNUR International Conference on Minority Religions, Social Change, and Freedom of Conscience, Salt Lake City and Provo (Utah), June 20–23, 2002. Available: http://www.cesnur.org/2002/ slc/lewis.htm

Licht, Michael. 1974. Some Automotive Play Activities of Suburban Teenagers. *New York Folklore Quarterly* 30:44–65.

Litvag, Irving. 1972. *Singer in the Shadows: The Strange Story of Patience Worth.* New York: Macmillan.

Long, Maud. 1955. *Jack Tales (II).* LP record (AAFS L48). Washington, D.C.: Library of Congress.

Magliocco, Sabina. 1985. The Bloomington Jaycees' Haunted House. *Indiana Folklore and Oral History* 14:19–28.

Maple, Eric. 1964. *The Dark World of Witches.* New York: A. S. Barnes.

250 • Sources Cited

——. 1966. *The Domain of Devils.* New York: A. S. Barnes.

——. 1973. *Witchcraft: The Story of Man's Search for Supernatural Power.* London: Octopus Books.

McClure, Kevin. 1995. Stars, and Rumours of Stars: The Egryn Lights and Other Mysterious Phenomena in the Welsh Religious Revival, 1904–1905. Self-published. Available: http://www.magonia.demon.co.uk/abwatch/stars/stars1.html

McGlasson, Cleo. 1941. Superstitions and Folk Beliefs of Overton County. *Tennessee Folklore Society Bulletin* 7:13–27.

Medway, Gareth J. 2001. *Lure of the Sinister: The Unnatural History of Satanism.* N. Y.: New York University Press.

Menefee, Samuel P. 1985. Circling as an Entrance to the Otherworld. *Folklore* 96: 3–20.

Meyer, Pastor David J. 2000a. Harry Potter? What Does God Have To Say? *Last Trumpet Ministries.* August 29, 2000. Available: http://www. lasttrumpet ministries.org/tracts/tract7.html

——. 2000b. Harry Potter Bewitches a Nation. *SIPL* [Southern Illinois Patriot League] *Freedom News.* 22 November 2000. Available: http://sipl.addr.com/feature_harrypotter.html

Michell, John. 1977. *Secrets of the Stones: The Story of Astro-Archaeology.* New York: Penguin.

Mikkelson, Barbara, and David P. 2001. Harry Potter. *Urban Legends Reference Pages* 2 December 2001. Available: http://www.snopes.com/humor/iftrue/potter.htm

Miller, Pamela A. 1982. Hair Jewelry as Fetish. In Browne, ed. 1982: 89–106.

Milspaw, Yvonne J. 1978. Witchcraft in Appalachia: Protection for the Poor. *Indiana Folklore* 11(1):71–86.

Minucius Felix, Marcus. 1931. Octavius. Translated by Gerald H. Rendall. In *Tertullian/Minucius Felix.* Loeb Classical Library, vol. 250, N. Y.: Putnam.

Muchembled, Robert. 1990. Satanic Myths and Cultural Reality. In Ankarloo and Henningsen, eds. 1990: 139–60.

Murray, Margaret A. 1921. *The Witch-Cult in Western Europe.* Oxford: Oxford University Press.

———. 1931. *The God of the Witches.* Oxford: Oxford University Press.

Newman, Paul. 2001. The Cambridge Crop Circles: What Do They Mean? *Cambridge (UK): Crop Circle web site.* October 2001. Available: http://www.cam.net.uk/home/nimmann/events/gogmagog.htm

Norris, Dr. Joel, and Jerry Allen Potter. 1986. The Devil Made Me Do It. *Penthouse* (January): 48+.

Olsen, Ted. 1999. Opinion Roundup: Positive about Potter. *Christianity Today.* December 13, 1999. Available: http://www.christianitytoday.com/ct/1999/150/12.0.html

Opie, Iona, and Moira Tatem. 1989. *A Dictionary of Superstitions.* Oxford: Oxford University Press.

OSUFA. Ohio State Folklore Archive. Department of English, Ohio State University, Columbus, Ohio.

Ouija Board, Bolshevik of the Spirit World, The. 1920. *Literary Digest* 64 (31 January): 64, 67.

Ouija Board Is Wartime Fad. 1945. *Science Digest* 17 (April): 30.

Owen, Alex. 1990. *The Darkened Room: Women, Power and Spiritualism in Late Victorian England.* Philadelphia: University of Pennsylvania Press.

Painter, Jacqueline Burgin. 1994. *An Appalachian Medley: Hot Springs and the Gentry Family, Vol I.* Asheville, N.C.: Biltmore Press.

Parson, Elsie Clews. 1917. Tales from Guilford County, North Carolina. *Journal of American Folklore* 30:168–208.

———. 1921. Folk-Lore from Aiken, South Carolina. *Journal of American Folklore* 34:1–39.

Pearson, Barry Lee. 1990. Vietnam Narratives. Paper read at the Annual Meeting of the American Folklore Society, Oakland, California.

Pedigo, Jess. 1971. *Satanism: Diabolical Religion of Darkness.* Tulsa, Okla.: Christian Crusade Publications.

Penn-Lewis, Jessie, with Evan Roberts. 1973 [1912]. *War on the Saints: The Full Text Unabridged Edition.* New York: T. E. Lowe. Available: http://www.marycraig.org/Books/WarOnTheSaints/Contents.html

———. 1993 [1912]. *War on the Saints (Abridged Edition).* Port Washington, Penn.: Christian Literature Crusade.

Peuckert, Will-Erich. 1957. Das Sechste und Siebente Buch Mosis. *Zeitschrift für Deutsche Philologie* 76:163–87.

Pietz, William. 1987. The Problem of the Fetish, II: The Origin of the Fetish. *Res* 13:23–45.

Pike, Albert. 1947 [1871]. *Morals and Dogma of the Ancient and Accepted Scottish Rite of Freemasonry.* Richmond, Va.: L. H. Jenkins, Inc.

Pimple, Kenneth D. 1985. "It's Because I Believe in It": History, Beliefs, and Legends of the Ouija Board. Unpublished graduate term paper (Bloomington, Ind.).

———. 1990. Folk Beliefs. In *The Emergence of Folklore in Everyday Life: A Fieldguide and Sourcebook,* ed. George Schoemaker. Bloomington, Ind.: Trickster Press.

Poggio Bracciolini, Giovanni Francesco. 1968. *The Facetiae.* Trans. Bernhardt J. Hurwood. N.Y.: Award Books.

Porter, Pastor Bruce. 2000. Occultic Influences on Our Children? August 2000. Accessed: http://www.familyfi.org/occultic_influences_on_our_child.htm (no longer available).

Price, Harry. 1945. *Poltergeist over England.* London: Country Life Books.

PSUHFA. Penn State University, Hazleton Folklore Archive. Hazleton, Penn.

Puckett, Newbell Niles. 1926. *Folk Beliefs of the Southern Negro.* Chapel Hill: University of North Carolina Press.

Pugh, Rusty. 2002. Parents Cautioned about Tarot Card Promotion. *AgapePress Christian News Service.* January 29, 2002. Available: http://headlines.agapepress.org/archive/1/292002c.asp.

Quarantelli, E. L., and Dennis Wenger. 1973. A Voice from the Thirteenth Century: The Characteristics and Conditions for the Emergence of a Ouija Board Cult. *Urban Life and Culture* 1:379–400.

Randolph, Vance. 1947. *Ozark Superstitions.* New York: Columbia University Press.

———. 1953. Nakedness in Ozark Folk Belief. *Journal of American Folklore* 66: 333–39.

———. 1992. *Unprintable Ozark Folksongs and Folklore.* Urbana: University of Illinois Press.

Raschke, Carl A. 1990. *Painted Black.* New York: Harper & Row.

Raupert, J. Godfrey. 1918. The Truth About the Ouija Board. *American Ecclesiastical Review* (November): 463–478.

Ray, Linda McCoy. 1976. The Legend of Bloody Mary's Grave. *Indiana Folklore* 9:175–86.

Rayburn, Otto Ernest. 1941. *Ozark Country.* New York: Duell, Sloan & Pearce.

Reimensnyder, Barbara. 1989 [1982]. *Powwowing in Union County: A Study of Pennsylvania German Folk Medicine in Context.* New York: AMS Press.

Riddle, Almeda. 1965. The Lady Gay. *The Max Hunter Folksong Collection,* ed. Dr. Michael F. Murray, Southwest Missouri State University. Cat. #0585 (MFH #672). Collected October 23, 1965. Available: http://www.smsu.edu/folksong/maxhunter/0585/

Roberts, Alexander. 1971 [1616]. A Treatise of Witchcraft. In *Witches and Witch-Hunters.* Menston, Yorkshire: Scolar Press.

Roberts, Jane. 1966. *How to Develop Your ESP Power.* New York: F. Fell.

———. 1970. *The Seth Material.* Englewood Cliffs, N.J.: Prentice-Hall.

Roberts, John W. 1989. *From Trickster to Badman: The Black Folk Hero in Slavery and Freedom.* Philadelphia: University of Pennsylvania Press.

Roberts, Leonard W. 1955. *South from Hell-fer-Sartin: Kentucky Mountain Folk Tales.* Lexington: University of Kentucky Press.

Rogo, D. Scott. 1987. *The Infinite Boundary: A Psychic Look at Spirit Possession, Madness, and Multiple Personality.* New York: Dodd, Mead.

Rowland, Robert. 1990. "Fantasticall and Devilische Persons": European Witch-beliefs in Comparative Perspective. In Ankarloo and Henningsen, eds. 1990: 161–90.

Rowling, J. K. 1998. *Harry Potter and the Sorcerer's Stone.* New York: Scholastic.

———. 1999. *Harry Potter and the Chamber of Secrets.* New York: Scholastic.

Rudkin, Ethel H. 1934. Lincolnshire Folklore: Witches and Devils. *Folklore* 45: 249–67.

Sachse, Julius Friedrich. 1954. Exorcism of Fire. *The Pennsylvania Dutchman* (15 January): 6–7, 9.

Santino, Jack. 1998. *The Hallowed Eve: Dimensions of Culture in a Calendar Festival in Northern Ireland.* Lexington: University Press of Kentucky.

Satire Mistaken for Truth. 2000. Available: http://home.swipnet.se/~w-49954/ English/Potter/onion.html

Sato, Ikuya. 1988. Play Theory of Delinquency: Toward a General Theory of "Action." *Symbolic Interaction* 11:191–212.

Scharpff, Paulus. 1966. *History of Evangelism: Three Hundred Years of Evangelism in Germany, Great Britain, and the United States of America.* Grand Rapids, Mich.: William B. Eerdmans.

Scholem, G. 1971. Kabbalah. In *Encyclopaedia Judaica,* 10:490–653. N.Y.: Macmillan.

Schults, Raymond L. 1972. *Crusader in Babylon: W. T. Stead and the Pall Mall Gazette.* Lincoln: University of Nebraska Press.

Schwarz, Luis H., and Stanton P. Fjeld. 1968. Illusions Induced by the Self-Reflected Image. *Journal of Nervous and Mental Disease* 146:277–84.

Scott, Beth, and Michael Norman. 1986. *Haunted Heartland.* New York: Warner Books.

Sebald, Hans. 1978. *Witchcraft: The Heritage of a Heresy.* New York: Elsevier.

Seth, Ronald. 1969. *Children against Witches.* New York: Taplinger Publishing Company.

Shaner, Richard H. 1961. Living Occult Practices in Dutch Pennsylvania. *Pennsylvania Folklife* 12, no. 3 (Fall): 62–63.

————. 1972. Recollections of Witchcraft in the Oley Hills. *Pennsylvania Folklife* 21 (Folk Festival Supplement): 34–44.

Shepard, Leslie. 1970. Introduction to *Borderland: A Casebook of True Supernatural Stories,* by W. T. Stead. New Hyde Park, N.Y.: University Books.

Simpson, Jacqueline. 1969. Legends of Chanctonbury Ring. *Folklore* 80:122–31.

————. 1994. Hecate in the Primrose Wood: The Propagation of a Rumor. *Contemporary Legend* 4: 91–118.

Simpson, Jacqueline, and Steve Roud. 2000. *A Dictionary of English Folklore.* New York: Oxford University Press.

Sixth and Seventh Books of Moses, The. 1916. Chicago: The de Laurence Company.

Smith, Betty N. 1998. *Jane Hicks Gentry: A Singer among Singers.* Lexington: University Press of Kentucky.

Smith, Robin. 1992. The Church of the Crooked Spire: St Mary and All Saints, Chesterfield. *Dear Mr Thoms* 28 (November): 1–12.

Smith, Susy. 1974. Confessions of a Psychic. In *Exorcism: Fact Not Fiction,* ed. Martin Ebon, 18–26. New York: New American Library.

Snellenburg, Betty. 1969. Four Interviews with Powwowers. *Pennsylvania Folklife* 18, no. 4 (Summer): 40–45.

Sparks, Beatrice. 1979. *Jay's Journal.* N.Y.: New York Times Book Co.

Stead, W. T. 1905. *The Welsh Revival: A Narrative of Facts.* Boston: The Pilgrim Press.

————. 1911. *How I Know That the Dead Return.* Boston: Ball Publishing Co.

————. 1970 [1892–93]. *Borderland: A Casebook of True Supernatural Stories.* New Hyde Park, N.Y.: University Books.

Stokker, Kathleen. 1992. Migratory Legend 3005: "The Would-Be Ghost"—Why Be He a Ghost? *ARV: Yearbook of Scandinavian Folklore* 48:143–52.

Stowe, Harriet Beecher. 1998 [1852]. *Uncle Tom's Cabin: or, Life Among the Lowly.* New York: Signet.

Summers, Rev. Montague. 1956 [1926]. *The History of Witchcraft and Demonology.* New Hyde Park, N.Y.: University Books.

ten Boom, Corrie. 1970. *Defeated Enemies.* Rev. ed. Fort Washington, Penn.: Christian Literature Crusade.

Terry, Maury. 1987. *The Ultimate Evil: An Investigation of America's Most Dangerous Satanic Cult.* Garden City, N.J.: Doubleday.

Tertullian. 1931. Apology. Trans. T. R. Glover. In *Tertullian/Minucius Felix.* Loeb Classical Library, vol. 250. Cambridge: Harvard University Press.

Thigpen, Kenneth A. 1971. Adolescent Legends in Brown County: A Survey. *Indiana Folklore* 4:141–215.

Thomas, Daniel Lindsey, and Lucy Blayney Thomas. 1920. *Kentucky Superstitions.* Princeton: Princeton University Press.

Thorpe, Benjamin. 1851. *Northern Mythology, Comprising the Principal Popular Traditions and Superstitions of Scandinavia, North Germany, and the Netherlands.* Vol. 3. London: E. Lumley.

Townsend, Barbara Ann. 1971. String Measurement: Additional Accounts. *Indiana Folklore* 4:89–94.

Townsend, Barbara Ann, and Donald Allport Bird. 1970. The Miracle of String Measurement. *Indiana Folklore* 3:147–62.

Trachtenberg, Joshua. 1943. *The Devil and the Jews: The Medieval Conception of the Jew and Its Relation to Modern Antisemitism.* New Haven: Yale University Press.

Trevor-Roper, H. R. 1969. *The European Witch-Craze of the Sixteenth and Seventeenth Centuries, and Other Essays.* New York: Harper & Row.

Turner, Patricia A. 1993. *I Heard It Through the Grapevine: Rumor in African-American Culture.* Berkeley: University of California Press.

Turner, Tressa. 1937. The Human Comedy in Folk Superstitions. *Publications of the Texas Folklore Society* 13:146+.

Turner, Victor. 1977. *The Ritual Process: Structure and Anti-Structure.* Ithaca: Cornell University Press.

Valiente, Doreen. 1973. *An ABC of Witchcraft Past and Present.* London: Robert Hale.

Van Arsdale, Daniel W. 1998. Chain Letter Evolution. Available: http://www.silcom.com/~barnowl/clevo/start.htm

Van Cleve, Janice. 2001. Traditions of the Dumb Supper. *Widdershins* 7:5 (Samhain, 2001). Available: http://www.widdershins.org/vol7iss5/02.htm

Victor, Jeffrey S. 1993. *Satanic Panic: The Creation of a Contemporary Legend.* Chicago: Open Court.

Waite, A.E. 1972 [1898]. *The Book of Black Magic.* York Beach, Maine: Samuel Weiser.

Warnke, Mike. 1972. *The Satan Seller.* Plainfield, N.J.: Logos International.

Watson, Lyall. 1991 [1980]. *The Nature of Things: The Secret Life of Inanimate Objects.* London: Sceptre.

Weinfeld, Moshe. 1991. *Deuteronomy 1–11: A New Translation.* Vol. 5. *The Anchor Bible,* vol. 5. New York: Doubleday.

Weird Science Page Database of Streetlight Interference, The. 2002. *Science Hobbyist,* ed. Matt Wright. Available: http://ww.amasci.com/weird/unusual/sli.html

Weiser, Rev. Daniel. 1954 [1868]. Braucherei. *Pennsylvania Dutchman* 5:14 (15 March): 6, 14.

Westcott, Marcia. 1969/70. Powwowing in Berks County. *Pennsylvania Folklife* 19, no. 2 (Winter): 2–9.

White, Charles, and J. C. Chinjavata. 1960. Myth and Social Separation with Reference to the Luvale and to Portuguese Africa. In *Myth in Modern Africa: The Fourteenth Conference Proceedings of the Rhodes-Livingstone Institute for Social Research,* ed. Allie Dubb. Lusaka: Rhodes-Livingstone Institute.

Whyte, H. A. Maxwell. 1973b. *The Kiss of Satan.* Monroeville, Penn.: Whitaker Press.

Wickland, Carl A. 1968 [1924]. *Thirty Years among the Dead.* London: Spiritualist Press.

Williamson, Tom, and Liz Bellamy. 1983. *Ley Lines in Question*. Kingswood, Tadworth, Surrey: World's Work.

Winstanley, Miss L., and H. J. Rose. 1926. Scraps of Welsh Folklore, I. Cardiganshire; Pembrokeshire. *Folklore* 37:154–74.

Wright, Travestine. 2003. The Harry Potter Books. *Gospel Warriors Ministries Inc.* January 4, 2003. Available: http://www.gospelwarriors.org/harry_potter_books.htm

Wukasch, Charles. 1991. The Seventh Book of Moses. *Tennessee Folklore Society Bulletin* 60:48–50.

Yarbro, Chelsea Quinn. 1986. *More Messages from Michael*. New York: Berkley.

Yoder, Don. 1965/66. Official Religion versus Folk Religion. *Pennsylvania Folklife* 15, no. 2 (Winter): 36–52.

———. 1974. Toward a Definition of Folk Religion. *Western Folklore* 33:2–15.

———. 1976. Hohman and Romanus: Origins and Diffusion of the Pennsylvania German Powwow Manual. In *American Folk Medicine: A Symposium*, ed. Wayland D. Hand, 235–248. Berkeley: University of California Press.

Zacharias, Gerhard P. 1980. *The Satanic Cult*. Boston: Allen and Unwin.

Index

Abrahams, Roger, 195
abuse, of children: "satanic ritual,"
174, 218, 227, 237n5; William
Thomas Stead and, 202
Adam and Eve, 144, 159, 211–12
adolescent(s): Anglo-American
culture and, 97–98, 112–14, 116,
143; automobile culture, 116;
gangs, 124; German, 86; girls,
play-rituals of, 6, 11–12, 142–73,
177, 236nn3–5; gravesite vandalism by, 97–98, 105–6, 112–13, 124,
134, 136–41, 140f; legend-tripping
rituals, 112–41, 130f, 133f, 140f,
153, 185, 201, 224; play ritual,
124–25, 136–41, 174–76, 181, 182,
185–89, 196, 223, 237n1; rebellion,
86, 124–28, 173, 176, 188, 196,
223, 224; Satanism and, 142–43;
suicide, 48, 61. *See also* children
African folklore, 4, 52
African Americans: culture of, 195;
folklore of, 92–95, 98–111, 114
aggression, social, 27, 32–37, 44
Ames, Julia, 202
amulets, 51, 83; biblical texts from,
49–50; blood and, 61–62; Bolivian, 5; chain letters as, 68, 233n9;
Jewish tradition of, 54–55, 60–64,
76; protective, 60–64, 72, 74. *See
also* rabbit's foot
Anglo-American culture: adolescents
and, 97–98, 112–14, 116, 143;
African-American folklore and,
92–95, 98–111, 114; Ouija Board
in, 175–76; sentimental folksongs
in, 104

animal(s): albino, 93; black cat, 100,
146, 149f; body parts/bones, 91–
95, 99–102, 109–11, 135; dog, 99,
134, 137, 209; mutilations, 123,
134, 137, 210; sacrifice, 134; white
wolf, 134. *See also* rabbit's foot
Antichrist, 20, 231n2
antioccult crusades, 9–11, 123–24,
134–35, 136, 142–43, 232n2;
American pioneer in, 30; counseling, 23–27, 29–30, 37–41, 42, 85;
four-tier model of, 143; of Kurt
Koch, 23–27, 29, 37–39, 41–42, 44,
77, 79, 85, 221, 224–25, 232n9;
"muggles" resemblance to, 14; as
political persecution, 12; *Raising
the Devil* on, 232n2; Welsh Revival
and, 199, 227; witches and, 19–20
Antiochus IV Epiphanes (Greek
ruler), 56
antiworld, 162, 167, 176, 223, 224
Apocalypse: year 2000 associated
with, 5, 90, 231n2. *See also*
Judgment Day
archaeologists, 120–21, 131
Armenian Orthodox religion, 35
astrologers, 17
Aubrey, John, 234n1
Augustine, Saint, 51, 119, 233n3
"Aunt Annie" (witch), 31, 33, 34, 73–
74
Austria, folk healing in, 23
automatic action/writing, 174, 179,
192, 200, 202, 205, 218, 220–21

babies: ashes of, 57–58; hexes on
crying, 30

259

Harry Potter books and, 1–4, 5–8, 7, 11, 13–15, 79, 89–90, 142–43, 190, 197–98, 228, 231n1; 237n1; v. Judaism, 52, 56–64, 77–78, 85; Latin mass in, 50–51; laying of hands in, 61; letters from heaven and, 64–66, 233nn6–7; literature and, 2, 49, 227; Ouija Board and, 176, 181, 182, 183, 188, 190, 218; v. Paganism, 38, 131; Satanism as protest against, 12; séances and, 172; Welsh Revival and, 197–222, 223, 226–27; witchcraft and, 44, 227. *See also* Catholic Church; Pentecostal religion; religions

Christianity Today, 1–2, 7

Church of Satan, 86, 185, 237n3

clairvoyants, 205

Cockrell, Amanda, 14–15, 228

Cohn, Norman, 9

college legends/play rituals, 119–22, 174, 181, 182–86, 236nn5–6

communitas, 186–87, 196

"confrontation" narrative, 225

conjuring: in Bible, 76; magic rooted in, 223; in Puritan Massachusetts, 144–45; secret seals in, 75–76, *75f, 77f,* 88; by youths, 148, 164

conspiracy theory: as response to occultism, 7, 12; Welsh Revival and, 7; witch trials and, 7, 16, 159–60, 173

Constantine (Roman emperor), 74

Copper, Arnold, 192

counseling: antioccult, 23–27, 29–30, 37–41, 42, 85; Christian, 222

Crawford, W.J., 178

crop circles, 118, 235n2

Crosby, John R., 35

Crowley, Aleister, 48, 185, 237n3

crusades, antioccult. *See* antioccult crusades

Cruz, Nicky, 10, 19, 171–72

cult(s): "cops," 47–48; devil/Satanic, 26, 113–14, 136–37, 141; "evil," 123; fertility, 8–9, 44; four

characteristics of, 183–85; Ouija Board, 182–88, 191, 198; raid, Pennsylvania, 48; sacrifice, 135, 143

cunning-folk, 10, 23, 33, 37–39, 40, 79–80

Curran, Pearl, 180

curses, 35–36, 126–27. *See also* hexes; spells

"dairy witch," 24–25, 32–33, 41

dares, supernatural, 131, 138, 167

Darwin, Charles, *The Origin of Species* by, 13

Daskam, Josephine Dodge, 207

Davies, Owen, 22–23

Dawkins, Richard, 67

Day, John A., 157–58

"Day of the Dead," 161

de Lexinton, John, 58

dead, communication with, 28

death: omen, 170; unexplained, 123, 210

Dee, John, 88

deformities, physical, 93

Deity Stone, 125

deliverance movement, 198, 199, 217, 221, 222

demonic obsession, in *Harry Potter* books, 227–28

demonic possession, 199–200, 216–17; of women, 189–96, 219–21

demonizing, of folk traditions, 27, 37–40, 227

demonology, in Welsh Revival, 199–200, 216–17, 224, 225–27

Depression, Great, 181

Der Lange Vergborgene Freund (Hohman), 70–73, 75–76, 81

devil, 6; barn with face of, 135; children and, 19–20, 26; cults, 26, 113–14, 136–37, 141; law v. theology in worship of, 83–86, 89–90; raising the, 12, 142, 173; reading linked with, 46–49, 50; selling soul to/pact with, 19–20,

191–92, 199, 214, 218, 222;
spiritualist influenced, 192, 237n5
Puckett, Newbell Niles, 93, 94, 99
Puritans, 144–45, 146

Qabbalah, Jewish, 52–56, 233n5;
Cabala version of, 55–56, 60, 61,
64, 74, 76, 87–88, 89, 223, 233n5
Quarantelli, E.L., 182–85, 188

rabbit's foot, 91–95, 99–102, 109–11,
122, 125, 136, 148, 223, 234n2,
234nn4–5; B'rer Rabbit and, 101–
2; witches and, 94, 100–101
Raber, William, 38, 39
race relations, 109–11
Raising the Devil (Ellis), 7; on
antioccult crusaders, 232n2; on
contemporary mythology, 4; on
demonization, 227; on organized
religion, 12; Ouija Board and, 174,
175–76, 190; on religious movements, 8, 198
Randolph, Vance, 20, 24, 31–32, 41,
42–44, 157, 170
rape, 190–91, 195
Raupert, J. Godfrey, 181
Rayburn, Otto, 157
reading, linked with devil, 46–49, 50,
73–74, 79, 85
rebellion ritual, 86, 124–28, 173, 176,
188, 196, 223, 224
Reformation, 56, 60
Reimensnyder, Barbara, 39, 80
reincarnation, 182
religion(s): alternative, 8, 197, 224;
defiance of mainstream, 123;
ecstatic, 10, 175, 211, 220; folk,
18–19, 201, 206; Luciferian
dialectic/occult and, 12, 224–25,
229; magic and, 229; nature, 8–9,
42–43. *See also specific religions*
revivalist movements, 226; Canadian,
224–25. *See also* Welsh Revival
Ringu (Japanese film), 233n9
rituals: backward, 153–54, 158–63;

Bible and key, 177; for charms,
100; children's play, 7, 11–12, 187,
225; defiance of supernatural,
122–23; dumb supper, 153–63,
167, 168–70, 175, 201, 218, 224;
hair, 103–5, 235n13; Halloween,
147–48, 150f, 153–54, 158; high
school/college, 119–22, 174, 182–
86, 236nn5–6; husband-divining,
145–63, 149f–152f, 177; "imaginary," 105–6; mirror-gazing, 150f–
152f, 158, 163–71, 224, 236nn3–5;
to neutralize hexes, 84, 145;
rebellion, 86, 124–28, 173, 176,
188, 196, 223, 224; "satanic ritual
abuse" and, 174, 218, 227, 237n5;
sieve-and-keys/sieve-and-scissors,
144, 145, 176, 178. *See also* legend-
tripping rituals; Ouija Board; play
rituals
Roberts, Evan, 201, 203–8, 210, 213–
14, 218, 220, 222, 226
Roberts, Jane, 181, 182, 183
Roberts, John W., 102
Roberts, Reverend Alexander, 144,
172
rocks. *See* stones
Rollright Stones, 128, 137
Romanusbüchlein (Gypsy's Little
Book), 70, 72
Roper Organization, 28
Rosemary's Baby, 87
Rowland, Robert, 161–62
Rowling, J.K. *See Harry Potter* books
(Rowling)

sabbats, 162
sacrifice: animal, 134; blood, 198; of
children, 9, 57–59, 60; cult, 135,
143
saints: life of, 160, 236n2; *War on the
Saints* and, 214–15, 221–22
Salem, Massachusetts. *See* witch trials
Satan, 6; battles with, 20; Church of,
86, 185, 237n3; fire controlled by,
62; as force v. person, 13; God and,

218; Welsh Revival and, 199–206, 212, 219–22
Stanton Drew (Neolithic site), 120
"stars and lights," 209–10, 214–15
Stead, William Thomas, 202–5, 215, 221–22
Stepp Cemetery, 127–28, 131, 134, 139; Warlock Seat in, 129, 139, 140f
stone(s): Bowing, 132; charms, 122, 123; Couch, 129, 130f; counting, 120; cursed, 115; Deity, 125; experiments, 137; formations, 119–24; grave, 119, 121–24, 128–36, 130f, 133f, 139; King Stone (Neolithic site), 122; Rollright, 128, 137; Thigh, 128–29; "Witches," 132, 236n8
Stone Couch (Pennsylvania), 129, 130f
Stonehenge, 120
storms, 120, 235n4
Stowe, Harriet Beecher, 103–5
suicide, 174; adolescent, 48, 61, 182
summer camp, institutional, 186–87
Summers, Montague, 9, 46
supernatural phenomena, 229; children's play and, 7; dares and, 131, 138; quasi-animate extensions of, 122; ritual defiance of, 122–23; in Welsh Revival, 199–200, 216–17, 224, 225–27. See also paranormal experience
Swing, William, 231n2
Switzerland, folk healing in, 23–24, 79

table-setting, backwards, 153–54, 158–63
table-tapping, 54, 177–79, 200, 237nn1–2
Taco Bell, 231n1
Talmud, 74, 76
tarot cards, 231n1
Taxil, Leo, 12–13
ten Boom, Corrie, 61, 65
Ten Commandments, 53, 64

Theodosian Code, 233n4
Theosophist circles, 182, 188
thieves, 80–82, 178–79, 234nn3–4
Thigh Stone, 128–29
Thigpen, Kenneth, 115, 185
Toledo Dig, 135–36
Tolkien, J.R.R., 2, 227
Tonbridge Free Press, 116
Tree of Life, 53
Trevor-Roper, H.R., 9
Trinity, charming in name of, 78, 86
Turner, Patricia A., 17
Turner, Victor, 186

UFO sightings, 210, 237n1
Uncle Tom's Cabin (Stowe), 103–5
United Religions Charter, 2, 231n2

Van Arsdale, Daniel, 66, 67–68, 233nn7–8
Van Cleve, Janice, 161
Vancouver Sun, 228
vandalism, graveyard, 97–98, 105–6, 112–13, 124, 134, 136–41, 140f, 223
Vietnam conflict, 108
village: cunning-folk of, 10, 23, 33, 37–39, 40, 79–80; "experts," 10, 21; folk culture, 10
violence, 227; sexual, 174, 190–96, 237nn4–7

Waite, A.E., 70–71
Wandlebury Mound, 118
War on the Saints (Penn-Lewis), 214–15, 221–22, 226–28
Warlock Seat. See Stepp Cemetery
Warnke, Mike, 105–6
warts, 78, 234n2
watches, stopping, 205, 237n1
Wayland, Hand, 106
Weasley, Ron, 48
Weiser, Daniel, 38–39
Welsh Revival, 8, 197–222; antioccult crusades and, 199, 227; Christianity and, 197–222, 223, 226–27;